BRISTOL: A PEOPLE'S HISTORY

BRISTOL

A People's History

PETER AUGHTON

Carnegie Publishing

To Julie Kathryn, a Bristolian

By the same author:
North Meols and Southport
Liverpool: A People's History
Endeavour

Bristol: A People's History

Published by Carnegie Publishing Ltd
Carnegie House, Chatsworth Road,
Lancaster LA1 4SL
01524–840111

Typeset and originated by
Carnegie Publishing

ISBN 1-85936-067-X

Cataloguing-in-Publication data
A catalogue record for this book is available from the British Library

Printed and bound in the UK by
The Cromwell Press, Wilts

Contents

Acknowledgements

Many people have helped during the research and writing of this book, including: Stephen Price and Ray Barnett, Bristol Museum and Art Gallery; John Williams, Bristol Record Office; Andy King, Bristol Industrial Museum; Bristol Central Library, College Green; Bristol University Library; Bolland Library, University of the West of England; Westbury-on-Trym Library; John Winstone (Reece Winstone Archive); Mrs Acford; Gerry Brook, Bristol Evening Post; Ian Beales, Western Daily Press; Rodney Sampson of Bristol University; the late Bryan Little of Bristol; and Dilys Aughton, my better half.

Illustrations

Most of the modern photographs reproduced in this book are the author's own illustrations. The following illustrations have been reproduced by kind permission of:

Bristol Record Office: p. 27, p. 34, p. 35, p. 102;

Bristol Museums and Art Gallery: p. 94, p. 111, pp. 114–15, pp. 116–17, p. 143, p. 153, p. 182, p. 183;

Bristol Industrial Museum: p. 83, p. 201, p. 209, p. 210;

GWR Museum (Swindon Museum Service): p. 169, p. 170, p. 173, p. 174;

The National Portrait Gallery, London: p. 108;

The Department of Archaeology, City of Bristol Museum and Art Gallery: (Millerd's Map and details) p. 52, p. 53, p. 54 (left), p. 56, p. 61, p. 73, p. 76, p. 77, p. 80, p. 81, p. 92, pp. 120–1; (Donne's Map and details) p. 3, p. 158, p. 159;

Bristol Postcard Club: p. 179, p. 186, p. 187, p. 188, p. 189, p. 190, p. 191, p. 192, p. 202, p. 203, p. 205, p. 206, p. 211, p. 212, p. 213 (top), p. 214, p. 220, p. 222, p. 232, p. 234, p. 235;

The Bristol Evening Post: p. 221, p. 223, p. 225, p. 233, p. 238, p. 239, p. 244;

The Society of Merchant Venturers: p. 156;

Dorothy Acford: p. 241;

Reece Winstone Archive: p. 145.

The extracts from *English Journeys* by J. B. Priestley on pages 218 and 219 were reproduced by kind permission of the publisher, William Heinemann.

'Bristol' from John Betjeman's *Collected Poems* on page 252 was reproduced by kind permission of John Murray (Publishers) Ltd.

The extract on page 236 from E. H. Skeeles' *Bristol in the 1940s* was reproduced by kind permission of The Reece Winstone Archive.

The figures quoted on page 100 from D. P. Lamb's *Liverpool: The African Slave Trade, and Abolition* (ed. Roger Anstey and P. E. H. Hair) were reproduced by kind permission of The Historic Society of Lancashire and Cheshire.

The extracts on pages 220, 224, 230–5 were reproduced by kind permission of *The Western Daily Press*.

Introduction

The foreigner sometimes has one slight advantage over the native. He remembers his first visit to the place.

The first time I saw Bristol was on a cold day in early January. It was late afternoon and overcast when the train rattled through the northern suburbs. Darkness was already falling as our locomotive screeched its way into Temple Meads Station. Our party numbered three adolescent schoolboys of the age that most people try to avoid – old enough to have outgrown the train-spotting phase, but still unable to resist the allure of the Castle Class locomotives of British Rail's Western Region.

I was already a Brunelophile and I knew I was seventy years too late to see a broad gauge flyer. I keenly felt some regret that only the ghosts of the broad gauge were there to greet me – but Temple Meads did not disappoint me. We alighted in the great curved hall full of the sights, sounds and smells of steam and smoke. Incomprehensible messages boomed out from the public address system. The shrill whistles of the engines echoed from the roof far above. On the neighbouring platform a live locomotive hissed with steam as it panted to haul its train up to speed. There was a glimpse of bright red fire, shining through the gloom from the cab of the locomotive as it headed for distant parts.

Outside the station we boarded a green bus with the word 'Bristol' emblazoned on its side in gold letters. I think it was route number one. It was quite dark, but we climbed to the upper deck, eager to see the sights of this maritime city. It was drizzling and the rain was turning into sleet. After negotiating a bridge over a dark river, we had a glimpse of a harbour and then the bus was labouring up a long steep hill surmounted by the silhouette of a tower so tall we thought it must be the cathedral. We consequently missed seeing the real cathedral which lay behind us on the left. The bus somehow reached the top of the hill but it growled on, still in low gear, and the road was still climbing. After what seemed an age we arrived at an open tree-lined space which we found was perversely called 'the Downs'. The conductor shouted up that the next stop was the 'White Tree' where we had instructions to alight. We looked in vain for a white tree but by this time it was too dark to see anything clearly. It had stopped raining but it felt cold enough to snow.

The reason for this wintry visit was to take the entrance examinations for Bristol University. The bitter pill of examinations was sweetened by two days off school. We spent only two nights in Bristol. Our accommodation was at Wills Hall of Residence, but there was time to see something of the city between the hours in the examination room. We saw the university and a few students wrapped in college scarves, but the term had not started and most of the students were still away on vacation. We saw the church of St Mary Redcliffe. We somehow found the way to Ashton Gate and saw an FA Cup tie (Bristol City 3–Accrington Stanley 1). One afternoon we followed our noses towards Clifton Village – the locals assured us that it was within easy walking distance. The merits of Victoria Square were lost on spotty adolescents with no appreciation of architecture, but as the houses gave way to the downs the stone pier of a bridge could be seen in the distance.

It amazed me how a city of this size could have a gorge so deep running right through it. The span of the bridge was so long; the towers were so high and the supports so light; the river so far below. I had read about it. I had seen pictures of it. But none of these could do it justice. I thought it was one of the wonders of the world! The motorists seemed to think it safe to drive across, but to a pedestrian the bridge seemed a very dangerous prospect, with a slender footpath, outside the chains, overhanging the fearsome drop. High above the entrance, near the top of the towers I could read the name of the designer, ISAMBARD KINGDOM BRUNEL, 1806–1859. Why was I applying for a place to study science? I decided that I wanted to be an engineer.

The university was foolish enough to offer me a place to read physics, but it was Manchester which ended up having to suffer my immature undergraduate years. I did not see Bristol again for nearly a decade, not until the time that I was offered the opportunity to work on the world's first supersonic airliner. I became a resident of the city and I spent the greater part of my working life there.

It is over forty years since I looked down, white-knuckled, from the Suspension Bridge to the Avon below. I wish that I could travel back and present the youth on the bridge with a copy of this book. That I cannot do. But what I can do is to take you back a thousand years to an older and more primitive bridge across the River Avon. It will take a long time to get back again through the centuries to the third millennium, but we will meet many interesting people on the way. Who knows? We may even be able to ride behind a broad gauge locomotive.

Peter Aughton
Bristol, July 1999

❦ CHAPTER ONE

The Bridge Place

The 1826 map by Donne shows as 'Roman encampment' at Clifton. A detachment of the 2nd Legion was encamped there. The defences are earlier, though – their concentric pattern being typical of Iron Age hillforts.

Nobody knew when the bridge was built.

It was long before living memory, perhaps as long ago as the time of Alfred the Great. Folklore claimed that Alfred himself had sheltered in the caves of the Red Cliff on the Wessex side of the river, but even if the great king did visit the place he would have found but the meanest of settlements at Bridge Stow.

About two miles to seaward was a ford where the river had cut a channel through limestone rocks which closed in on both sides to form a deep gorge; the same rocks made a hard bottom at the narrowest point of the muddy tidal stream. Swallows and skylarks soared with ease in the sky above, but the crossing was dangerous to the earthbound mortals at the river below. A small boy on top of the cliff, lying on his belly and daring to look over the edge, could watch the tidal waters rise rapidly far far below. Many a valuable animal had been lost at the ford. It was worth paying the toll to cross the river at the Bridge Stow.

Stone age man had chosen settlements high on the cliffs, at Stokeleigh to the south and Clifton to the north. The Romans had chosen to build their port downstream at Sea Mills where the diminutive river Trym flowed into the Avon, but the Saxons settled further inland at the point where the River Frome joined the same River Avon. The timber bridge lay right on the boundary of Wessex and Mercia and became part of the main trade route between the two kingdoms, with scraggy sheep and lumbering oxen being driven along the muddy road and across the bridge to the market. But there was a second trade route through Bridge Stow. The Avon was navigable by small craft to the Roman spa of Aquae Sulis and beyond and it carried much of the inland trade. The river also brought timber, hides and seafood from the coastal towns and villages of North Wessex and South Wales. To seaward the Avon had carved an impressive groove through the towering rocks to reach the estuary of the River Severn – an estuary so wide that men called it the Severn Sea. On Severn and Avon the tide was so strong it could carry seagoing craft right up the river to Bridge Stow, where the strangers to the town watched with awe at the rise of the tide which lifted the ships a full thirty feet.

The settlement lay in the parish of Barton Regis. In late Saxon times it had two simple stone churches but it consisted mainly of humble

Saxon Bristol

Tower Lane

Christmas Street

Broad Street

Head of the Quay

Quay

Conduit Tower

Christ Church

Wine Street

St Stephens

Small Street

St Leonard

Corn Street

High Street

Quay

Great Tower

Marsh Street

St Nicholas

Bristol Bridge

Early course of the Frome

Salk Street

Welshback

River Frome

Watergate [ex 1979]

Batten's Yard

Rackhay

River Avon

Tower

Marsh Gate

Marsh Gate

Marsh Wall

N
W   E
S

150   0   Feet   300

30   0   Metres   90

* M. W. Ponsford, 'Bristol Castle: Archaeology and History of a Royal Fortress' (M.Litt thesis (1979); R. H. Leech, *The Medieval Defences of Bristol Revisited* (1997); '"Almost the Richest City": Bristol in the Middle Ages', *British Archaeological Association Conferences Transactions*, xix (1997).

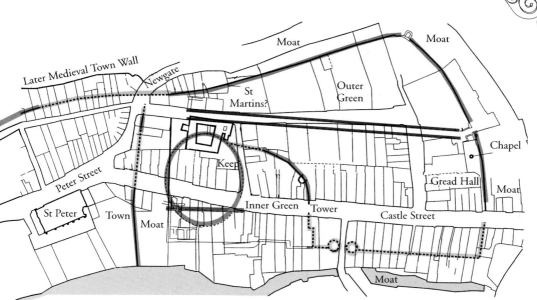

The area around Castle Park was destroyed by the Blitz in 1940 enabling more archaeological work to be done in this area. By 1980 a school of thought developed which put the Saxon town to the east of High Street and Bristol Bridge. This view is now being challenged.* The maps above and opposite subscribe to the view held by previous historians that the centre of Saxon Bristol was at High Cross. There is no doubt that late Saxon Bristol was a walled town. It is the extent of the wall which is in doubt. The whole of the inner wall is identified here as late Saxon.

Justification:

If the Saxon centre had been in Castle Park, then the bridge would have been built further upstream. It is illogical for the Saxons not to build on the west of High Street when it obviously offers a more secure defensive position than the east. There have been many Saxon finds to the west of High Street. St Werburg's may not have been the oldest church in Bristol but it is named after the Saxon saint buried at Chester Cathedral in the tenth century, implying a Saxon found-ation for the church. No Saxon wall has been discovered to the immediate west of Castle Park because it never existed. The Saxon wall enclosed the whole of central Bristol as we know it today.

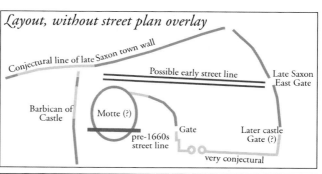

Layout, without street plan overlay

Conjectural line of late Saxon town wall

Possible early street line

Late Saxon East Gate

Barbican of Castle

Motte (?)

Gate

pre-1660s street line

Later castle Gate (?)

very conjectural

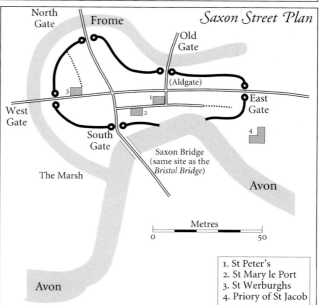

Saxon Street Plan

North Gate

Frome

Old Gate

(Aldgate)

West Gate

3

1

East Gate

2

4

South Gate

The Marsh

Saxon Bridge (same site as the *Bristol Bridge*)

Avon

Metres

0   50

Avon

1. St Peter's
2. St Mary le Port
3. St Werburghs
4. Priory of St Jacob

timber dwellings. At the end of the first millennium the trade and traffic had grown so much that by the reign of Cnut (1016–1035) coins were minted which carried the name of the place. The earliest coins carried the name 'Bric' or 'Bri', becoming 'Brics', 'Brist' or 'Bricsto' after the Norman Conquest. The local people seem to have had difficulty sounding the 'g' in 'Bridge' and they simply dropped it. The 'w' of 'Stow' gave them a similar problem so that the name became 'Bristo' and was destined to waver between 'Bristow' and 'Bristol' for several centuries before the spelling was finalised. The river Frome suffered a similar fate. It was pronounced 'Froom' but frequently spelt 'Frome', the only obvious reason being to confuse the foreigner! The contradiction seems destined to endure from Domesday to eternity.

It is in the *Anglo Saxon Chronicle*, the great work instigated by Alfred the Great, that we find the first written mention of early Bristol by name. In 1051 the *Chronicle* recorded that trade and traffic with Ireland was well established, and also gives the earliest description of a familiar problem encountered by sailors in the Severn Sea:

> Earl Harold and Leofwine went to Brycgstow to the ship which Sweyn had equipped and provisioned for himself. And the king sent Bishop Aldred from London with a force and they were to intercept him before he got on board, but they could not – or would not. And he went out from the estuary of the Avon, and had such sailing weather that he escaped with difficulty, and he suffered great losses there. He continued his course to Ireland when the sailing weather came ...[1]

The written records for Saxon Bristol are so few that the names of streets, gates and bridges are mere conjecture, but the street plan, with an east–west main street crossed by two streets at right angles, was probably laid down by the Saxons. As well as the Avon bridge near the south gate, there were two or possibly three smaller bridges over the Frome to the north and each bridge was reached by its own gate in the town wall. There is little doubt that Saxon Bristol was fortified by a wall, but the nature and the extent of the wall is in doubt. Gates existed near the bridges to the north and the south and an east gate was located at the north-east corner of the wall. There may also have been a west gate, but if so it did not seem to lead to anywhere except the river bank.

The momentous upheaval of 1066 initially made little impact on Bristol but the following year two illegitimate sons of the defeated King Harold Godwinson came unexpectedly from Ireland and plundered the area around the Avon.

> [1067] They went to Bristol, and meant to break into the town, but the town-dwellers fought against them hardily; when they could win nothing

from that town, they went to ship with what they had plundered, so fared to Somerset, and went inland there.[2]

The chroniclers give but a brief description, though even these few words show that there must be more to the event. First, it seems that Bristol must have harboured a strong Norman force for the residents were not prepared to parley with the Saxons. Second, it raises the question of how Bristol held out against the siege for there was no castle in 1067. The Saxon town had rivers bordering it on three sides but it also had its defensive wall, probably of stone, and it seems that these defences proved sufficient against the Irish invaders.

Soon after the Norman Conquest we find evidence of an unwelcome trade in Bristol, one which is usually associated with a much later century but which flourished for several generations even though it was illegal in a Christian country: slavery. The Normans, with their hated feudal system of serfs and villains, had no need of slaves as such, but in Ireland, where Norse rule was still in evidence, there was a strong demand for slave labour and England was seen as a good source of supply. This white slave trade is too early to be well documented but the parallels with the eighteenth century are striking. While some of the slaves were convicted criminals, others were innocent people captured and torn forcibly from their own homes and families. They were chained or roped together for sale, not on some distant Atlantic shore but for all to see in the very market place of Bristol. The details would be hard to credit except for the evidence of William of Malmesbury who wrote within living memory of the events. The writer had studied the life of Wulfstan, the bishop of Worcester who, for reasons which will become apparent, was a constant visitor to the port of Bristow which lay at the southern boundary of his diocese.

> ... he removed from among them an ancient custom, which had so hardened their hearts that neither the love of God nor the fear of King William had so far been able to abolish it. For many people, brought from all over England, were dragged off to Ireland in hope of greater profit; they offered for sale slave girls, both virgins and those already with child. One could see the lament over the ranks of the poor wretches roped together, young people of both sexes, with the beauty of free men and unspoiled by age, who would be the objects of pity to barbarians, they were daily exposed publicly for sale. An accursed deed, and infamous disgrace for those not mindful of their brutal condition to give over to slavery human beings ...[3]

Wulfstan was appointed to the see of Worcester in 1062 and he died in 1097, so that although the events described belong to the earliest period of Norman history, the white slave trade was probably a relict from Saxon times. It appears from William of Malmesbury that the slave trade passed down from father to son and it therefore covered two or more generations. Wulfstan's standing in Bristol was high, so much so that when a ship from Ireland was wrecked and the sailors' lives were saved, the locals attributed the rescue to a miracle worked by him. He used his credit to great effect in his efforts to suppress the trade.

> This very ancient custom, handed down in families from father to son, Wulfstan, as I have said, gradually abolished. Gradually, for knowing that their stubbornness was not easily to be bent, he often stayed with them for two or three months, coming to that place every Sunday and scattering the seeds of his godly preaching, which grew with the passing of time so strong amongst them that not only did they put away that vice but they were an example to the rest of England to do the same ...[4]

William of Malmesbury's account implies that Wulfstan's perseverance paid off, but there is evidence that on his death the trade was still not fully abated. Other west coast ports were also involved with the trade but Bristol was probably the worst offender.

It was during this period that the Domesday Survey was conducted. The manor of Barton Regis, which included Bristol, rendered the considerable sum of 110 marks of silver annually to the Crown. The details are confusing and the survey concentrates on the number of plough teams and the agricultural worth of the manor. This survey of 1087 does not mention a castle at Bristol but a passing mention appears in the Anglo-Saxon chronicle for the following year. It may therefore be assumed that 1088 was the year in which the earliest castle was built.

The first castle was of the typical motte-and-bailey construction favoured by the Normans. The motte was a conical earth mound with a base diameter of about 40 metres, rising to about 20 metres and surmounted by a fort. The bailey was the area surrounding the motte, consisting of open space and buildings; the bailey enclosed about two acres, with room enough for a garrison. Motte and bailey were surrounded by an earth embankment, a massive stone wall, and a ditch which was connected to both the Avon and the Frome. It is possible that the mechanism of the drawbridge gave rise to the name 'Winch Street' for a thoroughfare which became known as Wine Street about four centuries later. This first castle served for only about thirty years until on the same site the construction of a great stone keep began, built under Bishop Geoffrey de Coutance and Robert, Earl of Gloucester. The huge keep was five storeys high and built with square towers on each corner. The walls of the bailey were strengthened and permanent stone buildings were constructed to house the garrison inside the walls. The castle stood in a narrow neck of land between the Avon and the Frome, and was on the east side of the town, thus guarding the only side which was not protected by one of the two rivers. The town walls were rebuilt in stone at this time but the Norman walls followed the same lines as the Saxon walls, except in the neighbourhood of the castle where the east gate was replaced by the Nethergate about a hundred metres to the south. A 'New Gate' was added near the castle and the Saxon gate was renamed 'Aldgate' (Old Gate). Blind Gate and Aylward's Gate may both be Saxon but it seems more likely that they belong to this early Norman period. Bristol became a formidable town which, with a strong garrison inside the castle, could be held against all but the most determined siege.

The castle entered into national history soon after its completion and it played a major part in the civil war which broke out between Stephen and Matilda, the latter being half sister to Robert of Gloucester. Matilda's forces were marshalled at Bristol Castle under the command of Robert of Gloucester and for the first time Bristol entered the centre-stage of English history. When Stephen was captured in 1141 he was held hostage in the castle for a short time. An anonymous author under the name 'Gesta Stephani' gives an account of the incident. Even at this early period he describes Bristol as 'well-nigh the most opulent town in the country … the most impregnable of English towns'. He talks of the shipping and merchandise, the strong tide of the Avon and the defences, but he is a supporter of Stephen and he does not think highly of the Bristol people:

> From one part of it, where it is accounted to be more open to attack, and more approachable, a fortress rises upon a lofty mound, and this being fortified by a wall, by bulwarks and towers, and various engines, bids defiance to all attacks. Into this city they collected such a great and wonderful crowd of horsemen and their train of footmen, nay, so to speak more truly, a heap of highwaymen and robbers, that it appeared not only very great and fearful to the beholders, but even horrible and surpassing belief …[5]

The writer goes on to describe how the men of Bristol ravaged the neighbourhood 'like a pack of hungry dogs' for provisions and goods of any kind:

> The men of Bristol then, with unbridled licentiousness, scoured the country with avidity and haste in every direction, when they heard of any lands or possessions which belonged to the king, or to those who were not on his side, ravening like a pack of hungry dogs over the carcass which is laid before them. Yokes of oxen, flocks of sheep, whatever tempting object either saw their eye, or their proud heart desired, they seized and took away, sold or consumed … if they heard of any rich or opulent persons … they bound up their eyes and gagged them, either with a lump of something forcibly thrust into their mouths, or with a little instrument made to fit the head, and furnished with teeth, after

the fashion of a sharp cut curb or bridle, and so led them away blind-
folded, and brought them to the middle of Bristol, like as we read of
the sepulchre of Elisha; and, by means of either famine or torture, they
forced from them everything they possessed, even to the last farthing.[6]

The whole fiasco was blamed on the 'men of Bristol', but it must
be acknowledged that these were not local people at all, they were
soldiers garrisoned in the town, carrying out orders and scavenging for
war.

The castle and the strategic importance of Bristol always brought
her into the centre of conflict when the struggles involved the West
of England, South Wales or Ireland. In times of peace, however, the
security of the town walls enabled Bristol to develop her social life and
trade. After the building of the castle religious development in the area
was so rapid that it can only be described as phenomenal, growing
from two small churches in the Domesday survey to no fewer than
seventeen by the end of the twelfth century, including eight priories
and three hospitals. Churches existed at both Westbury-on-Trym and
Henbury from as early as the ninth century, but in the middle ages
these places were detached villages well outside the town.

It was in about 1189, towards the last year of the reign of Henry II,
that Bristol received its first charter giving certain trading rights and
privileges. The written records up to this time are very scarce so that
we know very little of the gossip, the characters and the merchants of
these early years. The dates of most of the churches and religious
establishments are fairly well known, however, and it is therefore
possible to obtain a good ecclesiastical viewpoint of Bristol in the
twelfth and thirteenth centuries, just before the major extensions to
the town in the 1240s.

Both the church of St Peter's and the nearby St Mary-le-Port have
Saxon remains, but the more central church of St Werburgh's was
probably also Saxon and any of these three could have been the earliest
church in Bristol. The priory of St James, north of the Frome, was of
Norman foundation, and was built by Robert of Gloucester at the
same time as the castle, which gave rise to the story that every tenth
stone from the castle went towards the building of the church. In the
1140s the Abbey of St Augustine's was founded, also north of the town
and outside the walls. The chapter house, dating from 1155, was an
exceptionally fine piece of late Norman architecture. Nearby was the
church of St Augustine's the Less, first mentioned in the twelfth century
but on the site of a Saxon tombstone. The central churches of All
Saints, St Ewen and Christ Church were all built in the middle decades
of the twelfth century, and all were small churches with tiny parishes
of several hundred souls living in the tightly-packed medieval streets
of Bristol. At the north end of the bridge St Nicholas church was built

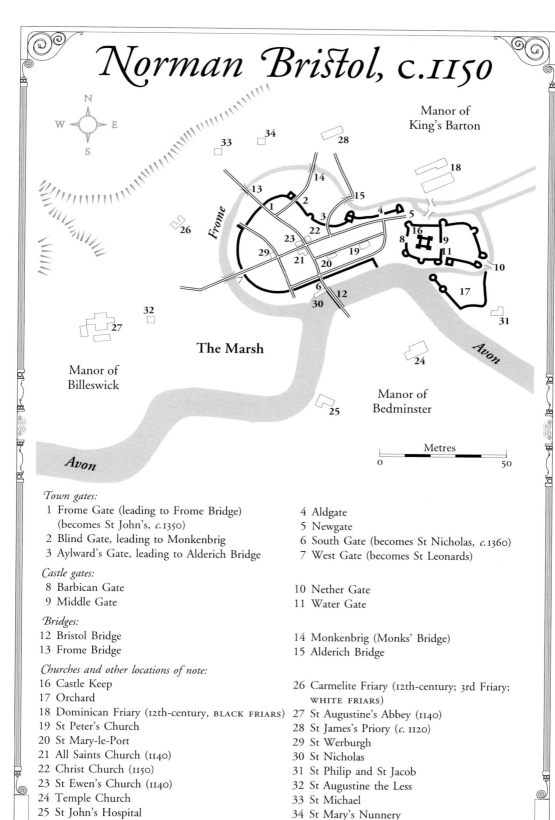

Norman Bristol, c.1150

Manor of King's Barton

The Marsh

Manor of Billeswick

Manor of Bedminster

Avon

Frome

Avon

Metres
0 — 50

Town gates:
1 Frome Gate (leading to Frome Bridge) (becomes St John's, *c.*1350)
2 Blind Gate, leading to Monkenbrig
3 Aylward's Gate, leading to Alderich Bridge
4 Aldgate
5 Newgate
6 South Gate (becomes St Nicholas, *c.*1360)
7 West Gate (becomes St Leonards)

Castle gates:
8 Barbican Gate
9 Middle Gate
10 Nether Gate
11 Water Gate

Bridges:
12 Bristol Bridge
13 Frome Bridge
14 Monkenbrig (Monks' Bridge)
15 Alderich Bridge

Churches and other locations of note:
16 Castle Keep
17 Orchard
18 Dominican Friary (12th-century, BLACK FRIARS)
19 St Peter's Church
20 St Mary-le-Port
21 All Saints Church (1140)
22 Christ Church (1150)
23 St Ewen's Church (1140)
24 Temple Church
25 St John's Hospital
26 Carmelite Friary (12th-century; 3rd Friary; WHITE FRIARS)
27 St Augustine's Abbey (1140)
28 St James's Priory (*c.*1120)
29 St Werburgh
30 St Nicholas
31 St Philip and St Jacob
32 St Augustine the Less
33 St Michael
34 St Mary's Nunnery

in 1148. It was no coincidence that this church was named after the patron saint of travellers and when the defensive walls were extended in the following century St Nicholas was rebuilt on the town wall. South of the Avon was the parish of Bedminster, where a chapel called St Mary's on the Red Cliff was commenced in 1158. St Thomas's church, named after Thomas a' Becket, and the church of the Knights Templar followed only a few years later. St Michael's (on the Mount)

Bristol Cathedral from the south, showing the east end of the cathedral, formerly the abbey church of St Augustine's.

The Chapter House of Bristol Cathedral, originally part of St Augustine's Abbey. The interlaced arcading, pillared and vaulted vestibule and ornate vault ribs make it one of the finest example of its kind in the country.

is first mentioned in 1147 and the chapel of St Brendon on 'Brendon' Hill also existed in the twelfth century.

The priories and friaries included St James (1120s), the Eremites (twelfth-century), the Dominicans (1227), the Franciscans (1234), the Carmelites (1245), and the Austin Friars (*circa* 1250). The nunnery of St Mary Magdalene existed in the twelfth century. The three hospitals were St John's (*circa* 1150), St Bartholemew's (*circa* 1220), and St Mark's, *alias* Gaunt's Hospital (1230).

The housing development and the trade of the port of Bristol obviously expanded as rapidly as did the ecclesiastical life, even though it is less well documented. Bristol became a thriving mercantile town with a population advancing from over a thousand towards two thousand by the year 1200. The centre of the Norman town was at the crossroads where Corn Street and Wynch Street met Broad Street and High Street, the latter being the route to the timber bridge across the Avon. The West Gate, Defence Gate and Pithay Gate all gave access to smaller bridges over the Frome. The New Gate was near the northwest corner of the castle wall and the Nether Gate, crossing the castle moat, gave access to the castle from the east, but did not give access to the town.

The shipping came right up to Bristol Bridge and cargoes were unloaded on both sides of the river. The Somerset side was not as well situated for the markets, but because of the bend in the river it had deeper water and was a better anchorage. Merchants on the Gloucestershire bank sought some means of expanding and improving their wharf space as the river traffic became progressively more and more chaotic. If Bristol was to expand its maritime trade a radical improvement in shipping facilities was needed. It was not only the wharf space which was inadequate; the old Saxon bridge could not cope with the amount of traffic crossing it. By the early thirteenth century the town had already outgrown its defensive walls and the prosperous expanding suburb of Redcliffe had no protection against invasion from the south.

An ambitious plan was formulated to build a trench 750 yards long — deep and wide enough to take ocean going craft — and to divert the river Frome from its course around the west wall of Bristol into this new channel. The new watercourse would provide as much mooring space as the Avon and it would double the number of ships which the port could service at any one time. The Redcliffe merchants, however, felt that they would not benefit from the new facilities and when they discovered that they were expected to shoulder part of the cost they became very much opposed to the scheme. The Gloucestershire merchants, on the other hand, were determined to have their way. They claimed that the works were of benefit to the whole town and

St James Priory church was founded in the twelfth century by Robert Earl of Gloucester, builder of Bristol Castle, who was buried in the nave. The church retains its original Norman nave and twelfth-century features on east and west walls.

Left: Norman masonry on the west wall.

they managed to obtain royal assent to go ahead with the plan. In 1239 the work was underway and the following year Henry III wrote personally to the Redcliffe men:

> ... Wheras our beloved burgesses of Bristol for the common good for the whole town of Bristol as of your suburb have begun a certain trench in the Marsh of St Augustine that ships coming to our port of Bristol may be able to enter or leave more freely and without impediment; which trench they will indeed be unable to perfect without great costs.

The gateway to St Augustine's Abbey still survives. The upper stages have been rebuilt, but the Norman stonework from about 1155 can still be seen with good examples of tracery and décor of the period.

We command you that, wheras from the betterment of the same port not only to the burgesses themselves but also to you, who are partakers of the same liberties which our aforesaid burgesses have in the town aforesaid and in scot and lot you are fellows with them, no little advantage ought to accrue. Moreover it may be very useful and fruitful for you for the work of the trench aforesaid to be perfected successfully according as it concerns you together with our aforesaid burgesses, to whom as sharers in the liberties aforesaid you shall give like efficacious aid as they themselves do, lest the aforesaid work, which we regard as our own, through your defection should receive delay.[7]

The Redcliffe men had some consolations. Their legal pleas were henceforth allowed to be heard in Bristol which saved them the long journey to the Somerset court at Ilchester – this was a forerunner of the application in the next century to make Bristol into a self governing unit. Other consolations were of a more practical nature. The old timber bridge was to be replaced by a new stone one with four arches, the new bridge to be bordered on both sides by shops and houses in a similar fashion to London Bridge. In addition, Redcliffe was to be protected by a new length of wall from a point on the Avon about three furlongs upstream of the bridge to a point about the same distance downstream. North of the river another new stretch of wall was planned over the marshy ground by the riverside to enclose the old course of

Left: St John's on the Wall. This is one of the best-loved churches in Bristol. It spans the only surviving medieval gateway.
Right: Temple Church: 'the leaning tower of Bristol'. The church was begun is 1398, and in 1586 Camden wrote that the tower 'has parted from the rest of the building, and left a chink from top to bottom three fingers broad, opening and closing as the bells ring.' Temple Church was destroyed in the Blitz, but the tower remained standing.

the Frome, thus extending the built up area within the protection of the walls both north and south of the Avon.

There is no contemporary account to describe Bristol at this time but in the 1240s it is unlikely that there was another town anywhere in the world which contained so much civil engineering activity. First a new channel was cut from a point on the Avon, above the Saxon bridge at the Temple meadows, to a point at Redcliffe Back. Then the whole river was dammed and diverted to flow through the new channel. A second dam was built just downstream from the bridge so that the townsfolk gazed down on a dry riverbed where their timber bridge had stood. The foundations for the new town bridge, to be built of stone, were under construction. In the bed of the Avon three central piers were built with a pier on each bank to give four stone arches supporting a road wide enough for houses and shops. When it was completed Bristol Bridge became a much sought after place to live, rentals being among the highest in the town – one of the main reasons for its popularity was probably the sanitary arrangements which were far more effective than anything in the heart of town!

In the south and the west of the town there were similar scenes of activity. Wooden scaffolding was erected in the Redcliffe area, and the ring of the masons' hammers and chisels clanged out day after day as the new walls took shape, complete with rounded towers at intervals and new gateways for the roads leading out of town to the south. But it was in the north, where the great new trench was being excavated to accommodate the seagoing maritime traffic of Bristol, that the most impressive works were underway. The River Avon had been diverted to give a temporary dry bed, and the river Frome was also to be diverted, but the new cut was a permanent feature and it was being excavated for a different purpose. Primitive cranes with wooden tread-mills were used for lifting the heavy stones to build the masonry quay on the Bristol bank, but the excavation of the trench must have been entirely manual. The ground was marshy and the work was excruciatingly wet and muddy. In the deep channel well below ground level hundreds of labourers scraped at the earth, shifting the mud and muck by barrow load up timber-lined ramps to the surface. Other workers hauled with ropes, rollers and levers to bring the cut stone from the local quarries to build the quay wall. It is rare to find harbour works on this scale in the middle ages with which to compare the new quay. The cost was five thousand pounds, an enormous sum of money for the times and comparable to that of the great castles and cathedrals, but the nature of the work was quite different: it was the work of man rather than the work of God. As such, it was much more in keeping with the canal and railway ages which lay far in the future.

By 1247 the great new trench was completed, the dam was broken

Bristol c.1250

after the diversion of the Frome

The 1240s represented a time of great expansion in Bristol. The diversion of the River Frome was completed in 1247 and was a major civil engineering feat which more than doubled the amount of wharf space in the port. The River Avon was also diverted so that a new stone bridge of four arches could be built on the dry riverbed. When the new bridge was complete the Avon returned to its old course and the diversion was retained as a moat for a new defensive wall.

Bristol was unusual in that it had not one but two sets of defensive walls at this time. The inner walls followed more or less the line of the ancient Saxon defences except that the new walls enclosed a much greater area as shown on the map. New gateways were constructed and fortified towers were

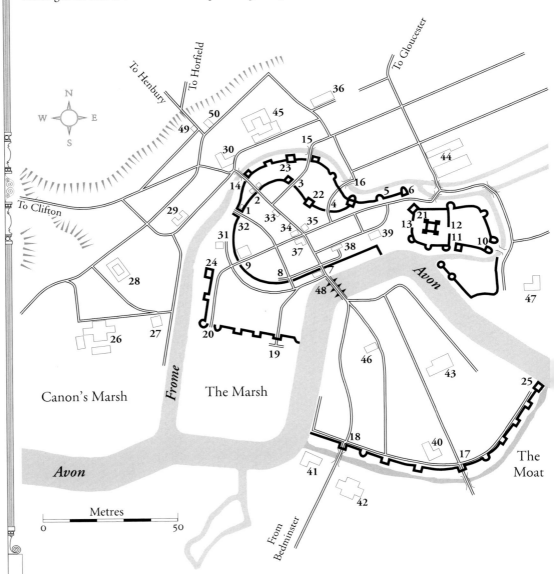

built at intervals along the wall. In the next century the inner wall was seen as almost redundant and the gateways had churches built upon them.

The wine trade was well established in the thirteenth century and represented the most valuable import into the port of Bristol. Bristol was a manufacturing centre for the woollen industry and the main export was cloth. Thomas Blanket from Flanders ran a weaving shop in Bristol and the blanket is supposed to be named after him. Lead from the Mendip mines was another important export which can still be found on the medieval roofs of cathedrals and castles across Europe.

The extra quay space created rapid maritime growth and the Avon became a very busy waterway. The re-developments proved very successful and Bristol became a trading centre comparable with York and Norwich. It was still more than a century, however, before Bristol became a county in her own right and nearly three centuries before she became a city.

Key

Gates on inner wall:
1 St Giles
2 North Gate (later St John's)
3 Blind Gate
4 Aylward Gate
5 Aldgate
6 Newgate
7 St Nicholas
8 Baldwin Steps (narrow footgate)
9 West Gate (later St Leonard's)

Castle gates:
10 Nether Gate
11 Water Gate
12 Middle Gate
13 Barbican Gate
    NB There was also Lawford's or Lafford's
    Gate to the east of the Castle

Gates on outer wall:
14 Frome Gate
15 Monkenbrig Gate and Bridge
16 Alderich Gate and Bridge
17 Temple Gate
18 Redcliffe Gate
19 Back Gate
20 Marsh Gate

Towers:
21 Castle Keep
22 Nightingale's Tower
23 Bagot Tower
24 Vyells Tower
25 Tower Harratz

Churches and other buildings of note:
26 St Augustine's Abbey (1140); Chapter House 1155)
27 St Augustine's the Less
28 Gaunt's Hospital
29 Carmelite Friary (12th-century; 3rd Friary; WHITE FRIARS)
30 St Bartholomew's Hospital
31 St Stephen's Church
32 St Giles Church (the name was also applied to the Gate, *see* number 1 above)
33 Guildhall
34 St Ewen's Church (1140)
35 Christchurch (1150)
36 St James's Priory (*c.* 1120)
37 All Saints Church (1140)
38 St Mary-le-Port
39 St Peter's Church
40 Austin Friary
41 St John's Hospital
42 St Mary Redcliffe (1158)
43 Temple Church
44 Dominican Friary (12th-century, BLACK FRIARS)
45 Franciscan Friary (1234, GREY FRIARS)
46 St Thomas (1195)
47 St Philip and Jacob (1174)
48 St Nicholas, *see* number 7 above)
49 St Michaels
50 St Mary's Nunnery

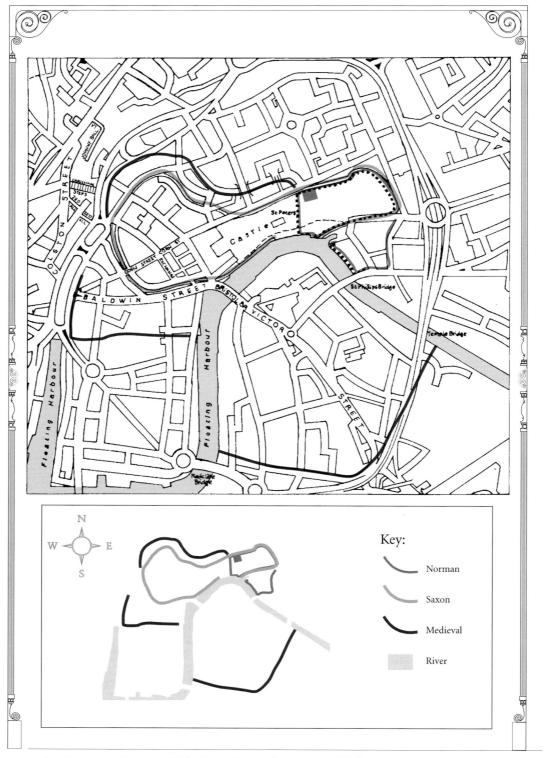

A plan showing ancient features of Bristol superimposed upon a simplified street map of the modern-day city centre.

and the waters of the Frome gushed into the new channel. The result was an immense success. It was a great day for Bristol when the first wooden vessels moored against the new quay. The new man-made harbour served the port for centuries to come and it must certainly be considered as one of the greatest civil engineering works of the middle ages.

CHAPTER TWO

Rebellion and Pestilence

It was the stronghold of Bristol Castle which dragged the West Country port, invariably against the will of the majority of its residents, into national politics. In the twelfth century the conflict between Stephen and Matilda was the first of these national incidents to involve Bristol. In the thirteenth century Princess Eleanor of Brittany was imprisoned in the castle until her death in 1241, the sole reason apparently being to prevent her from producing a legitimate Angevin heir to rival the Plantagenet dynasty. In 1254, the castle was granted as a marriage portion of Eleanor of Aquitaine, and it became an administrative headquarters for the region. A few years later Bristol became involved with the conflict between the barons, led by Simon de Montfort, and the Crown. De Montfort's army was stranded near Newport and he appealed to the Bristol merchants to send ships to transport his soldiers across the Severn. The merchants responded but the result was a disaster – the Bristol ships were trading vessels and were not equipped for war, so eleven were sunk in the Severn estuary near the Usk. De Montfort was forced to march north and cross the Severn near Gloucester, and the aftermath was his defeat at Evesham in August of 1265. Bristol was fined a thousand pounds for supporting de Montfort. The murage tolls, money used for the maintenance of the walls, were transferred from the town to the upkeep of the castle.

Thus the town and the castle were never amicable neighbours and it was early in the fourteenth century that friction between them reached a crisis point. A new royal constable, Bartholemew de Badlesmere, was appointed to the castle and the mayor and the residents were instructed to obey him 'in all things pertaining to his office'. The townspeople were expected to supply provisions for the castle, not simply food and fuel but also military supplies. A tallage tax was imposed and when the new duty was slapped on fish, the fishmongers refused to pay. The dispute grew from a point of principle to a major issue, the frictions increasing when the council of fourteen merchants who governed the town did not side with the fishmongers but gave their support to the new constable. The rebels found a leader in John Taverner, a merchant who had represented Bristol in the model parliament of Edward I and had twice been mayor of the town.

Taverner was elected Mayor in September 1312 and he quickly set about raising a local rebellion. Wooden barriers and siege towers were built at various points around the castle, and arrows and missiles were shot over the castle walls. The townsmen actually built a new crennelated wall, which they called the 'defence wall', between themselves and the castle. It crossed Wynch Street and Peter Street and lay along the line of what later became Dolphin Street. In 1313 John Taverner was captured by the king's men, taken to London and thrown into the Tower. This was very nearly the end of the rebellion before it grew to anything more serious, but for some reason the King released him on bail and he soon appeared back again in Bristol.

The Crown recognised that the Bristol merchants had a case and set up a royal commission of enquiry under Lord Berkeley to investigate the matter. However, the committee included many who had no connection with Bristol and the local people were very suspicious of the outcome. They did not wait for the findings of the enquiry. They took matters into their own hands, stormed the upper floor of the Guildhall where the meeting was taking place and held the commissioners prisoner. There followed an ugly scene with hand-to-hand fighting in the guildhall and the fighting spread to the streets outside. Some of the commissioners panicked and tried to escape by jumping from the first-floor windows, breaking their limbs on the street below. The fighting lasted for several hours and at the end of a bloody day twenty men were said to lie dead in the streets.

Edward II declared the Bristol men to be outlaws, but John Taverner still held power in the town and the rebels set up their own governing council. The Earl of Gloucester was instructed to march on Bristol with an army of twenty thousand. The force was easily large enough to re-take the town, but the date was 1314, the year of the English defeat at Bannockburn, so Gloucester's army never got to Bristol as it was quickly recalled to help defend the Scottish border. An extraordinary situation developed: the king's forces still held Bristol Castle, but Taverner's men held the rest of the town so that there was effectively a civil war within the narrow confines of the medieval walls.

The rebels had the support of some of the local barons but it was obvious that they could not hold out for long against the power of the Crown. Incredible as it may seem Bristol did in fact hold out as a rebel state for three years before any serious attempt was made to bring down Taverner's men. In 1316 a new enquiry was held, this time in London, and it came as no surprise that the enquiry found the Bristol men guilty. The rebels' defence was that they had merely been defending their rights. An account was given by Matthew of Malmesbury:

They had not been the beginners of the injustice, nor had they committed any fault as towards the king. Certain men had tried to take away their rights, and they, as became them, had on the other hand defended their rights; therefore, if their lord the king should remit the burdens laid on them, and should grant them their lives and limbs, their rents and goods, they would obey him as their lord and do all whatever he may command them; otherwise they would persist as they had begun, and defend their liberties and privileges unto death.[1]

The official report from the Crown describes the situation when the Sheriff of Gloucester arrived at Bristol in 1316 attempting to undertake his duties:

> The sheriff returned that he had gone in person to Bristol, and there in the guildhall had convoked the whole commonality, and had exposed them to the tenor of the king's orders, and all that the commonality answered unanimously that they would not allow any of the [guilty] men to be arrested and taken away; and when he had by word and imposition of hands arrested Henry le Shipman and many others, they forcibly broke the arrest ...[2]

The sheriff returned a second time with a larger posse of men from the county. This time he did not even gain entry, the castle ditch was drained and the castle mill was destroyed but the rebels had not actually taken possession of the castle. The sheriff described the scene as the great gates of the walls of Bristol were closed and barred in his face:

> ... the said sheriff, had gone again with a great posse of his county, when he found the gates closed against him, and the whole community, with a great multitude of evildoers, as well men of Bayonne as Welshmen, added to them, levied as for war against the king; that the commonality had drained and completely dried up the castle ditch, and broken down the castle mill, before the gate of the castle had made a ditch twenty-four feet broad and long, and fortified it with a strong [peel] tower, and there and elsewhere in the town had constructed barriers, chains, springalds,* and other engines to fight and attack the castle, so that no one in the castle could go out towards the town in any way, and they were preparing to hold the town against the king, and other open act of rebellion with banner raised.[3]

The king's officials had no option but to bring more forces to subdue the rebels. Lord Maurice de Berkeley blockaded the Avon and cut off all supplies by water. The sheriffs of Gloucester and Somerset together raised an army and advanced to the castle where heavy military catapults were installed to bombard the town. Huge stones soon reduced the defence wall to rubble and the townspeople found themselves under siege with their supplies cut off in what was a year of terrible famine and mortality. They surrendered.

---

* Something with a 'spring'. In this context probably a catapult.

Fines were levied, Bristol was forced to pay all the backlog of customs and tallage, but John Taverner was eventually given a pardon. Edward II appears to have treated the town with a consideration and leniency which seems out of character; either history has badly misjudged the king or he was not particularly interested in the rebellion and it was dealt with entirely by his subordinates. Discontent with the Crown simmered on, with several powerful local barons becoming so disenchanted with Edward II that they supported the insurrection and made Bristol a local centre of activity against the Crown. It was a losing battle, and in 1322 two rebels, Henry Wylington and Henry de Montfort, were captured and executed in Bristol. After the grisly fashion of the times their bodies were allowed to rot publicly for all to see – but local sympathisers reported that miracles happened at the gibbets where the bodies decayed.

The horror stories of Edward's reign continued as his supporters, the Despensers, were appointed constables of the castle. When Edward's fortunes collapsed Hugh Despenser the elder was ninety, but this did not prevent his enemies from butchering him and feeding his body to the dogs. Edward himself was imprisoned in Bristol Castle for a short time before being marched to his brutal murder at Berkeley Castle in 1327.

Even the Black Death, the worst of the great bubonic plagues of the middle ages, was a humane way to die compared to the sadistic horrors exercised in the name of justice by the inhuman power-mongers of the fourteenth century. The great pestilence devastated Bristol as much as any town in the country, and Samuel Seyer in his 'Memoirs of Bristol' gives a description from what he claims was 'one of our calendars':

> In 1348 the plague raged to such a degree in Bristol that the living were scarcely able to bury the dead. The Gloucestershire men would not suffer the Bristow men to have any access to them. At last it reached Gloucester, Oxford and London; scarce the tenth person was left alive, male or female. The churchyards were not large enough to bury the dead and other places were appointed. At this period grass grew several inches high in High Street and Broad Street; it raged chiefly in the centre of the city: this pestilence came from abroad and the people near the sea coast in Dorsetshire and Devonshire were first affected.[4]

The calendar from which Seyer quotes has never been found. Bristol was not a city at this time and the phraseology, even allowing for modernisation, does not have a fourteenth-century ring. Much as Seyer is respected as an historian he probably made this passage up. Replace the 'the tenth person' by 'one in two', however, and most of what he writes is probably true.

Weymouth is generally accepted as the port where the plague first came to England early in July of 1348. On the 15th of August Bristol became the first large town in England to suffer from the pestilence when the death of a priest was recorded at St Augustine's the Less. The town records for 1348 and 1349 are very few, partly because of the number of people who died in office. The most reliable sources are the ecclesiastical records and these show that in 1348–49 ten new incumbents were instituted out of a total of eighteen.[5] The Little Red Book makes no direct comment about the crisis, but on a list of 52 names representing the council in 1349, fifteen of the names are struck through. In another list of 52 names which appears in 1350, none of the names deleted from 1349 reappears and only three are struck through – it seems reasonable to assume that the names crossed through were victims of the plague.

The fourteenth-century population was reluctant to believe that their habit of using the street as an open sewer for human excrement, butcher's refuse and dead rats was a contributory factor to the plague. The authorities did have a vague notion of hygiene, however, and new laws were introduced to clean up the streets and to regularly cart away all ordure, entrails and rubble.

The Black Death was followed by a second outbreak of plague in 1361, which was said to differ from the earlier plague in that the wealthier classes suffered more than in the previous outbreak and the children were badly hit. The great plagues brought about a severe labour shortage and social conditions changed measurably in the latter half of the century. In 1377 a poll tax was levied on the whole population of England and for the first time it was possible to make reliable estimates of the population. The returns for Bristol show that 6,345 persons over the age of fourteen contributed, which implies a population of over 11,000. It is interesting to compare the Bristol returns with those of London (23,314), York (7,248), Coventry (4,817), Norwich (3,952) and Lincoln (3,412) – we see that at this time Bristol may claim to have been third largest town in the country.[6] It is also interesting to note how very rural England was at this time. Populous counties like Norfolk (88,797) and Kent (56,307) had rural populations far in excess of even London. If Bristol lost a third of its population through the two plagues then, allowing roughly for an increase after one generation, this implies a population of about 15,000 just before the time of the Black Death.

The daily life and business of the people had to continue in spite of the political upheavals happening around them. Most of the ships at this time plied along the English and Welsh coasts, with cloth and hides coming from Pembroke, tin from the Cornish mines and lead from the inland mines in the Mendips. Wine was imported from Portugal, Spain and France. There was also much Irish trade and fish came from as far away as the Icelandic coast. There was a lot of local

The Baker's Charter from 1347 shows the lockup and also the punishment for selling underwieght or poor-quality bread. The Bristol sled had evidently made its appearance as early as the fourteenth century.

inland traffic, the usual market produce, livestock and staple fare of the market town, but the most important of these was the woollen trade. The Cotswold towns and villages were the main suppliers of wool to Bristol and the Somerset towns were also major suppliers. The town itself was a manufacturing centre with weavers, tuckers, fullers, websters and tailors as common occupations and in 1337 we find Thomas Blanket from Flanders running a weaving shop in Bristol. At first there was some resentment at outsiders profiting from the Bristol trade, but the expertise of the Flemish weavers was instrumental in gaining a high reputation for Bristol cloth.* An illustrated manuscript from 1347 shows a baker, guilty of selling false measure, being dragged through the streets for public ridicule on a horse-drawn sledge. Thus the use of sledges in the narrow streets of Bristol dates from this time and probably earlier. Wheeled vehicles were banned because of a fear that they would damage the wine cellars and their valuable contents.

* The famed Bristol red cloth, however, belonged to a later century. The dye was imported from the New World.

Lord Mayor's Chapel.
The chapel was originally that of St Mark's Hospital, dating from about 1220. The tower can be dated to 1487. It became the church of Gaunt's monastery which was dissolved in the reign of Henry VIII. A few years later the chapel was bought by the new city council and became the Lord Mayor's Chapel.

Trade and regulations were incredibly well organised, and the guild system which jealously guarded the rights and privileges of all the trades and crafts was very highly developed for a provincial town. In 1344 the 'Little Red Book of Bristol' (so called because it was bound in a red deerskin) was commenced to record the rules and the trivia of day-to-day commerce. When the Little Red Book was found to be too small the Great Red Book was commenced in 1373, recording statutes and events very similar to its older but smaller brother.

There was one important issue, however, which the people found very frustrating. It was the boundary between Gloucestershire and Somerset – the old Saxon boundary between the ancient kingdoms of Mercia and Wessex. The Gloucester courts ruled north of the Avon, Somerset courts to the south, yet Bristol was obviously a single town and had functioned as such for more than three centuries. Towards the end of the long reign of Edward III the merchants put forward a petition for the whole of Bristol to be a self governing unit, to become effectively a county in her own right. This was a radical proposal, unprecedented in England, but the case was a good one. The king had suffered an expensive naval defeat at the hands of the Spaniards, and

The original
Bristol Cross may
have been erected
in 1373, when
Bristol was first
given county
status; it certainly
existed in the
fourteenth century.
The cross was built
up to its present
height in 1634 and
in 1736 it was
moved to College
Green. In 1764 it
was purchased by
Henry Hoare and
carted to his estate
at Stourhead.

John of Gaunt had wasted a fortune in a futile pompous parade from Calais to Bordeaux. Edward III desperately needed the money to continue the pointless war with the French which had only been going for a generation, but medieval mentality required it to keep going for a hundred years. The Crown needed the money, and the charter was granted in 1373 for the paltry sum of a hundred marks:

> 8th Aug., 47 Edward III [1373]
> We, at the supplications of our beloved mayor and commonality of the town aforesaid [Bristol], truly asserting the same town to be situate partly in the County of Gloucester and partly in the County of Somerset. We have granted by this our charter have confirmed for us and our heirs to the said burgesses and their heirs and successors for ever, that the said town of Bristol and its suburbs and the precinct of the same according to the limits and bounds, as they are limited, shall be separated henceforth from the Counties of Gloucester and Somerset equally and in all things exempt, as well by land as by water, and that it shall be a county by itself and be called the County of Bristol for ever ...[7]

The charter was written as an illustrated manuscript showing a merchant ship and the castle as the new coat of arms. It went on to describe the government of the town in great detail and to define the new boundaries, which included the islands of Steep Holm and Flat Holm in the Bristol Channel. It has always been assumed that the High Cross, which stood at the central crossroads of Bristol where High Street, Corn Street, Wine Street and Broad Street met, was erected to commemorate the event. The first mention of the cross is in the Little Red Book under the year 1403/4, when strangers selling smith-ware were required to 'stand in a place beside the high cross of Bristow openly so that the faults if any be of the said smith-ware may be overseen by the masters of the said craft'.[8] It is worth noting that the cross was already know as 'High Cross' even though it was originally only a fraction of its height in later centuries. An anecdote about the cross was recorded by William Wyrcestre in 1480:

> A certain Dynt, by craft a pumpmaker of the city of Bristol, told several men that he had heard from old people who used to tell him that they had seen a tree called in English a hawthorn growing in the High Street in the place where the splendid cross stands.[9]

If Dynt had heard the story fifty years earlier from a person aged eighty, then a date of 1373 is just possible for the cross.

It is a minor mystery why Bristol, the most belligerent and populous town in the West of England and with a history of rebellion and riot both before and after this period, did not support the Peasants' Revolt of 1381. Other West Country towns, notably Bridgwater, did have minor revolts. The reasons are complex, but one major factor seems to have been the general prosperity and high level of employment in Bristol at this period. Trade was excellent and was expanding rapidly, the great church of St Augustine's Abbey, destined to become Bristol Cathedral, was under construction and provided plenty of skilled and unskilled labour for local people. Across the river another great church was being rebuilt and provided almost as much employment; this was St Mary Redcliffe and we cannot help but feel that it reflected the old rivalry between the Gloucestershire and Somerset merchants, for the Redcliffe residents were determined to have the finest church in Bristol. St Mary's was already two hundred years old, but the Norman church was not grand enough for the Redcliffe merchants, so in the middle years of the century it was rebuilt in the new perpendicular and decorated style. The rebuilding was financed mainly by William Canynges, one of the wealthiest of the Bristol shipping merchants, and his grandson, also William Canynges, continued the work well into the next century. Other churches built at the same period were less opulent than St Mary Redcliffe but they were all quaint and attractive in their own unique way. St Stephen's was built in a prominent position on the quay in 1304, and was rebuilt and enlarged in the next century. The town had both an inner and outer set of defensive walls but neither set formed a closed circle because the quays and river banks were considered to be defensible without the need for a wall, which in any case would be a hindrance to trade. The inner wall was already seen as redundant and churches began to be built on it. The first of these churches was probably St Giles where the Jewish quarter had a synagogue in the disused crypt from 1275. St Nicholas was rebuilt on the wall soon after Bristol Bridge was completed and rebuilt again in about 1350 to include St Nicholas' Gate in its fabric. Soon afterwards the churches of St John the Baptist, St Leonard and St Lawrence were all built on the old inner wall and the gates were renamed after the churches standing over them.

To enter old Bristol for the first time was a moving experience. The town boasted nineteen churches, each with a spire or tower. Travellers from the north had a choice: there were two bridges – one led to the gateway beneath the church of St Giles and the other to the arches beneath the church of St John. Travellers from the south were obliged to pass over the Avon and beneath the imposing arch of a small but beautiful chapel, dedicated to the Assumption of the Virgin Mary, which was built to straddle Bristol Bridge. They entered the inner walls through the gate of St Nicholas. Inside the walls they found a busy town with narrow streets and overhanging upper stories, teeming with a population of over ten thousand. The massive keep of the castle overlooked the streets to the east of the town, while smaller towers occupied strategic points on the town walls. Dog sleds and horse sleds

Pie Powder Court. The plaque on the Stag and Hounds commemorates the last days of the Pie(d) Poudre Court (Court of the dusty feet). It was first mentioned in 1483 and was last held in 1850 on this site in Old Market.

rattled over the polished paving stones at great speed and every window and doorway displayed a trade or craft jealously guarded by the ordinances in the Little Red Book. Sometimes the fire of a baker's oven or a blacksmith's forge glinted from a yard at back of the shop. Food vendors abounded with cries of fresh bread, meat, fish and market produce for sale. Hooded friars walked the street in the white, grey or black robes of their order and churches and chapels stood on every corner. Beggars and prostitutes touted for money and custom. Housewives scrubbed at their washing on the slips by the riverside and others gossiped in the local accents as they drew fresh water from the wells and conduits. On the south bank of the Avon was a world of shipbuilding, of carpenters, shipwrights, smiths, rope-makers and sail-makers, with the a smell of hot pitch and newly-sawn timber. All the quaysides were hives of activity, especially when the tide chose to bring in the latest shipping from the wide world outside and foreign sailors leaned from the deck-rails to throw their hawsers over the bollards on Broad Quay. The flags of many nations flew from the masts in the harbour.

Towards the end of the fourteenth century the town records become more detailed and a clearer picture of local life emerges. Quaint customs appear, and although some of these are not recorded until next century they appear to originate from these times. One such custom was the 'Pie powder' court, a corruption of the Norman French 'Pied poudre', meaning the 'Court of the dusty feet'. The court was held on fair days at Old Market where the castle garrison came to purchase their provisions, and was a place where the poor could bring their grievances to the court and hopefully secure justice.

> They have hung the strips of crimson on the hostel porch to-day,
> Strewn the floor with sand and carpets where the Sheriff shall hold sway.
> Ranting rogues and pestering pedlars, rascals who have plagued the Fair,
> And the honest Bristol townsmen who have suffered will be there.
>
> Oyez! Oyez! Oyez!
>
> Pie Poudre Court is open to decide disputes arisen
> In the merry, merry Fair-time, and to cast all knaves to prison.
>
> When the court has meted justice, then great revellings begin,
> Pelting rascals up in Wynch Street, where in stocks they pay for sin,

To the top of Gallows' Acre, following them with song and shout,
Branding some and whipping others till the Curfew Bell tolls out.

Oyez! Oyez! Oyez!

Pie Poudre Court is open to decide disputes arisen
In the merry, merry Fair-time, and to cast all knaves to prison.

Rose Sharland: The Usher's Song

St John's Gateway.
The archway is
flanked by the
statues of Brennius
and Bellinus, the
legendary founders
of Bristol.

CHAPTER THREE

'New Founde Lande'

When Henry Bolingbroke, England's first Lancastrian king, deposed Richard II in 1399 the English found that they were not only fighting the French, they were fighting themselves as well. A town the size of Bristol had no option but to become involved in the civil war and three of Richard's West Country favourites, Scrope, Bushy and Green, were beheaded at the Bristol High Cross. The incident prompted Bristol's one scene in Shakespeare:

Richard II, Act III, Scene I: *Bolingbroke's Camp at Bristol.*

Enter Bolingbroke, York, Northumberland, Percy, Willoughby, Ross: Officers behind, with Bushy and Green, prisoners.

Bolingbroke. This and much more, much more than twice all this, Condemns you to the death. – See them deliver'd over To execution and the hand of death.

Bushy. More welcome is the stroke of death to me Than Bolingbroke' to England. – Lords, farewell.

Green. My comfort is, that heaven will take our souls, And plague injustice with the pains of hell.

By the middle of the century the Wars of the Roses were in full swing. Few people, even in Lancashire and Yorkshire, cared very much which of these great houses won the struggle for the throne; most of England wanted only a stable regime so that they could carry on their business in peace. This was certainly the case in Bristol where there was a lot of support for the Lancastrians at the outbreak of the war, swinging fickley towards the Yorkists as the latter gained the upper hand, and with full support for Henry Tudor when Richard of York was defeated at the Battle of Bosworth. Bristol contingents fought for the Yorkists at Towton in 1461 and again at the Gloucestershire battle of Nibley Green in 1470. When the Lancastrian Queen Margaret of Anjou arrived in 1471 the local people gave her gunpowder and supplies prior to the battle of Tewkesbury, which was fought only a few days afterwards.

In 1461 the Yorkist king Edward IV received a welcoming pageant from his Bristol supporters and he watched the public execution of

Mayor's Ceremony (Ricart). Ricart's *Kalendar* contains this valuable illustration of the swearing in of the mayor, with macebearers, councillors and public depicted in strict hierarchical order.

two Lancastrians at the High Cross in the town centre. Robert Ricart, the town clerk, recorded the event:

> This noble prince kynge Edward IV in the furst yere of his reigne came furst to Bristowe, where he was ful honuorably recyvid in as worshipfull wise as evir he was in eny towne or citee, And there was the same tyme hangid, drawen, and behydid Sire Bawdon Fulforde knyght and John Heyusaunt esquiere.[1]

In the fifteenth century there evolved a fashion to write up histories in a 'calendar' form. The calendar was not a day-by-day record but

Ricart's Plan of Bristol, from 1479, is the earliest town plan in Britain. The High Cross at the centre is easily recognisable as the top tier of the surviving cross at Stourhead. Four gateways are depicted – St John's, Newgate, St Nicholas' and St Leonard's.

rather a year by year record with events from national history thrown in for good measure between the more valuable local history entries.

'The Maire of Bristowe is Kalendar' is a well-illustrated document by the standards of the times. In it we see for the first time, in full colour, the new mayor standing beneath the royal arms and the Bristol coats of arms, splendidly attired in red scarlet cloth with fur trimmings, and the town clerk, Robert Ricart himself, reading out the oath. A sword bearer and eight mace-bearers stand in attendance. The councillors, also clothed in scarlet, are present and below are the burgesses, tradesmen and people of the town. The common crowd, although they are in the foreground of the picture, are depicted much smaller than the more important personages. Perspective was of no concern to the artist, it would have been unthinkable to depict the riff-raff as larger than their betters.

The same philosophy may be applied to Ricart's town plan of Bristol. The High Cross (Alta Crux) towers like a skyscraper above the tiled roofs of the town – Ricart saw the cross as the most important feature of Bristol. The gates of St John, Newgate, St Nicholas and St Leonard are shown, each correctly labelled and standing between grandiose oriental rounded towers with green conical spires surmounted by red globes. The plan would be of little use for finding Small Street but that is not the point. As the first ever town plan of Bristol, allowing for the times, it is a wonderful creation and the very first picture of the town.

In 1484 Ricart recorded a storm so violent that it was probably the greatest storm of the century. He claimed that over two hundred local people were drowned.

> This yere, the xvth day of Octobre, was the grettest flode and the grettist wynde at Bristowe and in the cuntrey there abouts the ever was seen, and grete hurt doon in merchaunts cellers in wode and salt; shippes lost at Kingrode, the Anthony of Bristowe and a ship of Bilbowe [Bilbao] set a lond at Holow bakkes, and other botes and cokkes lost; Saltmerssh drowned, corn, catell, and houses borne awey with the see, and moche people drowned, to the number of CC [200] and mo[re].[2]

Adam's *Chronicle of Bristol* describes the same storm but adds that there was an eclipse of the moon and gives a graphic description of an astronomical event:

> The moon being then eclipsed at the swelling of the seas gave but little light, appearing of diverse colours, viz. a strake of red beneath a strake of blue in the midst, a strake of green above that, so that at the top a little light appeared; and so she continued eclipsed and waxed clear again.[3]

Robert Ricart must have known his contemporary William of Wyrcestre who also wrote about Bristol at much the same time. Wyrcestre was a man of many interests and he had received the best education which Oxford could provide in his times. He was well informed on theology, medieval science, alchemy, astrology and mathematics – he was very skilled at calculating horoscopes from the positions of the planets. He was fond of herbs and the distillation of physic.

He calculated that 5189 years elapsed from Adam to the birth of Christ. He loved numbers and by some mystic process of cosmology he calculated the grand total of kingdoms in the universe as 18,446,073,709,551,615. He put his many talents to good use by becoming a writer, a traveller and a surveyor.

William Wyrcestre has a claim to be the first English topographical writer. He was born in Bristol, probably in 1415, and when in his sixties he paid two nostalgic visits to his birthplace, the first in 1478 and again in 1480 when he owned a house in the town. He must have been a conspicuous and eccentric figure always counting, pacing the streets and recording his findings to produce the most detailed of his many itineraries. He was, like everybody else, a prisoner of his times, but he was well ahead of his contemporaries in the Middle Ages in that he believed that his topological descriptions should include measurements

Tailor's Court. Hidden from view off Broad Street is Tailor's Court. The construction of the house shows it to be one of the oldest in Bristol, having been built possibly as early as the fourteenth century.

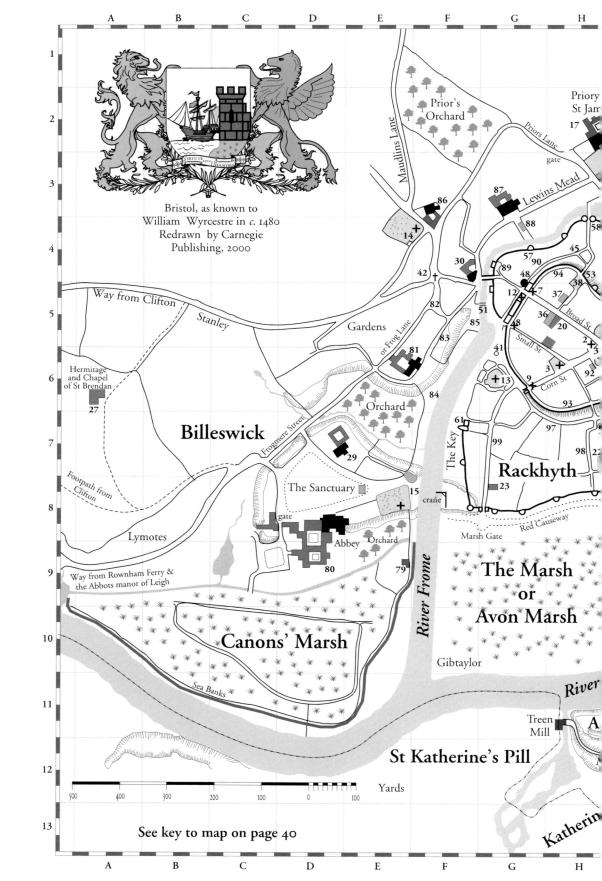

Bristol, as known to
William Wyrcestre in c. 1480
Redrawn by Carnegie
Publishing, 2000

Billeswick

Hermitage
and Chapel
of St Brendan
27

Way from Clifton

Stanley

Footpath from
Clifton

Lymotes

Way from Rownham Ferry &
the Abbots manor of Leigh

Frogmere Street

Gardens
or Frog Lane

Orchard

The Sanctuary

gate

29

Abbey
80

Orchard

79

15

crane

Prior's
Orchard

Maudlins Lane

Priors Lane

gate

Lewins Mead

Priory
St Jam
17

86
14

87

88

42

82

85

83

84

81

30

89
57 90
48
12
51

47 37
94
38
53
58
45

36
20
48
41

13

3
9

Corn St

Broad St

Small St

92

93

2
3

The Key

61
99

97

98 22

23

Rackhyth

Marsh Gate

Red Causeway

**The Marsh
or
Avon Marsh**

River Frome

Gibtaylor

Canons' Marsh

Sea Banks

River

Treen
Mill

A

St Katherine's Pill

Yards

500 400 300 200 100 0 100

Katherine

See key to map on page 40

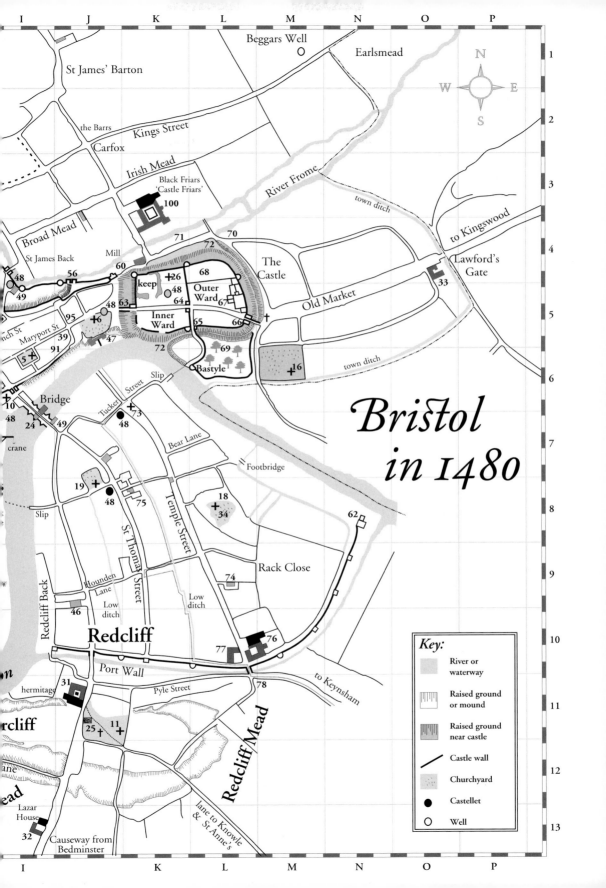

Bristol
in 1480

Key:

	River or waterway
	Raised ground or mound
	Raised ground near castle
	Castle wall
	Churchyard
●	Castellet
○	Well

Key to map of Bristol, 1480, on pages 38–39

Parish churches

1 H6 All Saints and the
       Kaledaries
2 H5 St Ewen
3 H6 St Werburgh
4 H5 Holy Trinity or Christ
       Church
5 I6 St Mary-le-Port
6 J5 St Peter

7 G5 St John Baptist & Gate
8 G5 St Giles & Gate
9 G6 St Leonard & Gate
10 I6 St Nicholas & Gate
11 J11 St Mary Redcliffe
12 G5 St Lawrence
13 G6 St Stephen
14 F4 St Michael

15 E8 St Augustine the Less
16 M6 St Philip and St Jacob
       (James)
17 H2 St James (Nave of Priory
       Church)
18 L8 Temple or Holy Cross
19 J8 St Thomas

Chapels

20 H5 St George (Broad St)
21 I7 St George (Welsh Back)
22 H7 St John Eucharist (Knapp's)

23 G8 St Clement
24 I7 St Mary on the Bridge
25 J11 Holy Ghost

26 K4 St Martin in the Castle
27 A6 St Brendan
28 H3 in St James's Churchyard

Hospitals

29 D7 St Marks
30 F4 St Batholomew
31 J11 St John Baptiste

32 I13 St Mary Magdalene
33 O4 Holy Trinity

34 L8 St Katherines (Weavers')
       (within Temple Church)

Centre

35 H6 The 'Tolsylle' (*see* Corn
       Street next to High Cross)
36 H5 The Guildhall
37 H5 Taylor's Hall
38 H4 Norman remains
39 J5 Bochery or Shambles
40 H6 Market Place
41 G6 Custom House

42 F4 Christmas or Knifesmith
       Street
43 H7 Baldwin's Cross and
       Steps
44 I7 Spicer's House and Chapel
45 H4 Lavanderies
46 J9 Canynges House
47 J5 Norton's House

48 G4, I4, K5, J5, I5, I6, K6, J8, Wells;
       castellets (*see* map key)
49 I5, J7 Public latrines
50 I5 Aylward Street
51 G5 Pillories
52 H5 High Cross

Inner Wall

53 H4 Blind Gate and Steps
54 H5 [Nightingales] Tower

55 I5 Pithay or Aylwards Gate
56 J4 Site of Aldgate (for gates

with churches *see* numbers 7,
8, 9, 10)

Outer Walls

57 G4 Bagot's Tower
58 H3 Monkenbrig & Gate

59 I4 Alderich Gate
60 K4 Newgate

61 F7 Vyells Tower
62 N8 Tower Harratz

The Castle

63 K5 Gate and Barbican
64 L5 Middle Gate
65 L5 Water Gate

66 L5 Nether Gate
67 L5 Hall and Chapel
68 L4 Great Garden

69 L5/6 King's Orchard

Other

70 L4 Ducking stool
71 K4 The Weare
72 L4/5, K4/5 Moat
73 K6 Stallage Cross
74 L9 Weaver's Hall
75 K8 Burton's Almshouses
76 M10 Austin Friars
77 L10 Spicer's Almshouses
78 L10 Temple Gate
79 E9 Grange
80 D8/9 Abbey of St Augustine

81 F6 White Friars (Carmelite)
82 F5 Steple Street
83 F5 Hare Street
84 F6 St Augustine's Back
85 G5 Prior's Slip
86 F3 Maudlin Nunnery
87 G3 Grey Friars (Franciscan)
88 G4 Spenser's Almshouses
89 G4 Frome Gate
90 G4 Grope Lane
91 J5 Worship Street

92 H6 Almshosues
93 H6 St Nicholas Street
94 H4 Tower Street
95 J5 Defence Lane
96 I7 Welsh Back
97 H7 Baldwin Street
98 H7 Baft Street
99 G7 Marsh Street
100 K3 Black Friars (Dominican)

to provide greater accuracy. He measured the length of Bristol Bridge to be 140 steps. The chapel of St Mary's on the bridge he paced out to be 36 steps long, which also gives some indication of the width of the bridge. He changed his mind, however, and reduced the former to 120 steps and increased the latter dimension to 40; then he reverted again to 36 steps for chapel length/bridge width but added the width of the chapel as 12 steps. The height of the bell tower he estimated as 90 feet and the spire above it as a further 18 feet. He paced out every street in Bristol. He gave the dimensions of every church. He counted the cellars street by street and gave the total number to be 130. He chatted to the porter of the castle to obtain its dimensions and he spent time gossiping with the hermit of Brandon Hill. He even watched the washerwomen scrubbing the clothes on the slimy slipways which led down to the River Avon.

William Wyrcestre died a few years after his second visit leaving his Bristol notes in a very haphazard form, but what he left was still a valuable contemporary record of a late medieval town. His interests also extended to shipping and he leaves us a marvellous and colourful description of the ships of all nations moored in the Severn, waiting for the tide to come in. When the tide covered the Black Rocks it was time for the sailors to hoist the sails for the last leg of their voyage. Some were arriving from distant realms and others were returning home to see again their wives and loved ones in Bristol:

> Black stones are in the Severn at Hollow Backs, 4 miles from Bristol [ie the Avon Estuary] beyond Hung Road, where ships and boats wait for the new tide. And the said small rocks are covered by the sea when the tide begins to flow from the Severn up to Bristol by King Road, Hung Road, Ghyston Cliff and —; no sooner has this flow of the sea begun than all the ships at the Hollow Backs from Spain, Portugal, Bordeaux, Bayonne, Gascony, Aquitaine, Brittany, Iceland, Ireland, Wales, and other parts weigh their anchors and set sail for Bristol.[4]

Wyrcestre gives us here a fair summary of the main shipping trade routes. Trade to the Mediterranean was rare, but he tells us that in 1446 Robert Sturmey despatched his ship, a cog called the *Anne*, through the Straits of Gibraltar with a typical West Country cargo of Cotswold wool, Cornish tin and Mendip lead. The *Anne* must have been a fair-sized ship for she also carried 160 very pious passengers, crusaders to the Holy Land. The first trading stop was at Pisa on the coast of Tuscany. The ship called at the port of Jaffa and the pilgrims eventually reached Jerusalem. On the return journey the *Anne* was sailing through the Pelleponese where she arranged to call at a Venetian-held fortress called Modon.* The pilgrims were looking

---

* The Methone of classical Greece.

forward to celebrating Christmas when the voyage ended in a sudden tragedy:

> ... the cog *Anne* was on the 23rd of December by a sudden storm and strong wind arising in the dark and dead of night suddenly and without warning driven on a rock and ashore, and 37 of the passengers and seamen were drowned, to the great grief of their friends in Bristol, and of their wives. But a certain devout bishop of Modon in Greece caused the bodies of the 37 dead to be honourably buried and he newly founded a holy chapel there to pray for their souls and for those of all the faithful departed.[5]

As the fifteenth century progressed the number and size of the Bristol ships continued to grow, and when the wealthy merchant Sir William Canynges died in 1474 nine ships are mentioned in his inventory, ranging from the *Galiot* of only 50 tons burthen to the *Mary Canynges* of 400 tons, the *Mary Redcliffe* of 500 tons and the massive *Mary and John* of 900 tons which cost him four thousand marks to build. Canynges employed 800 men in the Bristol shipyards where these ships were built. William Wyrcestre also recorded that one of Canynge's ships, of 160 tons burthen, was lost in the icy waters off Iceland. Was this ship a routine trader, or was it involved in a voyage of exploration? The answer may be significant in the light of later developments.

Trade between Bristol and Iceland was well established at this time. The outward cargo consisted mainly of cloth and manufactured goods, the return cargo was 'stockfish', a name given to dried cod from the Icelandic shelf. In 1477 a stranger from Genoa visited Iceland and started asking questions of the local people and also of the Bristol captains trading there. He had heard stories that the Bristol vessels were interested in exploring the seas beyond Iceland. The stranger picked up some curious stories: the Bristol sailors believed that islands existed in the seas to the west of Iceland; they had found a dark red wood floating on the Gulf Stream which they claimed was from a place they called the Isle of Brasil; they believed that another island called the Isle of the Seven Cities lay further west again. The stranger took due note, wanting as much information as he could gather. He had ambitions of his own to sail westwards into the Atlantic to try and find a new route to the Orient. His name was Christopher Columbus.

Unlike Columbus the Bristol merchants did not harbour romantic notions of a new route to the Indies. They had a more down-to-earth problem in that the powerful Hanseatic League was challenging their right to trade with Iceland for the stockfish. If islands did exist in the western seas then the Bristolians might be able to find new fishing grounds and make their trade independent of the Hanseatic League.

Cabot bronze,
by Stephen Joyce.
John Cabot
contemplates the
voyage to the west
in search of new
lands.

In July 1480 John Jay, a Bristol merchant who was related by marriage to William Wyrcestre, sponsored a ship of 80 tons to sail westwards into the Atlantic in search of the Isle of Brasil. William Wyrcestre was actually present in Bristol when the ship returned:

> On 15 July [1480] the ship belonging to —— and John Jay junior, of 80 tons burthen, began a voyage from the port of Bristol at King Road to the Island of Brasil to the west of Ireland, ploughing the seas for … Lloyd was master of the ship, the [most] competent seaman of the whole of England; news came to Bristol on Monday 18 September that the said ship had sailed the seas for about 9 months,* but had found no island and had been forced back by storms at sea to the port of —— in Ireland to rest the ship and the seamen.[6]

The next year there is a mention of two small ships, the *Trinity* and the *George*, setting sail on the same quest of 'examining and finding a certain island called the Isle of Brasile'. They were loaded with salt, which seems to imply that they hoped to make a good catch of cod. The Bristol records are silent about their fate. Later events indicate that they might in fact have discovered land but the evidence for this claim will be given when more of the story has unfolded. There is no doubt that the Bristol merchants were searching for land in the western ocean in the decade before Columbus and there is little doubt that the Genoese was well informed of their voyages.

It was in 1492 that Christopher Columbus made his epic voyage in the *Santa Maria*, with the *Pinta* and *Nina* in convoy. Columbus crossed the Atlantic and made a successful landfall but, as every schoolboy knows, he discovered the West Indies and not the American mainland. He returned to the Caribbean in 1494 and again in 1498, but it was not until this third crossing that Columbus reached the American mainland. He could not have imagined that his 1498 landfall was the same landmass as that of the cold northerly latitudes sighted by Bjarni Herjolfsson in 985, and where Lief Eriksson landed in about the year 1000. By the time Columbus landed on the American mainland he knew that at least one ship from Bristol had already crossed the Atlantic in northern latitudes.

In 1495 a Genoese merchant called Giovanni Caboto arrived in Bristol accompanied by his three sons Lewis, Sebastion and Sancius. He became known in England as John Cabot and he obviously knew of the Bristol voyages into the Atlantic sponsored by John Jay in the 1480s. Cabot, like Columbus, was interested in finding land to the west and in March 1496 he obtained letters patent from Henry VII 'to find, discover, and investigate whatsoever islands, countries, regions

---

* Seemingly an error meaning 9 weeks. Wyrcestre is correct in that 18 September 1480 was a Monday.

or provinces ... which before this time were unknown to all Christians.' Cabot lost little time and,
in the late summer of 1496 he made his first venture
into the Atlantic with a single ship. According to
the English agent John Day 'his crew confused
him, he was short of supplies and ran into bad
weather, and he decided to turn back.'

In the next year followed the most important
voyage ever made from the port of Bristol. On
about the 20th of May John Cabot sailed in a
three-masted caravel called the *Matthew* with a
crew of eighteen seamen. The days stretched to
weeks as the *Matthew* beat ever westward into the
setting sun, and the pole star lay to starboard as
she sailed through the Atlantic night. The voyage
was in midsummer; the longest day came and went
with still no sign of land. But on June 24th there
was great rejoicing aboard the ship; to the great
delight of the sailors the sea abounded with fish,
but far more significant was that a new coastline appeared on the
horizon. The *Matthew* approached the coast and searched for a place
to land. John Cabot went ashore and planted the English flag on the
new found land. The findings were described in a letter from John
Day to Christopher Columbus:

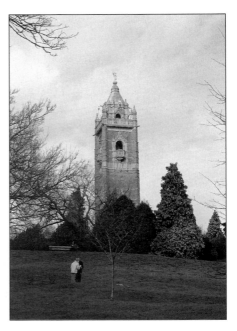

Cabot Tower, built
in 1897 to
commemorate the
400th anniversary
of John Cabot's
voyage to
Newfoundland.

> ... and they found tall trees of the kind masts are made, and other
> smaller trees and the country is very rich in grass. In that particular spot,
> as I told your Lordship, they found a trail which went inland, they saw
> a site where a fire had been made, they saw manure of animals which
> they thought to be farm animals, and they saw a stick half a yard long
> pierced at both ends, carved and painted with brazil, and by such signs
> as they believe the land to be inhabited. Since he was just with a few
> people he did not dare advance inland beyond the shooting distance of
> a cross-bow, and after taking in fresh water he returned to his ship. All
> along the coast they found many fish like those which in Iceland are
> dried in the open and sold in England and other countries, and these
> fish are called in England 'stockfish'; and thus following the shore they
> saw two forms running on land after the others, but they could not tell
> if they were human beings or animals; and it seemed to them that there
> were fields where they thought might also be villages, and they saw a
> forest whose foliage looked beautiful.[7]

The *Matthew* spent about two weeks exploring the coast to the
south. She then headed back to the east and with the help of the
prevailing winds swelling the sails she made a landfall in Europe after
a crossing of only fifteen days. Cabot's crew confused him again, as

they had done the previous year. His landfall was well to the south, in Brittany. This implies either that the skies were never clear enough to measure the sun's altitude or that Cabot was not skilled at finding his latitude. On the sixth of August Cabot was back in Bristol; by the tenth he was in London telling the king of his new discoveries.

John Cabot, like Columbus, was convinced that he had found a shorter route to Asia, and he made another voyage in 1498, this time with five ships. Little is known of the fate of this expedition. Only one ship returned, badly damaged, to Ireland and it is thought that Cabot died on the expedition. It was early in the same year that an Englishman called John Day, alias Hugh Say, wrote a letter to the Spanish 'Grand Admiral', none other than Christopher Columbus, with details of the Cabot expedition as quoted above. The letter, written in Spanish, lay undiscovered in the castle of Simancas, central Spain, until 1955. The account adds fascinating details related to the story. It implies that a landfall was made in the Atlantic Ocean by the Bristol men before Cabot and before Columbus! Furthermore Day implies that Columbus knew of this discovery:

> It is considered certain that the cape of the said land was found and discovered in the past by the men from Bristol who found 'Brasil' *as your Lordship well knows*. It was called the Island of Brasil, and it is assumed and believed to be the mainland that the men from Bristol found.[8]

Other adventurers followed Cabot, and in 1501 three Bristol merchants, Richard Warde, Thomas Assehurst and John Thomas, petitioned Henry VII to set off on a joint expedition with three Portuguese merchants to 'seek out and discover some islands lying in our sphere of influence'. In the same year the Bristol 'Company Adventurers into the New Found Lands' was formed and was granted letters patent for voyages of discovery and annexation.

The Bristol voyages leave a great many unanswered questions. Where was the land 'found and discovered in the past by the men from Bristol' mentioned in John Day's letter? Was this same land as that found by John Jay's second expedition of 1481? Where was the first point on the American coast seen by John Cabot's crew from the *Matthew*? Where did John Cabot first set foot on the American mainland?

The claim that Cabot was the first European to re-discover the American mainland is perfectly valid. There is no doubt about Cabot's crossing of the Atlantic, but his voyage is not well documented and we have to rely on secondary sources for information – in fact, we know more about it from the Spanish records than from the English.

The ships' logs, if they ever existed, have not survived. All information is second hand from letters, gossip, speculation and deduction. Cabot realised the possibility of a new sea passage to the Orient, but the Bristol men wanted no more than new fishing grounds for the humble cod. Their voyages are very poorly documented. They had no way of finding an accurate longitude and even the latitude of Newfoundland was not recorded.

The voyage of Columbus enjoyed royal sponsorship, it is well documented, and it had the glamorous attraction of being a new route to the Orient. Columbus used the power of the new printing press to advertise his discoveries, while his son Fernando wrote a biography which was widely read. John Cabot's son Sebastion is thought to have sailed on the *Matthew*. He lived for nearly sixty years after the voyage but at no time did he describe or write up the dramatic events of his father's voyage for posterity. Perhaps the English were jealous and secretive of their new fisheries. Perhaps they thought a new island in the cold Atlantic was no great discovery. But in 1509 Sebastion Cabot did venture to cross the Atlantic with two ships and three hundred men. He claimed to have sailed the east coast of the mainland both south and north further than any before him.

The extent of the new continent soon became very evident. Sebastion Cabot's account was published many years after the voyage but it is unconvincing and contains anomalies. The geographer Roger Barlow, writing in the sixteenth century when the Spanish treasure ships were carrying their gold back to Spain, summarised the English achievements:

> The New Founde Lande which was fyrst discovered by the marchants of Brystowe ... But whereas our Renglishe marchantes of Brystowe dyd enterpryse to discover and discovered that parte of the land, if at that season they had folowed toward the equinoctiall, no dowt but they shuld have founde grete riches of gold and perle as other nations hath done sence that time.[9]

In 1897 a hitherto unknown roll of accounts was discovered in the archives of Westminster Abbey. It showed that in 1498 one of the collectors of customs at Bristol was called Richard Ameryk. He was the man responsible for the payment of John Cabot's pension and the name has prompted much speculation about the naming of America, a claim which is very difficult to substantiate.[10]

One thing is clear; at the end of the fifteenth century neither Columbus nor Cabot knew that he had discovered the same new continent. It took another generation of exploration before the discoveries in north and south began to be pieced together and it was realised that the landfalls were not isolated islands in the Atlantic

John Cabot's ship the *Matthew* is thought to have been a three-masted caravel. On the five-hundredth anniversary of the voyage a replica was built to sail from Bristol to Newfoundland. It was built by traditional methods and is as close to the original as possible within the limits of our knowledge.

Ocean. It transpired that there was a whole coastline running almost from pole to pole – far out across the western ocean there was a whole new continent. The Tudor age was a reality by 1485 but it was not until the next century that Bristol merchants realised that their port was no longer a peripheral on the western boundary of the civilised world. It was destined to become a key point for the discovery, colonisation and trade with the new continent. Whatever the answers to the questions, one thing is clear. John Cabot, the Bristol seamen and the Bristol merchants played a critical leading part in the discovery of the New World. This contribution is seldom fully appreciated, even in Bristol, and certainly not in the rest of England.

CHAPTER FOUR

Tudor 'Brightstowe'

Our greatly to be dreaded defender of the faith, King Henry the Eighth, was firmly established on the throne of England. There were wars to be fought against the belligerent foreigners and Henry needed more money. The monasteries had plenty of money which didn't seem to circulate very much, so why not dissolve them to help fill the royal coffers?

Thus it was that in 1535, when Richard Layton arrived in Bristol from Glastonbury, he wrote to inform Thomas Cromwell that he had closed down Gaunt's House with four or five canons and St Augustine's Abbey, which had fourteen canons. He enclosed relics which included two holy flowers which would spring forth and bear blossoms on Christmas Eve, a bag containing 'Gode's cote, our Ladie's smock, parte of Gode's supper' and a fragment of stone from the manger at Bethlehem.

In Bristol the dissolution of the monasteries was effected with a minimum of disturbance and there was no rebellion to compare with the Pilgrimage of Grace which affected the northern counties. Bristol was not a central point for the religious conflicts of the times but it did not escape horrors such as the burning of Christian martyrs. In the previous century, when the Lollard movement was gaining support in Bristol, William Smith was burned at the stake for his heretical beliefs. In 1556, when Catholicism had been reinstated under Queen Mary, we have a description from Foxe's *Book of Martyrs* of William Saxton, a weaver who was burned at the stake on 18 September:

> … as he went to fire, he sung psalms. The Sheriff, John Griffiths, had prepared green wood to burn him; but one master John Pikes, pitying the man, caused divers to go with him to Redland, half a mile off, who brought good store of helme-sheaves, which indeed made good dispatch with little pain, in comparison that he should have suffered with green wood. In the mean space, whilst they went for the sheaves, the said Saxton made many good exhortations to the people, and died constantly and patiently with great joyfulness.[1]

When the traveller John Leland arrived at the gates of Bristol, the chapel of St Mark, which belonged to the monastery at Gaunt's House, had been bought by the corporation and was being used as the Lord

The gateway and some of the fabric of St Bartholomew's Hospital still survive near the bottom of Christmas Steps. In Tudor times the building housed Bristol Grammar School.

Mayor's chapel. Leland listed the churches and chapels in Bristol, and although much of his description echoes that of William Wyrcestre sixty years earlier, there were important differences. By Leland's time all the monastic houses were closed and had become Crown property. Equally significant was the fact that the new Bristol was no longer a common town; she had a cathedral and for the first time she could call herself a city. For a few decades Bristol seems to have re-acquired her Saxon name 'stow' and almost got the 'bridge' back into her name:

The Site of Brightestow
    The castle and moste parte of the towne by northe stondithe apon a

grownd metely eminent betwyxt the ryvers of Avon and Fraw, alias
Frome.

There ryseth an hill of an notable highte in respect of the plote of the
towne selfe from Frome bridge on, so goyeth up along onto Seint Austin's,
alias the Trinitie, the cathedrall church, and there endithe.[2]

Leland declined to give any details of the new cathedral. Perhaps
he was too polite. It had the finest Norman chapter house in England
but the church itself was the poorest cathedral in the country and it
bore little comparison to the magnificent edifices in older established
cathedral cities. The cathedral was formerly the church of the Abbey
of St Augustine's which was dissolved in 1539. At the time of the

Christmas Steps.
'Christmas Street'
was a corruption
of 'Knifesmith
Street', showing
the original trade
in this part of
Bristol. The street
was stepped in
1669 and it now
retains an
immensely quaint
character
reminiscent of old
Bristol.

dissolution a new nave was under construction around the old Norman church and the whole of the west end had been demolished – there was therefore only half a cathedral for John Leland to see. Time and money were needed to remedy the situation and to build a cathedral worthy of the new diocese, but in the chaos of the Reformation, and with the Tudor fashion of changing religion with each new monarch, neither Protestants nor Catholics were very enthusiastic about rebuilding the church only to see it change to a rival denomination a few years later. The situation was not helped by the creation of the new Bristol diocese which was an excellent example of the worst features of committee design and consisted of the Bristol parishes, a few token parishes in the south of Gloucestershire and the Archdeaconry of Dorset. It mostly comprised the parts that Gloucester and Salisbury dioceses found unprofitable, so consequently no money was forthcoming for the new cathedral and it was destined to be four centuries before the Victorians built a respectable west nave to balance the east.

A curious local ceremony is mentioned in Ricart's Kalendar (which was continued long after Ricart's death):

> After dinner, the said Mayor, Sheriff, and their brethren to assemble at the Mayor's compter, there waiting the bishop's coming, playing the meanwhiles at dice, the town clerk to find them dice, and to have one penny of every raffle; and when the bishop is come thither, his chapel there to sing, and the bishop to give them his blessing; and then he and all his chapel to be served there with bread and wine. And so depart the Mayor, Sheriff, and their brethren to hear the bishop's evensong at St Nicholas Church.[3]

This custom was known as the ceremony of the Boy Bishop. According to the historian John Latimer it was practised in 'all parts of the kingdom', but the Bristol version seems like an excuse for the council to play at dice while a madrigal boy paraded around in bishops' robes.

John Leland described the city walls and the gates. He gives a detailed description of the castle moat arrangement, the two courtyards and the ruined towers:

> The ryver Frome ran sumetyme from the were [weir] by the castle, where now is a stone bridge doune by the este syde of it; and so doithe yet a litle armelet of it brekynge out, and almoste the hole streme goithe by the northe syde of the castle, and there goeth by a New Gate under an arche.
>
> In the castle be 2 cowrtes. In the utter courte, as in the northe west part of it, is a greate dungeon tower, made, it is sayde, of stone browght out of Cane in Normandye be the redde earl of Glocestar.
>
> A praty churche and muche longging in 2 area. On the southe syde of it a great gate, a stone bridge, and 3 bullewarks *in laeva ripa ostium Fria.*

There be many towres yet standynge in bothe the cowrtes; but all tendithe to ruine.[4]

He lists the churches within and without the walls, the suppressed monasteries, the many hospitals, the 'greate bridge of 4 stone arches ovar the Avon' and the lesser bridges over the Frome. He was impressed by the efficient water supply and he gives a list of the pipes and conduits bringing water into Tudor Bristol. Leland was historian enough to discover the story behind the main quay; he gained access to Ricart's Kalendar and put together an excellent description of the three hundred year old works when the broad and narrow quays were built:

> The shipps of olde tyme cam only up by Avon to a place caullyd the Bak, where was and is depthe enowghe of watar; but the botom is very stony and rughe sens by polecye they trenchid somwhat a-lofe by northe west of the old key on Avon anno 1247 and in continuance bringyge the cowrse of From ryver that way hathe made softe and whosy harborow for grete shipps.[5]

Another traveller, Roger Barlow, described the town at almost the same time as John Leland. He too was impressed by the number of

Old Bristol Bridge.
Above: A detail of Millerd's Map of Bristol, 1673, showing the area around Bristol Bridge and the Chapel of the Assumption spanning the bridge. The height of the arches is not indicated, but Millerd's drawings imply that only small craft were to be found upstream.
Left: One of Millerd's marginal drawings showing the arches and the housing on Bristol Bridge.
The arches were about 30 feet high and the river banks a similar depth to allow for the exceptionally high tides that occur at Bristol.

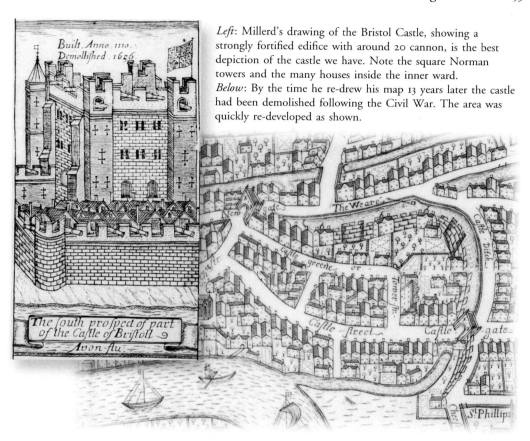

Built, Anno, 1110.
Demolished, 1656.

The south prospect of part of the Castle of Bristoll
Avon flu:

Left: Millerd's drawing of the Bristol Castle, showing a strongly fortified edifice with around 20 cannon, is the best depiction of the castle we have. Note the square Norman towers and the many houses inside the inner ward.
Below: By the time he re-drew his map 13 years later the castle had been demolished following the Civil War. The area was quickly re-developed as shown.

ships, the Quay and the Backs, and the obvious volume of trade in the town:

> ... a noble town of grete trade and many ships belonging to it. It hath a goodlie haven that cometh through the towne and a sumptuous bridge over it of lyme and stone after the manner the bridge of London. The shippes and botes comen in to ii partes of the towne, one is called the Backe, the other the Key, and ii leages from the towns is the river of Severne, ther is a goodlie rode called Kyngrode and another within that called Hungrode, wher ryde the shippes that liste not to come before the towne ...[6]

Bristol Bridge, with only four arches, was very small compared to London Bridge, but travellers frequently made comparisons. The bridges were built within sixty years of each other, both were built up as streets with housing on either side, both had chapels built on the bridge and both had such massive piers that they resembled a weir with the waters flowing through the narrow arches between the piers. The tides at Bristol Bridge were so high that to take a boat through

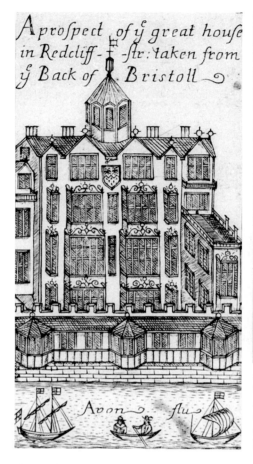

A prospect of y̌ great house in Redcliff-str: taken from y̌ Back of Bristoll

Avon ⁓ flu ⁓

Left: Canynges Great House was on Redcliffe Back, with acccess to the Avon at the end of the garden.
Above: This rear view of the Red Lodge in Park Row shows the house's antiquity. The lodge was built around 1590 by John Young at the end of the garden of his Great House at St Augustine's Back.

the arches when the tide was running strong could be compared to shooting the rapids. The records show that in 1548 the Council built two new houses on the bridge. They were of typical Tudor construction – timber-framed with brick chimneys and fireplaces, and with 258 square feet of expensive new glass costing sixpence per (square?) foot. Two of the newly dissolved Friaries provided ornamental stonework. The houses took 86 weeks to complete and cost £495 13s. 9d. but they became two of the most desirable residences in Bristol at a rental of £6 13s. 4d. per annum.[7]

If a picture is worth a thousand words then a map is worth five thousand. Discounting the artistic licence of Ricart's fifteenth-century town plan, the first contemporary map of Bristol was 'measured & laid in Platforme, by me, W. Smith, at my being at Bristow the 30 & 31 July Ano Dni 1568'. William Smith's plan shows the streets, city gates, walls and castle, houses with tiled roofs, the churches with their small plots of land, and even the little chapel on Bristol Bridge. The castle moat is depicted as too wide and too perfectly circular to be accurate and other minor details are imperfect, but as a piece of Tudor cartography the map is reasonably accurate and informative.

In 1581 came Hofnagle with his plan of 'Brightstowe', an enhanced view containing a little more detail than William Smith and populated by strolling Tudor residents in the foreground and cattle grazing on the outskirts of the city. His debt to Smith is obvious and it is difficult to identify any major changes in the intervening 13 years except that Hofnagle wrongly omits to show the chapel on the bridge. He shows that the city had expanded beyond the medieval walls, but that the number of houses outside was still very few. The outer walls from the thirteenth century are shown as almost complete but the inner walls are very fragmentary, with only the stretch from St John the Baptist to Pithay Gate still intact. A curious feature shown by both carto-graphers is the existence of a stretch of water between the walls on the west, clearly part of the old course of the Frome. Did Bristolians really retain a pool of filthy stagnant water in the midst of their town for over three hundred years, or was this a fanciful invention of the map makers to show a part of the past history? The question is difficult to answer.

On Saturday the 14th of August 1574 there was great excitement in Bristol. The Lord Mayor, Thomas Kelke, and his councillors waited in their ceremonial attire at Lafford's gate on Old Market for a royal procession to arrive. The occasion was the visitation of England's virgin queen, Good Queen Bess.

The queen entered the castle grounds through Lafford's Gate where the mayor presented the city's gilt mace to her majesty as a symbol of her sovereignty over Bristol. The queen graciously returned the mace. The mayor knelt meekly before the queen whilst the recorder, John Popham, delivered an oration and presented her majesty with a silk purse containing a hundred pounds in gold. Then there was a clanging of metal chains as the great barbican gate of the castle was opened and the procession entered the packed streets of Bristol where a cheering multitude of people waited to get a glimpse of their queen. The mayor rode proudly between two sergeants at arms, in front of the queen and her retinue. Then came the common council, followed by the nobility and a great fanfare of trumpeters. The procession was very long and at the rear were four hundred soldiers in livery, three hundred harque-busiers and a hundred pikemen attired in white corselettes.

It was well known that Elizabeth loved pageants and Bristol was determined not to disappoint her. A great fort had been constructed by the quay with a smaller fort standing on the hill beyond. A timber scaffolding was built in the Marsh to enable the queen and spectators to get a grandstand view of the proceedings. The smaller fort was taken in the first day but the larger fort was assaulted from land and water

'Among the fairest is St Mary de Redcliffe, without [i.e. outside]
the walls, with a grand ascent of steps, the whole so spacious and
well built, with an arched roof of stone and a lofty steeple, as to
exceed, in my opinion, all the parish churches of England ...'
(William Camden, 1586).

The small north porch (1320) can be seen bottom right.
Rebuilding of the church commenced in the mid-fourteenth
century in the new Perpendicular style, funded mainly by the
Canynges family. It took over a century to complete but the result
was magnificent, with flying buttresses not only on the nave but
also on the transepts. The spire fell in 1445/46 after it was struck
by lightning, but it was still some 200 feet high and Camden does
not appear to have noticed its truncated remains. Little says that
the 'thoroughfare' referred to (*bottom left*) ran under the floor of
the church!

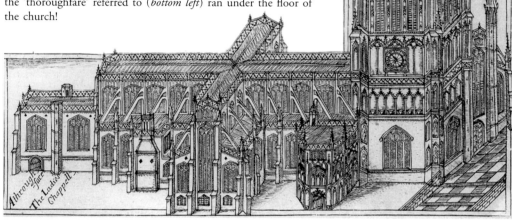

in a mock battle which lasted for four days. The queen had to listen to
boring speeches and bad poetry, which she suffered without complaint.
The military experiment cost a fortune in gunpowder but Bess was
well pleased with it. There is no doubt that she thoroughly enjoyed
her visit and the hospitality of the people and she 'gave Mr Maior and
his brethren great thankes for theire doinges'.

Queen Elizabeth is said to have described St Mary Redcliffe as 'the
fairest, goodliest, and most famous parish church in all England' – a
remark which is repeated *ad nauseam* every time St Mary's is mentioned. If the spire of St Mary's had not been struck by lightning
and fallen in the previous century then her remark would have
been closer to the truth. The source of her quotation has never been
found but it is suspiciously like that of a later Tudor visitor, William
Camden:

> Among the fairest of the latter [churches] is St Mary de Redcliffe, without
> the walls, with a grand ascent of steps, the whole so spacious and well
> built, with an arched roof of stone and a lofty steeple, as to exceed, in
> my opinion, all the parish churches of England that I have yet seen ...[8]

When the Spanish Armada set sail to invade England, only four ships sailed from Bristol to join Drake's fleet in the English Channel. This may indicate Bristol's low fortunes at the time, but it also indicates the very different nature of the seaports of Bristol and Plymouth. Where Plymouth was a naval port Bristol was a merchant port and the traders were very anxious to maintain good relations with the Spanish. When news of the defeat of the Armada reached Bristol there were some celebrations, but the wine merchants were not happy with their loss of trade and they did not see Drake as a national hero. The Spanish wars contributed measurably to the decline in trade, though it was not the only factor. In 1579 a quite different incident is recorded which seriously hindered the shipping in and out of Bristol for half a year. An accident at Hungroad involved two large ships and blocked the shipping lanes:

> In this yeere being the xxvth [of Queen Elizabeth, a mistake for xxi] the shipp called the Golden Lyon of Bristoll, beinge of the burthen of v c. ton [500 tons] and also accordinglie appoynted, came from Andoluzia but not all laden, and being in Hungrode, for lake of good attendance and want of ankers and suche like, was overthrowen and sonke in the river, and by her overthrowinge did sinke a new hulke which was mored by her, the which hulke was of iiij c. ton [400 tons], soe that the river was in greate dainger utterlye to have pirished, yfe great and diligent care had not bene presentlie executed by the Maior and Comminalitie, who gave great enterprises with shipps caskes, liters, and bootes, to recover the same, yet notwithstandinge all attempts coulde not in halfe a yeere remove her.[9]

There were other incidents which contributed to the Tudor recession in Bristol, some of which were largely the fault of the Council. It was fortunate that the queen did not choose to come a year later for in 1575 Bristol suffered one of the worst plagues in her history, and the discovery of three dead cats in the water supply indicates the most likely source of the infection. This plague was not an isolated incident, and in 1535 when Henry VIII planned to make a royal visit he was diverted to Thornbury because of the pestilence which was raging in Bristol at the time. Adam's *Chronicle* records a terrible plague in 1564 which was accompanied by a winter so severe that it was possible to cross the estuary of the Avon on the ice. The number of deaths is probably an exaggeration but it was still a terrible visitation:

> This year the 7th of October here was seen in the element red beams in length like the pole, and also fire like furnace: and after that here followed a very great plague, which endured a whole year; whereof here died above 2,500 people. From the 21 December to the third of January was such an exceeding hard frost, that the Thames of London was so hard frozen that men, women and children went upon it so boldly as upon the land,

and men did shoot at pricks,* and bowl upon it. And at Bristoll and
Hungrode it was so hard frozen that people passed over the channel
upon ice unto St George's side safely.[10]

To be fair to the council, they did get around to building new sewers
towards the end of the century and their improvements were noticed
by later visitors. 'The sewers are so contrived to carry and wash away
the filth, that nothing is wanting that can conduce to cleanliness or
health', wrote William Camden in 1586. He also remarked on the
leaning tower of Temple Church which was rapidly gaining in noto-
riety:

> [Temple] ... whose tower shakes so when the bells ring, that it has parted
> from the rest of the building, and left a chink from top to bottom three
> fingers broad, opening and closing as the bells ring.[11]

The sixteenth century was very eventful in the broader sense of
English history. By the end of Elizabeth's reign the rift between
Protestant and Catholic was as wide as ever, but many of the radical
changes of the century had worked out for the better. In Bristol three
grammar schools had been founded. Bristol Grammar School and the
Cathedral School both had claims to be the first, and Queen Elizabeth's
Hospital School was also a Tudor foundation. St Bartholemew's Hospital was reconstructed to house the Grammar School and new
elementary schools were founded to teach the elements of reading and
writing to young children – one of these occupied a room over the
Frome Gate which had previously been occupied by the Grammar
School. The Cathedral created a secular college for the education of
the clergy and its location became known as College Green. The
schoolboys worked at mastering their Latin grammar and the trainee
canons studied hard at their theology.

The land discovered by Cabot and those who followed him was
opening up to trade and there was much talk of colonisation. William
Camden noted that 'The citizens carry on a profitable trade all over
Europe, and send ships to the most distant parts of America'. If the
merchants were to profit from trade to the new continent then better
navigation was an essential requirement. Late in the sixteenth century
a very significant educational establishment was founded when the
Society of Merchant Venturers set up a school of navigation.

---

* Probably a target of some kind, the fair being held on the ice.

The Colonies

In 1519 able seaman Andrew of Bristol became the first Englishman to enter the Pacific Ocean. He did not sail on an English ship; he was a gunner on Ferdinand Magellan's epic voyage when the Straits of Magellan (the stormy passage between South America and Tierra del Fuego) was first discovered. Andrew, in common with his famous commander, did not survive the first voyage around the world and he never returned to his home town to tell the tale.

The exploration and mapping of the American continent no longer enjoyed royal patronage after the death of Henry VII. The Bristol merchants wanted to explore further, and in 1552 the Bristol Merchant Venturers were given a royal charter to search for the new lands. Not enjoying patronage from Henry VIII, they were expected to finance the ventures themselves. The Spanish and the Portuguese, meanwhile, continued to explore actively. Magellan's voyage had proved the existence of a south-west passage from the Atlantic to the Pacific and on to the Spice Islands. The passage was too long and too dangerous to be a practical trade route but the English optimists were convinced that if a south-west passage existed then a north-west passage must exist as well. The latter sea passage would lie entirely in the northern hemisphere; it would therefore provide a shorter route to the Orient and it would avoid coming into conflict with the Spanish who had a papal decree which allowed them to explore and trade in the tropical latitudes of the Atlantic.

There followed the voyages of Hawkins and Frobisher into the icy seas to the west of Greenland and the discovery of Hudson Bay with the wooden-walled Elizabethan ships sailing ever west and north to colder climes. The English galleons pushed further northwards as the ice froze on the sheets, yards and rigging. The hardships and the endurance of the Elizabethan sailors in the cold Arctic seas were unbelievable. The Bristol merchants had a stake in Martin Frobisher's voyages and they optimistically hoped that even if he did not find the North-West Passage he would discover gold or precious metals in North America. They were disappointed. In 1577 Frobisher returned from his second voyage with a heavy sample of ore which was 'so hard that it would strike fire like a flint', but it proved impossible to extract any metal from it. He put in at Bristol with two Eskimos from

Greenland, whom he had brought to England in the interests of furthering knowledge but also as a curiosity:

> They brought likewise a man called Callico, and a woman called Ignorth: they were savage people and fed only upon raw flesh. The ninth of October he [Callico] rowed in a little boat made of skin in the water at the Backe, where he killed two ducks with a dart, and when he had carried his boat through the march upon his back: the like he did at the weir and other places where many beheld him. He would hit a duck a good distance off and not miss. They died here within a month.[1]

The final sentence confirms that the story was a very sad one – of two humans taken completely out of their environment into a strange alien world in which they could not hope to survive, and providing a circus act for the gawking public.

In addition to the passage to the Orient there was much talk of forming an English colony in America. The elder Richard Hakluyt wrote his *Notes on Colonisation* in 1578 and his publication became a major factor behind Sir Walter Raleigh's unsuccessful attempt at establishing an English colony at Roanoke, Virginia, in 1584. In 1585 the younger Richard Hakluyt, cousin of the elder Richard, settled in Bristol to collect information for his classic work on *Navigations, Voyages and Discoveries of the English Nation.* The Newfoundland fishing banks were well frequented by the Bristol ships; though they no longer enjoyed a monopoly of the trade, Bristol was still the major port for voyages to North America. It is common to find Bristol merchants mentioned as sponsors for the Elizabethan voyages, but towards the end of the sixteenth century it was London which moved closer to the forefront of English exploration and colonisation.

After the turn of the century there was another period of interest from Bristol. Two small ships, the *Speedwell* and the *Discoverer*, of 50 and 26 tons respectively, sailed from Kingroad on 20 March 1603 when Elizabeth was still the Queen of England. The voyage was not destined to be Elizabethan, however, as weather conditions forced the ships to put in at Milford Haven, where they heard the news that the Tudor age had ended – Queen Elizabeth had died on the 27th.

The leader of the expedition was Martin Pring, and his backers were two Bristol merchants, Robert Aldworth and John Whitson. The latter is also remembered as the founder of Red Maids School. The ships were laden with agricultural tools, seeds, hats, clothes, mirrors and other trinkets. Their mission was to explore the northern part of Virginia, to trade with the Indians, to test the agricultural possibilities of the new continent and to bring back the bark from the Sassafras tree, which was supposed to be a cure for venereal disease. The expedition landed near Fox Island at the mouth of the Penobscot River

Opposite
Millerd depicts a busy quay and river at Bristol. Ship servicing facilities are in evidence in the graving area near the bend in the Avon, bottom left, while the crane, next to Marsh Street Gate, just downstream from Bristol Bridge, is also clearly shown. Trine [Treen] Mills can be seen, bottom left, powered by a small tributary of the Avon.

The map shows clearly the marsh as a promenade and recreational area, complete with avenues of trees and bowling green. This area became Queen Square thirty years later.

Note also Frome Bridge (*top right*), where Bristol Grammar School started life.

and the ships sailed along the coast of New England exploring the river inlets on the way. They crossed the Bay of Massachusetts and camped at an anchorage which they called Whitson Bay. They made contact with the Indians and an un-named youth had the redskins dancing to his music on the 'gitterne'. When the natives became too friendly the crew frightened them off with their two great mastiffs, one of which was big enough to carry a half pike in his mouth:

> One Master Thomas Bridges a Gentleman of our company accompanied only with one of these Dogs ... passed six miles alone in the Countrey having lost his fellowes, and returned safly. And when we would be rid of the Savages company wee would let loose the Mastives, and suddenly with out-cryes they would flee away.[2]

The explorers stayed for two months, long enough to become the first to grow 'Wheate, Barley, Oates, Pease and sundry sorts of Garden Seeds' in New England. Martin Pring's expedition therefore quite literally sowed the seeds of colonisation in the New World. Seventeen years later, in 1620, another English ship anchored in the same bay. The ship was lost and way off course. She had planned to make a landfall in Virginia but it was December and she had left it far too late in the season and the winter was well advanced. The *Mayflower's* company did not come as explorers, but as settlers prepared to work the soil and to face their first terrible winter in the New World. The Pilgrim Fathers urgently needed to find a suitable anchorage and a place to spend the winter. They scrambled ashore at Plymouth Rock. They renamed Whitson Bay and called the place Plymouth Harbour.

Martin Pring's next venture was as master of the *Olive Plant* on a London expedition to try to establish an English colony in Guiana. The expedition was a disaster and Pring had to beg a lift home on a Dutch vessel. In 1606 he sailed again from Bristol to New England under the sponsorship of Sir Ferdinando Gorges and Sir John Popham, the Lord Chief Justice of England. Gorges and Popham were well known promoters of the idea of colonisation and both had Bristol connections, Gorges was from Wraxhall near Bristol and Popham had held Ricart's old position as Recorder of Bristol. Little is known of the 1606 voyage but Gorges was well pleased with Pring's findings:

> ... the most exact discovery of that coast that ever came into my hands, and indeed he was the best able to perform it of any I met withal to the present, which with his relation of the country, wrought such an impression on the Lord Chief Justice and us all that were his associates, that we set up our resolutions to follow it with effect.[3]

Pring then turned his attentions to the development of trade with the east. Gorges remained an active promoter in a group called the Plymouth Company which represented the West Country ports of

Plymouth, Exeter and Bristol and in 1635 he was given a royal charter for the development of the province of Maine.

One man who knew and appreciated Bristol's contribution to the development of the New World was Thomas Fuller, an Anglican divine and a scholar who knew the city in the 1630s. His account gives an excellent summing up of the voyages to date:

> No city in England (London alone excepted) hath, in so short a time, bred more brave and bold seamen, advantaged for western voyages by its situation. They have not been merchants, but adventurers, possessed, with a public spirit for the general good; aiming not so much to return wealthier as wiser; not always to enrich themselves as inform posterity by their discoveries. Of these, some have been but merely casual; when going to fish for cod they have found a country, or some eminent bay, river, or haven of importance, unknown before. Others were intentional, wherein they have sown experiments, with great pains, cost and danger, that ensuing ages may freely reap the benefit thereof.[4]

The idea of a north-west passage to the Orient did not die with the Elizabethan age. Among the seventeenth-century explorers whose names are remembered in the northern territory were Hudson (1610–11), Button (1612–13), Gibbons (1614), Bylot and Baffin (1615–16), and Hawkridge in 1617.

Bristol's contribution in this field did not materialise until 1631 when Captain Thomas James, a skilled navigator and also a barrister, was chosen as commander of a new expedition. The start was delayed by the news that a rival ship from London was also seeking the North-West Passage in the same year. This was bad news for the Bristol merchants; from past experience they feared that any new trading rights from the venture would be granted to the Londoners and they would be excluded. Their fears were not unfounded as the Londoners already had a greedy eye on the lucrative Bristol soap industry and they were so close to the seat of power that they could control the industry to swell their own profits. A long correspondence ensued before the Bristol merchants felt assured of their equal rights, but it left some animosity between the two ships as they left for Hudson Bay. Thomas James left Bristol on the third of May 1631 in the *Henrietta Maria* of eighty tons:

> One Captain James, a man of great learning, experience in navigation, and well seen in the mathematical science, set sail from Kingrode, to discover the North-West passage to the East Indies ... [the ship] was well furnished with all necessaries, and victualled for 18 months; having but 20 men and 2 boys.[5]

By the end of June the *Henrietta Maria* was in Hudson Bay and navigating treacherous drifting ice. She cleared the ice floes and entered open water, but not for long. The further west she sailed the more numerous became the icebergs. Throughout July Thomas James explored north and west seeking a sea passage, but he found ice barring the way in every direction. Eventually, by the 11th of August, he sighted land on the western shores of Hudson Bay. Two days later the ship struck against a rock and the ship heeled over as far as the gun-whale, at which point the expedition very nearly perished but in due course they managed to free the ship and they got underway again with minimal damage. On the 29th there came what should have been an historic encounter: the *Henrietta Maria* met with the London ship captained by Luke Foxe. Reports state that there was no love lost between the captains, but James showed hospitality to his countrymen. Foxe appreciated James' efforts but he turned down the offer to winter with him in Hudson Bay.

> In The Morning Captain Foxe And His Friends Came Aboord Of Mee, Where I Entertained Them In The Best Manner I Could, And With Such Fresh Meat As I Had Gotten From The Shoare ... In The Evening, After I Had Given His Men Some Necessaries, With Tobacco And Other Things Which They Wanted, Hee Departed Aboord His Ship And, The Next Morning, Stood Away South-south-west Since Which Time I Never Saw Him.[6]

'I was well entertained by Captain James,' wrote Foxe. 'with varietie of such cheere as his sea provisions could aford, with some Partridges; we dined betwixt decks, for the great cabin was not bigg enough to receive our selves and followers ...' James still had time to return home before the cold weather set in, but he was determined to winter in Hudson Bay so he sailed to the south and found an anchorage in the bay that is now known as James Bay. He stripped his ship of the sails and rigging and partly submerged her so that she could not be carried away by the drifting ice. The ship had lost her rudder and they feared that they she may no longer have been seaworthy. The crew had to carry provisions for over a mile across the ice to winter in the primitive huts which they had built on the shore. Thomas James himself movingly described the scene as his ship was abandoned and left to survive the winter in the ice:

> Our men that were ashoare stood looking upon us, almost dead with cold and sorrowes, to see our misery and their owne. We lookt upon them againe, and both upon each other, with woeful hearts, Darke night drew on, and I bade the Boate to be haled up, and commanded my loving companions to goe all into her, who (in some refusing complements) expressed their faithful affections to mee, as loth to part from me. I told them that my meaning was to goe ashore with them. And thus, lastly, I forsook my ship.[7]

The ship was short of provisions, particularly fresh fruit and vegetables. Scurvy struck the crew. It was difficult to find firewood. The ground was frozen to a depth of ten feet. Many were sick and four men died in the bitter northern winter. When at last the spring came and the ice began to melt they were greatly relieved to find that the ship was still seaworthy and they managed to recover the rudder from the seabed. James sailed north to latitude 65° 30' but he found himself surrounded by ice. He spent the summer months exploring Hudson Bay, but finally, to the great relief of his weary men, he gave up the search and decided to return home. Foxe had returned the previous year, having chosen not to spend the winter in the North West territory. Both James' and Foxe's voyages were full of courage and hardship, but like their predecessors both were failures in their quest for the elusive passage to Cathay. They were the last of their generation to search for the North-West Passage.

As we have already seen, Bristol was a merchant port. Ships and men were frequently supplied to the royal navy in times of war but enemy action was rare. In the 1630s, when war with Spain broke out again, a Bristol ship called the *Angel Gabriel* was involved in an action against three Spanish ships. Seyer, in his *Memorials of Bristol*, published a ballad which seems to have been greatly influenced by Tennyson's *Revenge*, claiming that the *Angel Gabriel* chased the Spanish back to Cadiz with losses of five hundred dead against only three on the Bristol ship. The figures are fiction and so is most of the action. It is certainly not contemporary and appears to be an early nineteenth-century fabrication. However, it still records a real incident and is worth repeating:

The Honour of Bristol

Attend you and give ear awhile
And you shall understand,
Of a battle fought upon the seas
By a ship of brave command:
The fight it was so famous
That all men's hearts did fill
And make them cry 'to sea
With the Angel Gabriel.'

The lusty ship of Bristol
Sail'd out adventurously
Against he foes of England
Their strength to with them to try:
Well victual'd, rig'd, and man'd,
And good provision still,
Which made them cry 'to sea
With the Angel Gabriel.'

Our Captain to our Master said,
Take courage Master bold;
The Master to the seaman said,
Stand fast my hearts of gold;
The Gunner unto all the rest,
Brave hearts be valiant still,
Let us fight in the defence
Of our Angel Gabriel.

Then we gave them a broadside
Which shot their mast asunder,
And tore the bost-spret of their ship
Which made the Spaniards wonder:
And caused them to cry,
With voices loud and shrill,
Help, help, or else we sink,
By the Angel Gabriel.

With that their three ships boarded us
Again with might and main,
But still our noble Englishmen
Cried out 'A fig for Spain';
Though seven times they boarded us
At last we shewed our skill
And made them feel the force
Of our Angel Gabriel.

Seven hours this fight continued,
And many brave men lay dead,
With purple gore and Spanish blood
The sea was coloured red.
Five hundred of their men
We there outright did kill,
And many more were maim'd
By the Angel Gabriel.

We had within our English ship
But only three men slain
And five men hurt, which I hope
Will soon be well again:
At Bristol we were landed
And let us praise God still
That thus hath blest our men
And our Angel Gabriel.[8]

Admiral Sir William Penn (1621–1670) was the son of Giles Penn,
a merchant of Bristol. He rose to the rank of Admiral and was second
in command to Blake in the first Dutch war. William Penn supported
Parliament during the Civil War, but he was not an active anti-royalist

and he was present on board the *Naseby* in 1660 when Charles II returned to England to claim his throne. Penn was a very wealthy man and became a major sponsor of the new king, to such an extent that Charles could find only one way in which to pay off his debt. The king granted William Penn a large tract of land in America, 47,000 acres to the west of the Delaware River. William Penn (the elder) died in 1670 and was buried at St Mary Redcliffe and his son, also called William, became very involved with the Quaker movement which was making great ground in Bristol at this time.

The Quakers had their meeting places at Temple and also in the old Dominican Friary near Broad Mead. Their meeting place was known by the curious name of Quaker's Friars, which seemingly combines two widely different religious movements. William Penn the younger was able to use his father's land in America to experiment with ideas of religious, social and political freedom. He founded a new colony, formed by English Quakers, mostly originating in the Bristol area, but soon joined by Swedish, German and Swiss families eager to partake of the new freedom. The name of Pennsylvania, originally the name of sixty square miles of land near the Delaware River, became the name of a whole colony and a whole American state. The fact that it was named after the father and not the son is proved by a letter from the younger William Penn dated 5th of January 1681. He honoured his father, who had been dead for ten years, but he felt it pretentious to use the Penn family name for the new colony. King Charles over-ruled William Penn II and pushed the name through by Royal assent. A private letter describes Penn's feelings on the matter:

> Dear Friend,
>
> ... after many waitings, watchings, solicitings, and disputes in council, this day my country was confirmed to me under the great seal of England, with large powers and privileges, by the name of Pennsylvania; a name the king would give it in honour of my father ...
>
> [I proposed] ... Sylvania, and they added Penn to it, and though I was much opposed to it, and went to the king to have it struck out and altered, he said it was past, and would take it upon him; nor could twenty guineas move the under secretary to vary the name; for I feared lest it be looked upon as a vanity in me, and not as a respect in the King, as it truly was, to my father, whom he often mentions with praise ...
>
> Thy true friend,
> Wm Penn.[9]

Thus Bristol figures very prominently in the early history of the colonisation of America. London was an east coast port whereas Bristol faced to the west and during the seventeenth century and most of the eighteenth the latter was the leading port for trade with the New World. When the tide rushed in and the Pill boatmen heaved on the oars to pull the tall ships up the Avon, there was invariably a vessel returning from the Americas to anchor and unload on the quay with news and merchandise from the colonies. Emotional scenes were common on the Broad Quay as the ships brought timber and tobacco, news of friends and relatives across the ocean and sailors pining to see their homes and families after months of hardship at sea.

Very few English ships entered the Pacific Ocean in these times and the circumnavigation of the world by Captain Woodes Rogers was therefore an exceptional voyage. Rogers was little more than a buccaneer, but he was sponsored by a consortium of Bristol merchants who hoped to gain from his privateering activities. In August 1708 Captain Rogers sailed from Kingroad with two ships, the *Duke* of 320 tons, 30 guns and 150 men, and the *Duchess* of 300 tons, 24 guns and 120 men. His navigator was a Somerset man, William Dampier, who had already sailed to the Pacific and was the first Englishman to set foot on the coast of New Holland (Australia).

The voyage was relatively uneventful until the ships reached the Pacific. As they passed near the island of Juan Fernandez a fire was spotted with a tall column of smoke. The ships approached the island to find a shipwrecked mariner, a Scotsman called Alexander Selkirk, who had been living alone on the Pacific island for four and a half years. Selkirk had been master of a ship called the *Cinq Ports* and his story was that the ship was so un-seaworthy he had actually chosen to take his chances on the island rather than sail any further in her. Other reports say that he had a violent quarrel with Dampier who was in charge of the former expedition – the rescue cannot have been entirely by chance for Dampier knew that Selkirk had been left on Juan Fernandez. Selkirk was an experienced seaman and when the ships reached the Philippines and began to plunder the Spanish treasure ships he was put in charge of a prize, a captured galleon which was renamed the *Marquis*.

Woodes Roger's voyage was the most successful privateering voyage ever made from Bristol – claims were made that the booty amounted to £170,000. The figures were grossly exaggerated but when the ships returned in October 1711 the sponsors had made an enormous profit and interest in the voyage was so high that two accounts of the voyage around the world were published. Alexander Selkirk's story as the shipwrecked mariner made a great impression on the popular imagination and the published accounts were used by Daniel Defoe in his fictional work *Robinson Crusoe*.[10]

Roundheads and Cavaliers

> ... this yeare uppon the fowerth of October was the greatest snow that
> ever was knowne by the memory of man, which continewed fower dayes,
> and by reason that the leaves were then uppon the trees many trees of
> all sorts, espeachially of fruite trees, were throwne downe by the roots,
> and the limbes and boughes of many others were broken in pieces.[1]

The date was 1604. It is an accepted fact that the English winters were
very severe in the seventeenth century, but snow as early as the 4th of
October, as far south as Bristol, the heaviest fall in the memory of
man, and before the leaves had fallen from the trees; this was surely
something which nature could never repeat.

It was the first year of the reign of James I. The century was still
young, and it was destined to bring many social and economic changes.
There was the periodic visitation of the plague. The calendar records
a hundred deaths in the year before the snowstorm and an incredible
2,950 in the same year. In 1606 came a great gale from the south west
and extensive flooding in the Severn Estuary. People and cattle were
drowned near the river. Cellars were flooded in Bristol, with many
merchants losing their stock.

When the plagues and the weather had done their worst, trade in
the city recovered rapidly. Many visitors came and recorded their
findings and we can build up an accurate, fascinating and sometimes
amusing picture of Bristol in this century. In 1634 three soldiers, a
Captain, a Lieutenant and an 'Ancient', journeyed from Norwich, a
city which competed with Bristol to be the second in the kingdom.
Lieutenant Hammond was generous in his findings:

> This Citty stands sweetly in a pleasant Cock-pit valley, yet with an ascent
> to the heart thereof where stands a fayre cross on the midst between
> both Bridges, lately and richly beautify'd, and not much inferior to that
> in Coventry. To it comes 4 large and fayre streets from the 4 chiefe
> quarters of the city, viz. High Street which is the fayrest from the great
> Bridge in Somersetshire; Broad Street from the Key bridge in Glouces-
> tershire; Wine street from the Castle; and Corne Street from the Marsh.[2]

His account as yet adds little to our knowledge, but the 'fayre cross'
he describes really was a 'high' cross at this time. The original height
of about 15 feet became over seventy feet, with gothic arches at ground

level. It was brightly painted and gilded in gold with niches above containing effigies of no fewer than eight monarchs. Adam's *Chronicle of Bristol* gives a detailed description:

> The high cross of Bristol, which was taken down in the month of May 1633, was enlarge, beautified, and ended in December 1634. Whereas formerly was placed the pictures of 4 kings that had been good benefactors to Bristoll viz. King John, who gave us a charter, was placed, and yet standeth, facing and looking due north: Henry the third was his son, who confirmed the same charter; is placed with his face towards the east; King Edward the third renewed and enlarged our said charter and with more privileges than did his predecessors; was, and is yet placed and facing towards the west: and king Edward the 4th, who likewise confirmed all former privileges was placed, and yet standeth, faced towards the south.
>
> Now as this cross is enlarged and made higher, so above those aforesaid kings are place four other famous princes. The first of these is King Henry the 8; whose picture is placed facing to the east: the second is Queen Elizabeth of famous memory, whose picture is placed facing toward the west, as well she deserved by her careful and vigilant eye over her and our enemies in Rome and Spaine: the third new picture presenteth King James, whose placed looking towards the south; and lastly is the picture of King Charles who is placed due north. And all of these have renewed and confirmed our said charter. The charge in new building, gilding and painting, with iron-works about the said cross (of which

The Hatchet (*left*) is one of Bristol's oldest surviving public houses, in an area which has undergone several major re-developments. It is a seventeenth-century building, with the earliest fabric dating from 1606.

The Shakespeare (*right*) was built in 1636. This timber-framed building retains much of its seventeenth-century character.

iron-work some is bestowed about the building which now cannot be discerned) did in all amount to the sun of 207s. Before this time was no defensive grates of iron-work as now it hath but it lay all open. The very iron-work with the said grates and other bolts and bars to cramp it together, cost above 36£, and the stuff for gilding thereof cost 48£.[3]

Lieutenant Hammond describes the efficient sewage arrangements, an indication that some action had been taken after the plagues in the early part of the century. He writes at great length about the city churches:

> The city is very sweet and cleane in respect of the quotidian tydes that wash and cleanse her lower parts, and the vaults and sewers that are under all, or most the channels of her upper parts. In her wee found (besides that fayre and strong Fabricke of the Cathedrall which was newly finished) 18 Churches which are all fayrely beautify'd, richly adorn'd and sweetly kept, and in the major part of them are neat, rich and melodious Organs that are constantly played on. Their Pulpitts are most curious in which the Citizens have spared no cost nor forwardnesse to beautify and adorne (a pious and religious example for all our kingdom) ...[4]

The churches were well kept but the castle was in a terrible state of decay. Although this was of no importance at the time it became a point of great concern a few years later when the Civil War broke out. The land between Avon and Frome was still known as the 'Marsh' and it was still undeveloped for housing, but it had been well drained and provided an excellent recreational area for Bristolians to take their leisure. Here the merchants and citizens enjoyed a stroll beneath the trees, surrounded by water and shipping on three sides. There was a bowling green, a military band with fife and drum 'which causeth a sweet and pleasnt Eccho of their martiall Musicke'. The visitors enjoyed watching the local militia drilling and practising their shooting skills.

Visitors noticed that it was common for small dogs to be employed in a wooden treadmill to turn a spit for roasting meat, later in the century the dogs became victims of technological change and were replaced by clockwork. Outside the exchange in Corn Street was a curious arrangement of brass pillars. Peter Mundy from Cornwall gives a good description:

By the High Crosse is the Exchange where

Westbury College. The college building at Westbury-on-Trym dates from about 1460 when it was well outside Bristol. It was used by Prince Rupert as his headquarters during the royalist siege of Bristol. It has long been swallowed up by the city.

are many curious and costly pillars of brasse, about 3 or 4 foot high, broad at the foote and toppe, sett off purpose for men to leane on, pay and tell money, etc.[5]

These were the famous 'Bristol nails' which generated the saying 'to pay on the nail'. The first nails were late Elizabethan and by the seventeenth century they were a well established feature in Corn Street.

The peace of the early decades did not last. When the Civil War broke out between the king and parliament both sides knew that it would be impossible for them to control the West Country without the support of Bristol. Most of the merchants were loyal to parliament but their unsuccessful attempts to break into the monopolies and privileges of the Londoners created a large minority with royalist sympathies. It was impossible to be neutral, however, and at the outbreak of the war Bristol declared for parliament and three ships were supplied to support the parliamentarian cause.

Rupert's Gate. It was here on 10th September 1645 that Prince Rupert surrendered from the Royal Fort. He rode out through this gateway 'clad in scarlet, very richly laid with silver, mounted upon a very black Barbary horse'.

The castle was in a sorry state of repair; the city's medieval walls were non-existent in many places; and in any case Bristol had long outgrown its ancient boundaries. It was decided to build a new outer defensive wall to the north, joining Brandon Hill, Windmill Hill and Prior's Hill at Kingsdown. A fort was to be built on each hill, the greatest of which was the Royal Fort built on the highest point of Windmill Hill. The city was held under the command of Colonel Nathaniel Fiennes, whose father was one of the few among the peerage to openly declare against the king.

The surrounding country was predominantly royalist, and as Prince Rupert mustered his forces it was only a question of time before Bristol came under siege. In July 1643 Rupert was quartered at Westbury-on-Trym with an army of twenty thousand royalists and planning an assault on Bristol. He moved closer and encamped at Clifton, encountering no resistance on the way. He began to attack the hastily built defensive wall. Soon after Rupert's siege began, the long perimeter wall was breached at its weakest point, the saddle between Brandon Hill and Windmill Hill. As the Roundheads tried to re-group their forces the Cavaliers made ready to advance on Bristol – they were perfectly placed on high ground with a long slope before them. There followed the famous 'Washington Charge' led by Colonel Washington,

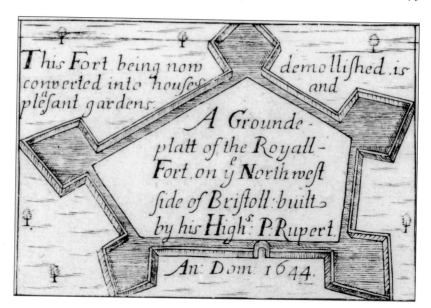

This Fort being now demollished, is converted into houses and plesant gardens.

A Grounde-platt of the Royall-Fort on ye Northwest side of Bristoll:built by his High⁵: P.Rupert. An: Dom 1644.

A plan of the 'Royal Fort' built by Prince Rupert in 1644. It was demolished after the war but the land was redeveloped as a residential area.

of the same family as the first President of what was much later to become the United States of America. The royalists charged easily down to College Green and advanced to the Frome Gate. Inside the walls of Bristol there was a great state of panic and confusion.

Within the city the royalists had many supporters who were more than willing to open the gates to them, and even as Rupert's soldiers approached men were wading across the muddy waters of the Frome to join ranks with them. But some of those inside the walls had other ideas. Mrs Dorothy Hazard was married to the Anglican vicar of St Ewens, but she became a fanatical Puritan and set up what was effectively the first non-Anglican congregation in Bristol. She was a woman who put up with no nonsense and she strongly disapproved of Cavalier excesses. During the siege she used her considerable organisational abilities to pile up obstacles on the inside of the gates. With the rank and file deserting to the other side Bristol could not hope to hold out much longer against Prince Rupert, and Colonel Fiennes surrendered. It was claimed that a thousand of his troops changed sides, but even as Prince Rupert crossed the Frome Bridge into Bristol Dorothy Hazard and the grocers' wives were still offering spirited resistance and building up the barricades.

The royalists were jubilant. Charles I came to visit on 3 August and there was even talk of moving the court from Oxford to Bristol. But elsewhere things were going badly and the next year the action moved to the North and culminated with the Roundhead victory at Marston Moor in 1644. The royalist defeat at Naseby in the following year was effectively the end of the royalist cause. After Naseby, Bristol was the

A few seventeenth-century gabled houses survive at the upper end of Colston Street. They are now an attractive and well preserved group.

last hope for the King's supporters, and in 1645 the city found itself again under siege, although the positions were the reverse of two years earlier. Fairfax and Cromwell arrived with a parliamentarian force in August. It says much of the medieval defences from 1240 that the assault at Redcliffe failed, but the flimsy northern defences were easily broken and on the 10th of September 1645 Rupert surrendered from his headquarters in Royal Fort. Thus neither the parliamentarians nor the royalists were able to hold Bristol against a determined siege. It was the 'cock-pit' geography of Bristol, noted by Lieutenant Hammond, with the many surrounding hills providing perfect siege positions, which made it so difficult to defend. A local newsletter described Fairfax escorting the defeated but proud Prince Rupert respectfully through the streets to the castle:

> The prince was clad in scarlet, very richly laid in silver lace, mounted upon a very gallant black Barbary horse; the general and the prince rode together, the general giving the prince the right hand all the way.[6]

Charles I was tried and executed, but the royalist cause was not finished. The most fleeting visit ever made by royalty to Bristol was that of Charles' son after the battle of Worcester. In 1651 the future Charles II passed through Bristol disguised as a servant, accompanied only by the loyal Jane Lane, fleeing from the Roundhead army. He took refuge with the Norton family at Abbots Leigh and eventually made his way to the south coast and to exile in France.

It was amazing that Bristol, with its close-packed timber houses and its many open fires, never had a conflagration to equal the great fire of London. In February 1647, however, a most destructive fire broke out when an apothecary named Edwards accidentally started a fire on Bristol Bridge. Within a few hours 24 houses were burning ferociously, from St Mary's Chapel to the northern end of the bridge. Other houses had to be pulled down to create a firebreak and this luckily prevented the fire from spreading to the rest of the city. For many years the chapel had been used for housing and trade but the fabric was so badly damaged by the fire it was deemed to be very dangerous and it was pulled down in 1649.

It was during Cromwell's commonwealth years that the diarist John Evelyn paid a visit and noted that the castle had been virtually destroyed after the Civil War. He made the usual rounds and made the usual comparisons with London. He witnessed the sugar manufacture and sampled the Spanish wine and he was most impressed by the Avon Gorge:

> ... Bristol, a city emulating London, not for its large extent, but manner of buildings, shops, bridge, Traffique, Exchange, Marketplace, etc. The Governor shew'd us the Castle, of no great concernment. The City wholy Mercantile, as standing near the famous Severne, commodiously for Ireland and the Western world ... but what I saw was most stupendous to me, was the rock of St Vincent, a little distance from the Towne, the precipe whereoff is equal to any thing of that nature I have seen in the most confragose cataracts of the Alpes, the river gliding betweene them after an extraordinary depth.[7]

In 1665 came Marmaduke Rawdon, a merchant from York. We know that the cathedral remained half built for four centuries, but most of the visitors were too polite to say as much. Rawton was the exception. He disliked the cathedral; he disliked the sledges in the city centre; and worst of all he disliked the people. His account of Bristol provides a balance to the usual polite eulogies:

> This is a cittie well populated, of greate trade, hath a cathedrall, but I think the meanest in England; they have convenient havens for ships; they imitate London very much in their hospitall boys in blew coats ...
> In this cittie are many proper men but very few handsome women, and most of them ill bred, being generally men and women very proud,

nott affable to strangers, but rather admiring themselves, soe that an ordinary fellow that is but a freeman of Bristol, he conceits himself to be as grave as a senator of Rome, and very sparinge of his hatt, in soe much that their preachers hath told them of it in the pulpitt ...

They use in the cittie most sleds to carry their goods, and the drivers such rude people, that they will have their horse uppon a strangers back before they be aware ...[8]

Some of the conceited freemen to whom Rawton refers thought that the comparison with Rome could be justified. Over-enthusiastic Bristolians tried to match the hills around Bristol with the seven hills of Rome. For those who prefer fairy tales to fact statues of the legendary founders of Bristol – Brennius and Bellinus – were displayed on St John's gate for all to see, a clear parallel with Romulus and Remus.

Only three years later, in 1668, Samuel Pepys came to visit. He mentions not only horse-drawn sleds, but also dog-carts as sleds, both of which were a menace to the pedestrian. The sleds were confined to the central area of the old town where the merchants disliked wheeled vehicles because they thought the wheels could do damage to the wine cellars. Pepys, in his capacity as secretary to the Admiralty, was greatly interested in the shipping and was delighted to find the new warship, the *Elgar*, almost completed in Francis Bailey's yard. His visit to Bristol was not business, however; it was purely for pleasure. He made no more than a day trip from his lodgings in Bath and he might not have made the trip at all had it not been for his maid Deborah Willet who was Bristol born and bred and dearly wanted to see her hometown again.

It was a three-hour journey by coach from Bath but Pepys was in no hurry and he didn't get underway until eleven. The summer evening was long and the return journey would be made by moonlight. Deborah was born in Marsh Street very close to the Quay. Her name appears in the baptismal records of St Stephens on 12 December 1650, so we may assume she was seventeen in 1668 when she arrived with Pepys. Her uncle was a Bristol merchant called William Butts. Thanks to the greatest diarist of the century we are taken right into the heart of a Bristol home. It was June and there were strawberries on the menu. Bristol was a sailor's town, tearful farewells were commonplace and so were joyful homecomings. Deborah Willet was no sailor, but Pepys' description of her welcome is one of the most moving incidents in his long diary:

... Then walked with him [William Butts] and my wife and company to round the key and to the ship and he showed me the Custom House and made me understand many things of the place and led us through Marsh Street where our girl was born but Lord the joy that was among the old poor people of the place to see Mrs. Willet's daughter it seems

The Bristol High Cross stood at the junction of High Street, Corn Street, Broad Street and Wine Street. Note the railings and the poor miscreant in the stocks.

The Tolsey. A seventeenth-century view of the merchants' Tolsey in Corn Street, showing the Nails, where the merchants made their transactions.

her mother being a brave woman and mightily beloved. And so brought us a back way by surprize to his house where a substantial good house and well furnished and did give us good entertainment of strawberries a whole venison pasty cold and plenty of brave wine and above all Bristoll milk. Where comes in another poor woman who hearing that Deb was here did come running thither and with her eyes so full of tears and heart so full of joy that she could not speak when she came in that it made me weep too I protest that I was not able to speak to her (which I would have done) to have diverted her tears.

CHAPTER SEVEN

A Long Street Full of Ships

Wool was the oldest manufacturing industry in the city. Bristol Red cloth was first produced using Brazil wood or red sandalwood dye, and later using a dye produced from cochineal. The woollen industry required a good supply of clean water and this became progressively more difficult to obtain in the city. The result was that cloth manufacture moved out from Bristol to surrounding villages and the Cotswold towns. The industry survived longer south of the river in Temple and St Thomas, and in 1698 the Quakers opened a new workhouse for unemployed weavers, although this was towards the end of cloth manufacture in Bristol.

The Nails are on the pavement in Corn Street, outside the Exchange. They are the origin of the phrase 'to pay on the nail'. Two are Elizabethan (1594); the others date from 1625 and 1631.

The soapmakers were a very old established trade and at one time there were 27 soaphouses in Bristol. Soap was manufactured from olive oil but as the Atlantic trade developed it became common to use train oil which was imported from Newfoundland. The train oil produced an inferior product and because of this in 1618 the soapmakers were required to use only olive oil, the penalty for using 'noisone and unwholesome' materials being a stiff fine of forty pounds. Some of the soapmakers became very wealthy, and a good example is John Carr who left land to Queen Elizabeth Hospital in 1586, and who had interests in London as well as Bristol. It was the soapmakers who were the more vociferous of the anti-London faction. In 1634 the Londoners issued a proclamation giving themselves the sole rights to manufacture soft soap and banning an industry which was already four hundred years old in Bristol.

From September to the month of December 1637 our city was never free from commissions, commissioners and pursuivants of sundry sorts, which lay in several parts of our city to make enquiry not only against merchants but against other tradesmen, who were

The Llandoger
Trow dates from
1663. It had five
gables until 1940
when two were
destroyed in the
Blitz. Robert Louis
Stevenson stayed at
the inn to imbibe
atmosphere for his
novel *Treasure
Island*: 'I saw ...
many old sailors,
with rings in their
ears, and whiskers
curled in ringlets,
and tarry pigtails,
and their
swaggering, clumsy
sea-walk; and if I
had seen as many
kings or arch-
bishops I could
not have been
more delighted.'

examined and sent up to London, and great impositions laid upon them
to the grief of many: insomuch that all shopkeepers stood in much [fear]
of them, especially soapmakers, who were constrained to pay 40£ custom
for every ton of soap they made, and every man rated what quantity he
should yearly make; and account for every mans doings was weekly taken
by some appointed for oversight thereof. Some were known to make
more than they were allowed or paid for, whereupon above 30 of them
were served up to London, where (against their wills) they were retained
long with great expense, imprisoned, and fined in above 200£, and were
bound to more inconveniences before they could be discharged ...

   Those foresaid commissioners for merchants were so extreme, that they
examined clerks belonging to ye merchants, to hear what they could
inform, of whom one clerk they here imprisoned for not giving them
satisfaction, and then carried him to London and imprisoned him again.
Another clerk being from home, they came about midnight into his
house and bed chamber to take him away, where not finding him they
searched his house for books.[1]

The monopoly greatly angered the Bristol merchants and after an
appeal they were granted the right to manufacture 600 tons of soap
per annum, but this was far less than they had been producing. They
made five visits to London to plead their case but with little success,
and when a tax of four pounds per ton was levied on the soap they

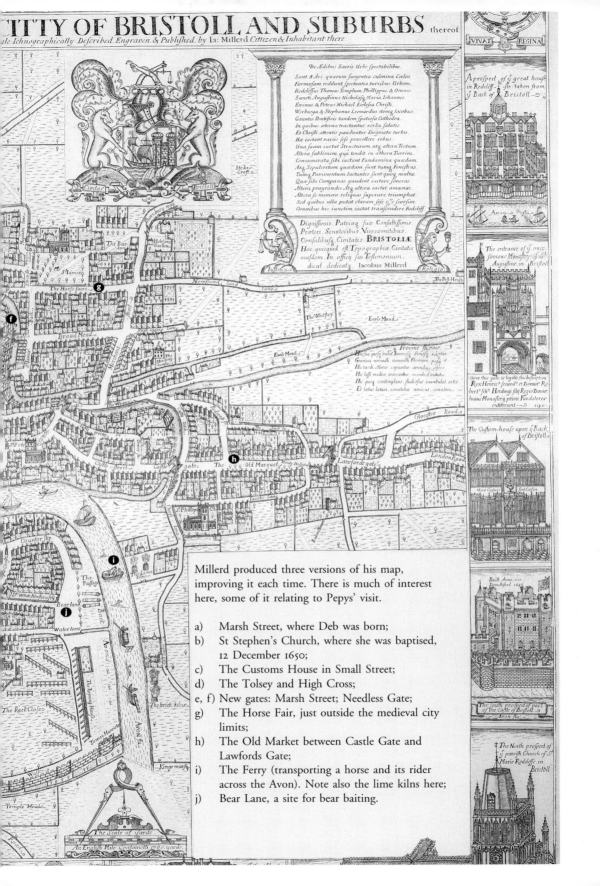

Millerd produced three versions of his map, improving it each time. There is much of interest here, some of it relating to Pepys' visit.

a) Marsh Street, where Deb was born;
b) St Stephen's Church, where she was baptised, 12 December 1650;
c) The Customs House in Small Street;
d) The Tolsey and High Cross;
e, f) New gates: Marsh Street; Needless Gate;
g) The Horse Fair, just outside the medieval city limits;
h) The Old Market between Castle Gate and Lawfords Gate;
i) The Ferry (transporting a horse and its rider across the Avon). Note also the lime kilns here;
j) Bear Lane, a site for bear baiting.

were even more outraged. Twelve soapmakers ended up in the Fleet prison for non-payment of the new tax.

Sugar and tobacco were imported from the New World. Sugar manufacture existed in 1612 and had grown to be an important industry by the middle of the seventeenth century. A brief account is given by the diarist John Evelyn who witnessed the manufacture in 1654:

> ... I first saw the manner of refining sugar, and casting it into loaves, where we had a collation of eggs fried in the sugar furnace, together with excellent Spanish wine ...[2]

A few years later the parishioners of St Thomas's complained about the sugar house of John Hinds, which they considered to be a dangerous fire risk, and he was ordered to move his refinery to safer premises within two months. John Evelyn must also have seen glass manufacture, but this industry was still in its infancy at the time of his visit and did not begin to expand until later in the century. Glass bottles were manufactured and were used to export the Hotwells water and the beer brewed from it. Spun glass was made for domestic windows and a reference to a glass grinder appears in 1683.

Both sugar and glass were dependent on the coal industry and the existence of a local coalfield was a very significant factor in the industrial development of Bristol. The coal was mined at Kingswood during the middle ages for domestic heating and by the seventeenth century it was being used extensively for manufacturing industries. In August 1606 the Chamberlain took the unprecedented step of riding out to the coalfield to check the measure of the miner's bushels. Kingswood was considered a lawless region, a world apart from Bristol, even retaining its own dialect which was reputed to be 'rich in Anglo-Saxon words'. The chamberlain had to bribe the miners two shillings to take the measure but we are told that the job was successfully performed.[3]

The city records show cases where the price of coal rose to beyond the reach of the poor and in 1642 several shiploads were imported from South Wales to be sold at cost price to the needy. Travellers from Bath often came via Kingswood along what was not the most salubrious route by which to enter Bristol. Celia Fiennes gives a few details from 1680 which show that the pack horse was the main means of transportation for the coal:

> ... from the Bath I went westward to Bristol over Landsdown 10 mile and passed thro' Kingswood, and was met with a great many horses passing and returning loaden with coals dug just thereabout; they gave 12 pence a horse load which carryes two bushells, it makes very good fires, this is the cakeing coale.[4]

Merchants' Dock (near Cumberland Basin) was a place where ships were built and repaired. It was about a mile downstream from the centre.

When tolls were introduced on the first turnpike roads the miners objected strongly to the payment of tolls on their coal. They assembled together in great numbers, pulled down the tollgates and threw them into the Avon. 'They are a set of ungovernable people, regardless of consequences', claimed the mayor. 'They extort money of people as they pass along the road, and treat them very rudely unless they give them some. They have passed through this city with clubs and staves in a noisy manner, but committed no violence here. I am persuaded, had any opposition been made, the consequences would have been fatal.' The tollgates were re-erected but within a few hours the miners pulled them down again and refused to supply any coal into Bristol. Troops were brought in and four of the rioters were taken captive. The gates were replaced a second time. As soon as the soldiers had left some strange-looking women arrived wearing high-crowned hats and pulled down the gates yet again – the women were the Kingswood miners in disguise! Packhorse coal was then allowed free carriage, but the affray dragged on for years before the miners accepted tolls for wheeled vehicles.[5]

In 1680 when Celia Fiennes visited Bristol she was impressed with the Colston almshouses but she disliked the cathedral and she found the old part of the town narrow and dingy, with the overhanging upper stories keeping out the light. Her comments may well be coloured by the criticism against her father, Colonel Nathaniel Fiennes, who had defended Bristol during the Civil War:

> Bristol lyes low in a bottom the greatest part of the town, tho' one end of it you have a pretty rise of ground; there are 19 parish churches beside the Cathedrall which has nothing fine or curious about it; the buildings of the town are pretty high most of timber work, the streetes are narrow and something darkish, because the rooms on the upper storys are more jutting out, soe contracts the streete and the light; the suburbs are better buildings and more spacious streetes; there are at one place as you enter the towne 2 almshouses 6 men and 6 women apiece each, there is also at another part of the town a noble almshouse more like a gentlemans house that is all of stone work, a handsome court with gates and pallisodos before four grass plots divided by paved walks and a walk round the same; the one side is for the women the other for the men, the middle building is 2 kitchens for either and a middle roome in common for washing and brewing, over all is a Chappell; they have gardens behind it with all things convenient, they have their coal and 3 shillings per weeke allowed to each to maintain them; this is for decayed tradesmen and wives that have lived well, its set up and allowed to by Mr Coleson [Edward Colston] a merchant of London.[6]

St Michael's Hill still contains good examples of seventeenth-century, timber-framed, domestic buildings.

After the fiasco with the London soapmakers the Bristol merchants were very keen to assert their independence from London and Daniel Defoe was very aware of this on his visit in 1720. Eighteenth-century visitors were not in general as complimentary as their predecessors from the previous century. The Industrial Revolution was still in its infancy and they did not know what to make of the smoking chimneys of the glass kilns which shared the skyline with the church spires. The number of conical glass houses was growing steadily and in 1720 Daniel Defoe counted fifteen of them:

> ... [Bristol] ... The greatest, richest and best port of trade in Great Britain, London only excepted. The merchants of this city not only have the greatest trade, but they trade with a more entire independency upon London, than any other town in Britain. And 'tis evident in this particular, that whatsoever exportations they make to any part of the world, they are able to bring the full return back to their own port, and can dispose of it there ...
>
> ... the Bristol merchant as they have a very great trade abroad, so they have always buyers at home, for their returns and that such buyers that no cargo is too big for them. To this purpose, the shopkeepers in Bristol who in general are all wholesale men, have so great an inland trade among all the western counties, that they maintain carriers just as the London tradesmen do, to all the principle counties and towns from Southampton in the south, even to the banks of the Trent north; and

King Street is the most cosmopolitan street in Bristol. Buildings from four centuries harmonise well together; they include pubs, almshouses, warehouses, theatres and a library.

tho' they have no navigable river that way, yet they drive a very great trade through all those counties

... There are no less than fifteen glass-houses in Bristol, which is more than there are in the city of London: they have indeed a very great expence of glass bottles, sending them fill'd with beer, cyder, and wine to the West Indies, much more than goes from London; also great numbers of bottles, even such as is almost incredible, are now used for sending the waters of St Vincent's Rock away, which are now carry'd, not all over England only, but, we may say, over all the world.[7]

When Alexander Pope came to Bristol he too was undecided about the smoking chimneys. Where Defoe counted fifteen in 1720, Pope counted twenty in 1739. Their number had grown to exceed that of the church spires. Pope's description of the forest of masts in the harbour is unparalleled by any other visitor:

I hardly knew what I undertook when I said I would give you some account of this place. Nothing can do it but a Picture, it is so unlike any Scene you ever saw. But I'll begin at least and reserve the rest to my next letter. From Bath you go along the river, or its Side, the Road lying generally in sight of it, on each Bank are steeping rising Hills cloathed with Wood at top and sloping towards the stream in Green Meadows, intermixed with white Houses, Mills & Bridges, this for 7 & 8 miles, then you come in sight of Bristol, the river winding at the bottom of steeper banks to the Town where you see twenty odd Pyramids smoking over the Town (which are Glasshouses) and a vast Extent of Houses red and white. You come first to old walls, & over a bridge built on both sides like London Bridge, and as much crowded, with a stronge mixture of Seamen, women, children, loaded Horses, Asses, & sledges with Goods dragging along, all together, without posts to separate them. From thence you come to a Key along the old Wall with houses on both sides, and in the middle of the street, as far as you can see, hundreds of Ships, their Masts as thick as they can stand by one another, which is the oddest & most surprising sight imaginable. This street is fuller of them, than the Thames from London Bridge to Deptford, & at certain times only, the Water rises to carry them out; so that at other times, a Long Street full of ships in the Middle & Houses on both sides looks like a Dream ...[8]

The centre of Bristol, inside the old walls, was a very crowded place in which to live and work. The narrow streets had overhanging upper storeys, with danger appearing both from chamber pots overhead and the sledges underfoot. Those who could afford it had moved over the Frome to the roomier properties on St Michael's Hill or to the new houses in Queen Square. The latter was named after Queen Anne in honour of her visit in 1702, but the Bristolians paradoxically erected an equestrian statue of William III in the centre. Pope did not know bronze from brass but he still gave an excellent description of Queen Square:

> The city of Bristol itself is very unpleasant and no civilised company in it. Only the Collector of the Customs would have brought me acquainted with the Merchants, of whom I hear no great Character. The streets are as crowded as London but the best Image I can give you of it is 'Tis as if Wapping and Southwark were ten-times as big, or all their people run into London. Nothing is fine in it but the Square, which is larger than Grosvenor-Square and wellbuilded, with a very fine brass statue in the middle of King William on Horseback; and the quay which is full of ships and goes half round this Square. The College Green is pretty and (like the Square) set with trees, with a very fine Old Cross of Gothic curious work in the middle, but spoild with the folly of gilding it, that takes away all the venerable Antiquity. There is a cathedral very neat and 19 parish Churches.[9]

Rysbrack's statue of William III, Queen Square. The equestrian statue dates to 1736, by which time the square had already been named after Queen Anne. The statue witnessed and survived the Bristol Riots of 1831.

Metal working was a local industry which began with copper and brass parts for the shipbuilding industry and which grew in importance to serve many other industries. It was not strictly located within Bristol but about six miles away near the coalfield at Warmley where zinc, copper and brass were smelted. In 1707 Abraham Darby, an important member of the Quaker community, was made a freeman of Bristol and he intended to set up in business manufacturing iron pots at Baptist Mills where he had previously run a malt mill. Darby had experimented for years with the problem of casting iron and his eventual success was partly due to the suggestion of a Bristol boy called John Thomas, and partly to his own reverberating furnace which was based on the designs of the Bristol glass furnaces. Hannah Rose, daughter of John Thomas, described how Abraham Darby had first tried to cast iron pots using Dutch expertise before her father solved the problem; she also describes how closely the trade secrets were guarded:

> After some time he had a mind to set the Dutchmen to try to cast Iron Pots in sand. They tried several times but could not do it, so he was at a great loss in paying Wages for no result. At length John Thomas, my Father, then a young Man who came on trial to learn the trade of Malt Mill making, seeing the Dutchmen try and could not bring to perfection, asked his master to let him try, so with his leave he did it, and afterwards his Master and him were bound in Articles in the year 1707, that John Thomas should be bound to work at that business and keep it secret and not teach anybody else, for three years. They were so private as to stop the keyhole of the Door.[10]

William Reeves' Black Castle was built of slag from the zinc works around 1765 with dressing of Bath stone. Walpole, when he first saw it, called it the 'Devil's Cathedral'. In fact the Black Castle is a well-liked building with a unique charm of its own.

The Bristol coal was of poor quality and this was probably the main reason why Abraham Darby moved to set up business at the other end of the River Severn, at Coalbrookdale in Shropshire. It was there that the first cylinders for the Newcomen atmospheric engines were cast in iron, many of which were transported down the Severn and installed at the Cornish tin mines. The earlier Newcomen engines had expensive brass cylinders and it seems likely that these may have been cast in

Bristol, the largest centre of brass making at the time. Abraham Darby's trade connections with Bristol were maintained and Newcomen engines could be seen pumping water from the mines at Warmley. Latimer mentions an 'ingenious machine' near Crewe's Hole for raising water to supply Bristol. If this was a primitive steam engine, as he supposes, then it deserves further research because it appears to predate the first known Newcomen engine erected near Dudley in 1710.[11] In 1731 there was a 'water engine' at Castle Mills. No details of these engines are known but in 1749 the *Bristol Journal* gives an account of the new 'fire engine' installed at William Champion's brassworks at Warmley. The amazed public watched with wonder as the water raised by the engine was used to turn a water wheel and provide power for the factory:

> The machine is the most noblest of its kind in the world; it discharges upwards of 3000 h[ogs]h[ea]ds of water in an hour. The water is bouyed up by the several tubes in a hemisphere of a conical form, and falls into a pool as in a cascade, and affords a grand and beautiful scene.[12]

The secrets of the glass-making and metal industries were jealously maintained and in the 1750s foreign visitors came to learn more about the industrial processes. A Mr Ferrner from Sweden arrived in 1759. He bribed the workmen with drinks and money in return for trade secrets and he left a detailed account of both the glass and the metal industries. On the 7th of January 1760 the morning was so cold that the river was frozen over. He successfully gained access to the warm interior of a glass-house. He seems to have confused Redcliffe Gate with Temple Gate for he found himself in the wrong glass-house!

> In the morning all was covered with snow and the river was frozen. I went out through Radcliffe Gate towards Bedminster-cum-Capellis, which is a small village or suburb of Bristol, where I was told they blow the best English window-glass. But when I entered the glass house they had nothing else there but coarse drinking glasses.
>
>   Here I found out that the window-glass house was outside Temple Gate. I therefore went there and saw the whole process; but despite giving drinking money I could not discover the composition of the glass which the workmen in this place do not know themselves. With further questioning I found out that there was a crystal furnace or glass house not far inside Temple Gate.[13]

The next day he gained access to a third glass-house and he had more success with his findings:

> I was again at the crystal glass house, where they were blowing white cups with white enamel in the foot or the handle and also flasks of the same type with white stripes. Here I heard which ingredients make up the composition, which consists of fine white sand from the Isle of

Glass kiln. The Prewitt Street glass cone was originally ninety feet tall and the largest in Bristol. After serving as a chemical factory for a century and decaying for another fifty years it now survives as a restaurant of great character.

Whight [Wight], of red lead, of potash, of arsenic and of a kind of black metallish material, of which the workmen said they did not know the name.[14]

On the 18th he went to Warmley to try and discover more about the metal industry. He gives many fascinating details of William Champion's works:

This day I went again out to Warmly 5 miles from Bristol, after the first [visit] did not give me the expected information it was now urgent to see something. Here are 14 brass furnaces, 10 copper furnaces, a brass wire drawing mill, 10 brass battery hammers and a spelter works. The mixture used for brass I was told was 20 pounds of calamine to 45 to 50 pounds of copper. In all this there was nothing peculiar or different from the Swedish methods, as far as I could see except only that they employed reverberatory furnaces here for the smelting of copper and other uses with coal as the heat with charcoal was insufficient. This is common in all works here in England. That which was unusual and also clever here was that the same water was used again and again for driving the brass hammers, which runs through leats to these hammers, is collected in a deep pond right under the pump house, in the same was as in London and in years past in Dannemora. Here the water is pumped into a wide pond which lies higher than the battery mill or the works and then it runs into the works again. The boiler, in which water was boiled was strips of iron, riveted together . . .[15]

He was impressed with the steam engine which drove four pumps and was supplemented by a windmill. Here he gives the dimensions of the iron cylinder:

> The cylinder on top of it was 9 foot long and 4½ wide and cast of pig iron. There were 4 pumps, of which 2 come up at a time bringing with them at each stroke 5 hogsheads of water. Apart from this water engine there was at the other end a windmill, which pumped up water in this large pond from the area below it and built in the same way as all those similar mills in Holland.
>
> In the production of the brass they do not mix the calamine into the copper before it is pulverised in mills which look just like ordinary flour mills.[16]

We are now told something about William Champion himself, a master who was held in great awe by the workmen. The 'spelter' was impure zinc but this was refined to produce a much purer zinc – 'a white metal, which is nearly as good as silver; but no man is allowed to see the production'. Champion guarded the secret of the zinc manufacture so jealously that his workmen were not even allowed to talk to their wives about it:

> The spelter works was built right in front of Mr Champion's windows, who is the most important shareholder in this works, manages it himself and lives mostly there. He is so fiery in his surveillance that the workers there will hardly whisper his name. The wives of those who are employed in the works may never enter it and it is said that the workmen were sworn never to tell them what they were doing. No other workman from Warmly may put a foot inside that door. This Mr Champion has himself, with much cost, trouble and risk brought or stolen this art from Holland to England. He made two journeys there for this purpose and still has three Dutchmen here at the works; but has since then so much improved the metal that this is now almost of a different kind. It is sold at 18 pence per English pound.[17]

The fame of Bristol as a manufacturing centre was well known. In the early decades of the eighteenth century she was one of England's leading industrial centres and it was only the lesser quality of the coal which prevented Bristol from becoming a centre for the smelting of iron. The waters of both the Avon and the Frome worked hard on their passage to the sea and a great variety of industries developed on the riverbanks. There is little doubt that Bristol made an important contribution to a British revolution which was greater and more significant than all the other social and political upheavals of the eighteenth century. Here was large scale manufacturing; here was the black coal extracted from the bowels of the earth. Here were the bright orange fires of the furnaces. Here were the flowing molten metals of the foundry. Here were the black smoking chimneys of the kilns and here was the hissing white vapour of the panting steam engine with its red hot fire and its perpetual motion. Bristol was one of the birthplaces of the Industrial Revolution.

CHAPTER EIGHT

The Hot Wells

When Lieutenant Hammond and his colleagues visited Bristol in 1634 they made a short excursion up the hill to the manor of Clifton. Having reached the edge of the cliffs they descended again to the bottom of the gorge. Hammond described the object of the expedition:

> A strange hot well, which comes gushing out of a mighty stony Rock ... To it we descend by ... near 200 slippery steps; which place, when the tide is gone, never wants good store of company to wash in this well, and to drink of that warm and medicinal water.[1]

The Hotwell in its early years, showing primitive accommodation, piped spring water to an open pool, and a stone quay giving access by boat at high tide.

The well had always been a feature of the gorge and it was noted by William Wyrcestre in the fifteenth century, but there is no mention of its use for medicinal purposes until the seventeenth century. Having descended the slippery steps it was necessary either to ascend them all again or to wait for high tide and a boat to carry the visitors back to Bristol – consequently the gouty patrons of the Hot Well had to be reasonably fit to make the journey to the waters in the first place. In spite of this problem of accessibility it was not long before the Hot Well acquired great fame and a reputation for effecting some incredible cures in the best quackish traditions of the times.

For 33 years, from 1610 to 1643, Hotwells water was sent regularly around Land's End and the Straits of Dover to Dr Thomas Ward, the master of Sidney Sussex College in Cambridge, who took it for an unknown complaint. By 1629 Lord Poulett, writing to Lord Dorchester, was making the claim that the waters could cure leprosy. The waters acquired a reputation for gall stones and, as the fame of the Hotwell grew, claims were made for curing skin diseases, ulcers, scurvy,

The South prospect of a part of St Vincents rock & ye Hot well neer Bristoll

Avon flu

diabetes, gout, rheumatism, dysentery, hot livers, feeble brains and red pimply faces. Claims to cure venereal disease and cancer came later. Before rushing off to take the waters, however, it should be mentioned that the medical profession were divided about it efficacy. In 1628 Thomas Venner MD wrote a learned treatise on 'The Baths of Bath' in which he added a piece 'concerning the water of St Vincent's Rock, near Bristol'. He wrote that the waters were used against the stone but added a few provisos. 'In consequence of this peculiar virtue', he wrote, 'people of all sorts repaired to the place, and so abundantly glutted themselves at the spring that few were benefitted and many hurt, seeing that they had weakened the stomach, subverted the liver, annoyed the head, occasioned cramps and pain of there joints, and bred crudities, rhumes, coughs, dropsy and consumption.'

As the number of visitors grew there became an obvious requirement for a level road which would give better access to the springs along the river. In July 1662 William Schellinks from Amsterdam visited Bristol, travelling down the Avon by boat and noted the Hotwell as he passed by:

> On the 17th July in the morning we went with Mr. John Pietersen Reyers in a small boat with the ebb tide 4 miles down river to Hungroad or the roadstead, at 3 miles is the roadstead for the ships, which come in from the sea and mostly unload there. Downstream the river is very twisted and turning, and flanked in some places on both sides by very high and precipitous rocks, so that, as one travels through the narrow twisting passage, one fears that one will be driven against them, a strange experience. On the cliffs a lot of goats were feeding. At the foot of these steep rocks, several feet under water at high tide, are, almost on top of each other, two springs or wells, one giving hot and the other cold water in abundance and very clear, wheras the river water is opaque and cloudy because of the rapid rise and fall of the tides ...
>
> Going back up river with the tide, we came to the hot well and drank from it; the water was milk-warm, but is hotter in winter; a very good ale is brewed from it.[2]

The local brew which he mentions was claimed to be 'wholesome against the spleen'. The next day Schellinks visited the Hot Well again, this time he travelled on foot along the river bank to the gorge and he climbed up the two hundred slippery steps to Clifton. He noted in passing that a new road was under construction to take carriages:

> On the 18th of July in the morning we went for a walk along the river to the top of the town; in the afternoon we went on foot to the great well, which is a 3 miles walk, got into a heavy rain shower, and went up the hill to Clifton to refresh and dry ourselves. The landlord showed us some Bristol diamonds, amongst them a piece of rock in which were a lot of crystals, by nature very strange with angles and corners as if they

had been cut like that, mostly so hard that one can write with them on glass. They were hewn out of the rocks near the hot spring.

Note: By the water near the well the rocks are being cut away to make a roadway for carriages[3]

The new road did much to improve the accessibility and popularity of the spa and in 1677 a royal visitor arrived by coach: she was Queen Catherine of Braganze, the wife of James II. The Earl of Ossory and numerous courtiers attended her as she drank the waters. Queen Catherine, in common with many visitors, was making a day trip from Bath. The new spa was hardly a serious rival to Bath, and it made little impression on the number of visitors to the spa town. If anything it probably increased Bath's popularity by providing the additional attraction of a day out in the Avon Gorge. The converse side was that Bath contributed greatly to the number of visitors to Hotwells and the local and resident clientele were supplemented by many day trippers.

In 1687 Celia Fiennes visited the Hot Well. She drank the waters and bought a piece of Bristol Diamond:

> ... I went a 2 miles to the hott spring of water which lookes exceeding cleer and is warm as new milk and much of that sweetness; this is just by St Vincent's Rocks that are great clifts which seeme as bounds to the river Aven this channel was hewn out of those rocks they digg the Bristol Diamonds which look very bright and sparkling and in their native

The Old Hotwell House was built in 1696 by Thomas Callowhill and Charles Jones. It survived until 1822. A few of the 200 'slippery steps' to Clifton can be seen on the right. This lithograph is by Samuel Jackson, and dates from the 1820s.

THE OLD HOTWELL HOUSE, BRISTOL.

rudeness have a great lustre and are pointed like the diamond cutting; I had a piece just as it came out of the rock with the rock on the back side, and it appeared to me as a cluster of diamonds polish'd and irregularly cut; some of these are hard and will endure the cutting and polishing by art and soe they make rings and earings of them ...[4]

The Bristol diamonds were nodules of quartz which could be found in the rock formations hidden beneath the patches of vegetation.

At this point in time there was a bath house at the Hotwells but no accommodation. A few years later the Bristol Merchant Venturers bought up much of Clifton, including the land occupied by the Hotwell in the Avon Gorge. In 1695 they leased the well for 90 years to Charles Jones, a soapboiler, and Thomas Callowhill, a draper, and these two built a pump room and lodging houses for the comfort and accommodation of the visitors. The new building cost five hundred pounds and it became known as Hotwell House. It was built to enclose the hot spring and to screen the spring waters from the muddy tides of the Avon. Hotwell House was a substantial building with four floors and a basement. It had nothing of the elegance of Bath but it served the purpose for which it was intended and in the early decades of the eighteenth century the number of visitors increased steadily.

Before long the Hotwell waters were being shipped regularly to London. The sea voyage usually took four to six weeks but in 1726 Richard Bristowe, a London goldsmith, advertised the water at 6s for a dozen bottles, newly arrived after only eight days transit from Bristol. Three years later there were two ballrooms and three large taverns at the Hotwell and the well was so crowded from noon until two that it was impossible to get near enough for a drink. Alexander Pope visited in 1739, and described the avenue of trees which led to Hotwell House:

Passing still along by the river you come to a Rocky way on one Side, overlooking green Hills on the other; On that rocky way rise several white Houses, and over them red rocks, and as you go further, more Rocks above rocks, mixed with green bushes, and of different coloured stone. This is at a Mile's end, terminates in the House of the Hot well, whereabouts lye several pretty Lodging Houses open to the River with Walks of Trees.[5]

Pope then paid a mixed compliment to the waters:

I believe the Bristol waters at the well, would be serviceable if I could stay long enough, viz. six weeks or two months, for as they are an Alternative, and of no great strength, they require a longer time to operate than the warmer and more impregnated Mineral-Waters such as Bath etc. The place is so Exposed, and so inconvenient for want of Chairs, Coaches at all easy, etc., that there is no living long here in winter for such thin bodies as mine.[6]

Dowry Square was built in 1725 and offered a better class of
accommodation for long-term patrons, but it was half a mile upstream
from Hotwell House. The well waters were connected by an underground passage to the Avon and a very high tide could cause the spa
water to become polluted by river water. In hot weather a low tide
exposed the mud and visitors complained of the smell. The fortunes
of the Hotwell varied greatly throughout its lifespan and in the middle
years of the century the spa suffered a decline.

In 1754 a new tavern was opened in Dowry Square by a Ms Trinder
of Bath. 'Elizabeth Trinder, from the Lebeck's Head Tavern Bath, has
opened a house at the Hotwells for the reception of company as a
tavern or eating house. An ordinary every day at three o'clock, at half
a crown a head ... the house being the first of its kind attempted
here'. John Wesley's journal shows that in the same year he took time
off his travels to rest at the Hotwells and to sample the waters. A local
preacher called Dolman wrote that 'when he [Wesley] first came ...
his countenance looked as if a greedy consumption had determined to
put an end to his days. But in less than three weeks ... he was enabled
to set out on his Cornish circuit ... preaching every day'. This was
good publicity material but the place had declined in popularity and
Dolman admitted that the only visible signs of humanity were the
gibbeted remains of two murderers visible across the water.[7]

In 1755 the water table fell to an exceptionally low level and the well
waters ran 'as red as blood'. This was seen as a strange omen but the
'scientific' community was easily able to explain it when news came
through of an earthquake at Lisbon on same day. The spa's fortunes
picked up again and many improvements were made from the 1750s
to the 1770s, when the 'New Vauxhall Gardens' were laid out to give
riverside walks and public breakfasts were served to visitors. Balls and
concerts were given at regular intervals. In 1776 a 'New Vauxhall' was
opened up which enjoyed a very brief popularity. An anonymous
Bristolian wrote a satirical poem about it:

> They have here furnished up an old family seat,
> And built a saloon, in length seventy-five feet,
> The gardens were luckily laid out before,
> So some lamps stuck about there now needed no more.
> Six days out of seven in business begun
> Is ended in jollity, feasting and fun.[8]

Latimer's account summarises the character and the atmosphere very
well – it needs only a Hogarth to illustrate the scene:

> Scarcely a trace of the downright honest trading class remains. Folly has
> taken possession of all, and the modest shopkeepers that formerly con-
> tented themselves with decent bob-wigs now parade about with tails

down their backs, like monkeys, while their wives, starched out in silk and lace, rattle along in fine coaches ...

On Sundays the vanity stricken throng [repair] to College green to display their fine dresses. The nights are given up to fine suppers, upon which tradesmen squander all their profits. After this denunciatory exordium, the author proceeds to describe his visit to Vauxhall, where he beholds a breeches maker defending his fair cheeks from the sun with a pink silk umbrella, and another shopkeeper, renowned for his drinking, mirth and song swaggering

> With a large oaken stick, a slouched hat, and black stock,
> Cropt hair, leather breeches, and jockey-cut frock.

A drunken parson, a gouty alderman dubbed Turtle, and other personages receive similar irreverent treatment; the illuminations are ridiculed; and the voices of the singers are said to have been drowned by the uproar made by 'the Bucks' in the neighbouring bowling green.[9]

In May 1777 *Felix Farley's Journal* noted that there was a new fashion for taking the waters. 'We are informed from the Hotwells that it is there the prevailing *ton* for gentlemen to go and drink the waters at the Pump Room with their nightcaps on; and that this innovation of the head dress somewhat alarms the ladies'. Two weeks later the fashion had evolved to the wearing of two watches! 'We are informed that no considerable alteration in dress has taken place since the Revolution of the Nightcap, except the seemingly extravagant appendage of an extraordinary watch; as the gentlemen of the true *ton* wear one in each fob.' The newspaper then went on to describe yet another fashion of the moment. 'The season at the Hotwells is now truly brilliant, but no considerable alteration in polite amusements has taken place, except that ladies and gentlemen have formed a resolution of going to the balls undressed.' The contributor never re-appeared to clarify the meaning of his final word!

The spa reached its greatest popularity at this period, but the lease ran out in 1784 and the Merchant Venturers advertised for a new leaseholder. A lot of money was needed for improvements. It was estimated that £1000 was needed to repair the quay wall and £100 for tidal protection. In 1786 the Colonnade was built in a small quarry against the rocks and in 1790 Samuel Powell took over the lease, although he had to increase the rents and charges to pay for the repairs. The Colonnade was an attractive and high-class development with a covered walk, shops and a circulating library, and with accommodation on the upper floors. The library was run by the poet Ann Yearsley, a milkwoman who was sponsored by Hannah More. In June of 1789 a visitor to the Hotwells complained about the arrangements in a letter to the local journal. At this time there existed both an old and a new long

room and visitors were frequently confused about which function was to be held in which room. A dispute arose between the two parties as to which room would hold breakfast on which day. The Clifton residents came to the rescue with an impartial arrangement, a public breakfast and dance were held every Monday, a ball on Tuesdays, and a promenade with dancing was held on Thursdays in alternate rooms. Breakfast and promenade cost 1s. 6d. per head. The ball cost a gentleman a guinea at each room for the full season, and for this sum he was allowed to introduce two ladies.

Trade was booming in the 1780s but it was followed by an inexorable decline in numbers. By the next decade Clifton had grown considerably both as a high-class residential suburb and as a fashionable spa in its own right. It seemed that walking and horse riding on Durdham Downs was a far more appealing pastime to the young and active. In a different era the rise of Clifton might have been the saving of Hotwells but the rise came too late. The first seaside resorts had appeared at much the same time and bathing in the seawater became a far more popular pastime than drinking the mineral waters at the inland spas.

Thus the Hotwell lingered on into the nineteenth century but the old Hotwell House was demolished in 1822. This was not the end, however. A new Tuscan-style pump room was built and it survived until 1867. The Hotwell always had a precarious existence. Its greatest days were the later decades of the eighteenth century but it was unable to survive the rapid changes which came with the nineteenth century.

The Colonnade at Hotwells dates from 1786–87 and is a remarkable survival from the Hotwell Spa. The ground floor originally contained a shopping arcade which included Ann Yearsley's circulating library.

CHAPTER NINE

'Deepest Deadliest Guilt'

Edward Colston. 'This great and pious benefactor was known to have done many other excellent Charities,' reads his memorial in All Saint's church. 'And what He did in Secret is believed to be not inferior to what He did in Public.' Edward Colston did more than any other individual to bring the slave trade to Bristol.

Colston School, Colston's Arms Houses, Colston Charities, Colston Place, Colston Hall. Edward Colston (1636–1721) was a wealthy merchant and in financial terms he was probably the greatest of all Bristol's benefactors. He had endowments and charities, not only all over Bristol but also in London, Surrey, Devonshire and as far away as Lancashire. 'This great and pious benefactor was known to have done many other excellent Charities', reads his memorial in All Saint's church. 'And what He did in Secret is believed to be not inferior to what He did in Public.' So is posterity allowed to ask what Edward Colston did in secret? Yes. He amassed a fortune in sugar. He owned plantations in the West Indies. He was a member of the Royal African Company in London. There is no secret. Colston was quite open about his activities, it is simply that later generations found it hard to accept that one of their greatest benefactors built his fortune on the back of the African slave trade. Edward Colston probably did more than any other man to bring the slave trade to Bristol.

In the seventeenth century the slave trade was just another example of the London monopolies which angered the provincial ports because the latter were not allowed to share in the trade and the profits. It was the demand for cheap labour on the sugar plantations and in the Virginia tobacco industry which created a trade in human slaves. In the early days Virginia was used as a penal colony and it was common for criminals to be given a reprieve from the death sentence in exchange for transportation to the plantations as slave labour – the classic fictional case was that of Daniel Defoe's heroine Moll Flanders. Bristol was a centre for the transportation activity, and there is a disturbing record in 1651 of five hundred Scottish loyalists who were sentenced to forced labour in the Virginia plantations because they supported the king at the battle of Worcester.

After the bloody assizes of 1685 Judge Jeffries, the most hated man in the West of England, not only sent hundreds of innocent soldiers to the gallows after the Duke of Monmouth's defeat at Sedgemoor, but also sentenced an estimated 850 men to transportation. When Jeffries arrived in Bristol he seemed most put out that he could find only three men to send to the gallows, so he launched a tirade against the mayor for kidnapping children and transporting them to the colonies. His facts were wrong; the mayor had transported under age felons to the colonies but he had acted quite legally, saving their lives by commuting death sentences to transportation. There are records of child kidnapping in Bristol for transportation to the colonies, but these were isolated criminal activities and were usually dealt with by the law.[1]

In 1698 the London monopoly on the African Trade was lifted. Several outports immediately began trading to the African coast. Bristol was the best-placed port to take advantage of the new laws and it took only two decades for Bristol to overtake London's dominant position in the trade, a place which she held for about two more decades until the middle of the eighteenth century. In the 1750s it was Liverpool which took the lead and which handled the bulk of the trade until abolition in 1807. The table shows the mean number of vessels leaving the three major English slaving ports throughout the eighteenth century. The size of the ships varied greatly. Sometimes just a few slaves were carried on a merchantman to add a little profit on the side, with a small slaver carrying about thirty slaves. Later in the century a large slaver could carry four hundred or more.

Mean number of clearances per year
from English ports to West Africa in the eighteenth century

Year	London	Bristol	Liverpool
1710	24	20	2
1725	87	63	not known
1730–39	25	39	21
1750–59	13	20	49
1771	58	23	107
1772–75	40	22	95
1776–82	17	6	35
1783–92	31	25	88
1793–1804	18	5	107
1805–07	0	0	101[2]

Many ships traded directly from Bristol to Jamaica for sugar, and to Virginia or South Carolina for tobacco. Both these products depended heavily on slave labour but the direct traders did not carry slaves. It was on the dreaded middle passage of the three-legged voyage, from Europe to Africa, Africa to America and America to Europe, that the live cargoes were carried. The trade has always been held to be very lucrative, with profits to be made on each of the three legs, but there were great risks involved and the gains were offset by frequent losses. Bristol was a great manufacturing centre and the outward cargo to Africa would typically contain metal pots from the Warmley foundry, often second hand pots and pans bought at the local markets, copper and iron bars, cotton goods, firearms and gunpowder. The firearms were sold to the slave traders on the African coast. These were the unsavoury dealers who scoured the African interior to capture Negroes and bring them to the coast manacled together for sale to the slaving captains.

In 1774 the snow *Africa* left Bristol for New Calabar on the Gold Coast. She was a prize from the French wars, a two-masted square rigger of a hundred tons burthen. The captain, George Merrick, was experienced in the African trade, and he carried with him all the necessary trading certificates and instructions from the ship's owners:

The slave trade on the west coast of Africa, showing slaves arriving at the trading post already manacled for transportation.

[barter for] ... good healthy young negroes and ivory, and ... not to buy any old slaves or children but good healthy young men and women, and buy all the ivory you can and when you are half-slaved don't stay too long if there is a possibility of getting off for the risk of sickness and mortality then become great ... let no candle be made use of in drawing spirits or to go near the powder ... We recommend you to treat the negroes with as much lenity as safety will admit and suffer none of your officers or people to abuse them under any pretence whatever, be sure you see their victuals well dressed and given them in due season ... We recommend you to make fires frequently in the negroes' rooms as we think it healthy and you have iron kettles on board for that purpose. We recommend mutton broth in fluxes, so that you'll endeavour to purchase as many sheep and goats to bring off the coast for that purpose as you conveniently can.[3]

The owners were full of good intentions for the health of the Negroes once they had forcibly torn them away from their homes and families, but the slaves were packed and shackled so tightly that it was impossible to keep them healthy. The space allocated was typically 66 inches by 16 inches per slave. Only the captain and the crew of the slaving vessel witnessed the atrocious hell-hole of the middle passage, with the slaves chained together and crammed like sardines in the stinking hold of the ship. Alexander Falconbridge, one of the ship's surgeons, described the conditions between the decks:

... having occasioned the port-holes to be shut, and the grating to be covered, fluxes and fevers among the negroes ensued. While they were in this situation, my profession requiring it, I frequently went down among them, till at length their apartments became so extremely hot as to be only sufferable for a very short time. But the excessive heat was

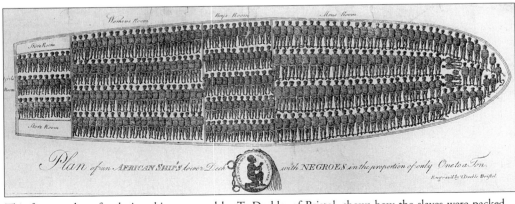

This famous plan of a slaving ship, engraved by T. Deeble, of Bristol, shows how the slaves were packed between the decks on the dreaded middle passage across the Atlantic. Note the roundel, bottom centre, which is surrounded by a cat-of-nine-tails, and shows a begging slave boy with the caption, 'Am I Not a Man and a Brother'. The illustration was obviously prepared as evidence in favour of the abolitionist cause. Nevertheless the overcrowding depicted here is not far wide of the mark.

not the only thing that rendered their situation intolerable. The deck, that is the floor of their rooms, was so covered with blood and mucous which had proceeded from them in consequence of the flux, that it resembled a slaughter-house. It is not in the power of the human imagination to picture to itself a situation more dreadful or disgusting. Numbers of the slaves having fainted, they were carried up on deck, where several of them died and the rest were, with great difficulty, restored. It had nearly proved fatal to me.[4]

For eight weeks the Negroes, torn forcibly from their homes and families and tossing on the stormy Atlantic with little idea of their fate, had to endure this terrible depravity. When the weather allowed they were taken on deck to exercise – this was not a humane concession, it was done merely to keep the cargo in a fit condition for the market.

> Packed in close misery, the reeking crowd,
> Sweltering in chains, pollute the hot abode,
> In painful rows with studious art comprest,
> Smoking they lie, and breathe the humid pest:
> Moistened with gore, on the hard platform ground,
> The bare rub'd joint soon bursts the painful bound:
> Sinks the obdurate plank with racking force,
> And ploughs, dire task, its agonising course.
>
> *James Stansfield*

In 1727 the *Castle* loaded 271 slaves at Andony in Africa who were purchased at about £2 15s. a head. In the following year the *Virgin* arrived in Jamaica with 262 slaves who were sold at £30 17s. 6d. per head – these prices were very typical and they show that the profits were enormous. 'Surely negroes were never so much wanted', reads a letter from R Assheton to Isaac Hobhouse. 'Nor can that want be supplied for two years to come, which the Days [a Bristol slaving partnership] are very sensible of, and push all they can. The general terms Pratten buys at is £30 to £32 per head for men, women, boys and girls.' In 1729 Assheton wrote that he could only obtain £19 10s. a head for his cargo because they were mostly 'children or grey headed'. In this particular case over a third of his shipment died only a few weeks later because they were so weak and depressed from the Atlantic passage. It was not an isolated incident; in the same year the *John and Betty* of Bristol arrived in Jamaica with 150 slaves, having lost a hundred on the passage and buried eleven more after her arrival in port. The slaver *Greyhound* left Bonny with 339 slaves, but only 214 were still alive when the ship arrived at Barbados. In 1737 there was a mass suicide attempt on the slaver *Prince of Orange* commanded by Captain Japeth Bird, when a hundred Negroes jumped overboard:

I thought all our troubles of this voyage were over; but on the contrary

I might say that dangers rest on the borders of security. On the 14th of March we found a great deal of discontent amongst the slaves, particularly the men, which continued till the 16th about five o'clock in the evening, when to our great amazement above an hundred men slaves jumped overboard ... out of the whole we lost 33 of as good men slaves as we had on board, who would not endeavour to save themselves, but resolved to die and sunk directly down. Many more of them were taken up almost drowned, some of them died since, but not to the owner's loss, they being sold before any discovery was made of the injury the salt water had done them.[5]

There were victories for the Negroes; these were rare and so are worth recording. There is an account of a slave revolt in May 1728 when a Captain Holliday and 'all his crew except the cabin boy' were murdered off the coast of Africa. In 1753 the slaver *Marlborough* sailed from the Gold Coast carrying 400 slaves. Three days out of Bonny many of the crew were taken sick and 28 slaves had to be unchained to help man the ship. The Negroes grasped their opportunity and managed to seize the firearms, they killed the captain and 35 of the crew, but they had to keep the boatswain and a few other whites alive to navigate the ship back to Bonny. Another Bristol slaver, the *Hawk*, tried to recapture the *Marlborough* but the Negroes determinedly held them off by firepower. *Felix Farley's Journal* records a 'furious quarrel' between the blacks with a hundred thrown overboard – but the Bristol newspapers were not exactly impartial where slavery was involved, so it would be nice to balance this part of the story with the Negroes' version of what happened. They struck a blow for black freedom and they forced six of the captive English sailors to guide them back to their home shore.

A terrible case of infanticide appears with the trial of Captain William Lugen who was bound for Carolina on the middle passage with 200 slaves. A Negro mother died leaving a very young child which was left critically ill on deck in the burning sun. The Negroes refused to care for the infant, fearing that it had an infection, and the ship's surgeon declared that it could not live through the day. Captain Lugen ordered the child to be thrown overboard. He was brought to trial for his actions but the bigotry against the blacks was so bad that he was acquitted on the grounds that he had shown no premeditated malice.[6]

When the slaves reached the plantations their problems were not over. One of the saddest cases was that of a young girl who survived the passage to South Carolina, but she was so depressed and sickened by the passage that she had no desire to live on in slavery. She hanged herself with a piece of small vine, so slender that her carcass must have weighed very little.

When the fierce sun darts vertical his beams,
And thirst and hunger mix their wild extremes;

When the sharp iron wounds his inmost soul,
And his strained eyes in burning anguish roll;
Will the parch'd negro own, ere he expire,
No pain in hunger, and no heat in fire?

Hannah More

The Georgian house of John Pinney, owner of the Nevis sugar plantation in the West Indies. The house dates from about 1790 and is the work of William, son of Thomas Paty.

Many merchants in Bristol were also owners of the sugar plantations and therefore owners of large numbers of slaves. They all admitted that cruelty existed on the plantations but they all went to great pains to point out that their own slaves were given the best possible treatment. They all professed to look after their slaves in an exemplary fashion, it was always somebody else who was maltreating the slaves. Much of our knowledge of the conditions comes from the papers of John Pinney who lived at the Georgian House in Great George Street – he owned the Nevis plantation in the West Indies. By the standard of the times Pinney was one of the better masters; he looked after the elderly Negroes on his plantation and he paid for medical treatment when it was required – just as long as it wasn't too expensive:

Avoid as much as possible the calling in of a Doctor to the Negroes; they are so exorbitant in their charges, it is impossible for an estate to support it. Simples, good nursing and kitchen physic are the only requisites to recover sick negroes; I was very successful in my practice, and have no doubt that you will be equally so.[7]

Medical practice was very primitive, full of eighteenth-century folk-lore, and lacking in sound scientific knowledge, but when an epidemic of smallpox broke out on Pinney's plantation the isolation techniques were well known and slaves were innoculated against the disease. The incident also serves as a good illustration of the hypocrisy of the slave dealers. The blacks responded to the vaccine in exactly the same way as the whites, yet the slavers frequently tried to justify their actions with the pathetic excuse that the Negroes were a different species from the whites. Pinney actually refers to them as 'human' flesh but he still tries to appease his conscience in a way which was typical of all the merchants in the trade:

Since my Arr[ival] I've purch[ase]d 9 Negroe Slaves at St Kitts and can assure you I was shocked at the first appear[an]ce of hum[a]n flesh expos'd for Sale. But surely God ordain'd 'em for ye use and benefit of us: other[wi]se his Divine Will, would have been manifest by some part[icula]r Sign or Token.[7]

The obvious signs of distress and suicide amongst the slaves were conveniently not seen as 'God's Sign or Token'. The dealers had no problem about easing their conscience with their religion and their correspondence frequently refers to captives 'shipped by the grace of

God' and uses phrases of the form 'God sent the ship to her desired port in safety'.

It was customary for the ship's captain to be allowed to keep one or more slaves as part of his salary and this meant that a few Negroes sailed on the third leg of the triangular voyage and became residents of eighteenth-century Bristol. The sea captains would usually sell their Negroes to wealthy families as domestic servants and advertisements were therefore quite common in the local newspapers. Latimer gives many examples:

Farley's Bristol Newspaper 13 August 1728
Captain John Gwythen offers for sale 'a negro man about 20 years old, well limb'd, fit to serve a gentleman or to be instructed in a trade'.

Bristol Intelligencer 12 January 1754
For sale to 'any gentleman or lady who wants a negro boy', a lad of 14 just landed.

Felix Farley's Journal 2 Auguest 1760
To be sold, a Negro Boy about ten years old. 'He hath the small pox.'

The Negroes frequently ran away from their masters and adverts for lost or runaway slaves were more common than new sales:

London Gazette 17 January 1713
Captain Foye of Bristol offers £5 for the capture of a negro called Scipio aged about 24.

London Gazette 5 July 1715
Mr Pyne, the Bristol postmaster, undertakes to pay two guineas and expenses for the recovery of Captain Stephen Courtney's negro, aged about 20 'having three or four marks on the temple and the same on each cheek'.

Bristol Journal 15 November 1746
Captain Eaton announces the evasion of his negro Mingo, whom he had owned for eight years, for whose recovery he promised a guinea. 'All persons are hereby forbid entertaining the said Black at their peril.'

Bristol Journal 12 March 1757
The elopement of a young negro called Starling, who 'blows the French Horn very well'.

Very few people in England were entirely free of guilt. The farm labourer, stuffing his clay pipe with tobacco, would feel offended at the suggestion that his smoking habit was supporting the slave trade.

'Here Lieth the Body of Scipio Africanus Negro Servant to ye Right Honourable Charles William Earl of Suffolk and Bradon Who died Ye 21 December 1720, Aged 18 years.'

The tea, drunk in the fine china cups in the homes of the wealthy, was sweetened by sugar grown with slave labour and the cotton industry, which grew to clothe the world, depended on the slaves for its raw material.

The first bank in Bristol, trading from 1750 in Broad Street, was founded by African merchants and was very willing to finance new ventures in the trade. The whole trade of Bristol became directly or indirectly involved, and it was impossible for anybody to refuse dealings with the African merchants or to deny them services when they had the money to pay handsomely at more than the going rate. In the early years of the trade the public were simply not informed of the happenings on the middle passage; the only eyewitnesses were the sea captains and the sailors and their yarns were easily passed off as being highly exaggerated. The plantation owners were careful to assure the public that they treated their slaves with the utmost kindness and consideration, sentiments which they repeated *ad nauseam.*

But the truth will out, and by the middle of the century it was obvious to many people that there was something terribly wrong about the whole concept of slavery and the way it was executed in practice. The most active anti-slavery people were undoubtedly the Quakers, and they included William Champion who withdrew from the sugar trade and sold off his lucrative plantations in the West Indies. The Quaker-controlled banks changed their policy and refused credit to companies directly involved in the slave trade. Thomas Clarkson was himself a Quaker and when the abolitionist movement gained ground Dr Long Fox and James Harford were just two of many Quakers who opposed slavery on the very just principle that it represented a gross violation of human rights. Later in the century the Methodist movement was also active in abolition and John Wesley was outspoken in his condemnation of the trade. In 1788 he was preaching against slavery when his sermon was interrupted by what he deemed was a supernatural occurrence:

> A vehement noise arose, and shot like lightning through the whole congregation. The terror and confusion were inexpressible. The benches were broken in pieces, and nine tenths of the congregation appeared to be struck with the same panic. In about six minutes the storm ceased. No one can account for it without supposing some preternatural influence. Satan fought lest his kingdom should be delivered up.[8]

Slavery was one of the issues over which Dr Johnson and his biographer James Boswell could not agree. Boswell subscribed to the view that slavery had been practised since biblical times and was a necessary evil, but it was Samuel Johnson who coined the phrase 'how is it that we hear the loudest yelps for liberty amongst the drivers of

Thomas Clarkson arrived in Bristol in 1787 and became the most active local abolitionist. He spent years gathering information and talking with local people about the horrors of the slave trade.

negroes?' On one occasion, when in the company of some 'very grave men of Oxford', Johnson put the cat amongst the pigeons by proposing a toast to 'The next insurrection of the negroes in the West Indies'.

In 1787 Thomas Clarkson described his feelings as he approached Bristol near the start of his long campaign towards the abolition of the slave trade:

> The first place I resolved to visit was Bristol ... On turning a corner within about a mile of that city, at about eight in the evening, I came within sight of it. The weather was rather hazy, which occasioned it to look of unusual dimensions. The bells of some of the churches were then ringing; the sound of them did not strike me, till I had turned the corner before mentioned, when it came upon me at once. It filled me, almost directly, with a melancholy for which I could not account. I began now

to tremble, for the first time, at the arduous task I had undertaken of attempting to subvert one of the branches of the commerce of the great place which was now before me …[9]

Clarkson found that many Bristolians were willing to talk to him openly about the trade. Many of them condemned it, but when it came to giving him active support they were not very forthcoming. The ship-owners would not see him, neither would the slaving captains for fear of losing their jobs. To find out more about it he decided to visit the downbeat taverns and alehouses in Marsh Street, behind Broad Quay and in the worst parts of the city. He wanted to meet and talk with the common seamen who had sailed the middle passage and witnessed the horrors with their own eyes.

The life of the common sailor was amongst the hardest in a time of great hardship. If the sailor was lucky enough to have a home he was away from it for many months at a time. The honest sailor was always outnumbered by his dishonest and drunken shipmates. The bullying and the cruel punishments of shipboard life bred a body of hardened and disillusioned seamen. They were nearly all illiterate so that first hand accounts of their life are virtually non-existent. They were frequently recruited by press gang methods and forced into signing on for a voyage when they were too drunk to know anything about the commitment which their mark implied. But Thomas Clarkson sought their company. He soon discovered that they hated signing on for a slaving ship; they not only disliked the trade but their wages were lower and they were nearly always bribed, threatened or forced to sign on after accepting too much alcohol. He drew them out to give their accounts of the slave trade. The sailors told him of the terrible numbers of slaves who perished on the middle passage, but they told him too of the death rate among the sailors, which was even higher than that among the Negroes. Even as they unfurled their tales to Thomas Clarkson a ship called *Brothers* was moored at Kingroad, aboard which 32 sailors had died from ill treatment during her recent voyage. The captain of the slaver *Alfred* had been on trial for murdering a sailor at Barbados but he bribed one of the witnesses and was openly boasting of his escape from justice. Thomas Clarkson wanted to take the case to the Bristol magistrates but the deputy town clerk would not get involved – he knew that the merchants would bribe the witnesses to leave on another voyage before their testimony could come before the court.

Clarkson befriended the landlord of the *Seven Stars* tavern in St Thomas Street. There he talked with more seamen and he found that the trade was even worse than he had suspected. After much hard pondering on his findings he formulated an idea. The public was wary of supporting the blacks, but what they could be made to support was the privations of the sailors. If the death rate amongst the sailors was even higher than amongst the slaves, then this was nearer to home than the middle passage and he knew that he could use the evidence of the sailors to prove his point.

Prominent amongst the local abolitionists was Hannah More, who was born in the village of Fishponds in 1745, the fourth child of the village schoolmaster Jacob More. Hannah became a philanthropist with a wide spread of interests and she developed a very cultured social circle. She read the Cardiphonia, written by the reformed slaving captain John Newton, and she heard him preach at St Mary Woolnoth in the City of London. Hannah More and John Newton found they were kindred spirits and a long correspondence developed between them. It was Newton who first raised Hannah's interest in the question of abolition, but her social circle was so wide that she soon befriended practically all the leading abolitionists. In 1776 she met William Wilberforce for first time at a dinner party and a few years later she was responsible for introducing Charles Wesley and William Wilberforce to each other. She knew Edmund Burke, the Bristol MP, and she knew Thomas Clarkson. She circulated Clarkson's reports and his plan of a slave ship amongst her Bristol and London circles. She quarrelled with Lord Monboddo over his defence of the slave trade. To help further the cause Hannah wrote an epic poem on The Slave Trade, which includes:[10]

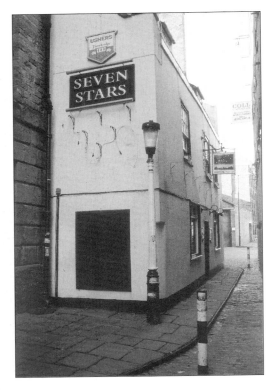

This is the pub where Thomas Clarkson, the Quaker anti-slavery campaigner, obtained much of his information about the conditions endured by the sailors. It played a major part in the ending of the slave trade.

> Shall Britain, where the soul of freedom reigns,
> Forge chains for others she herself disdains?
> Forbid it, Heaven! O Let the nations know
> The liberty she loves she will bestow.
>
> *Hannah More*

Thomas Clarkson gained the support of Dr Edward Long, James Harford, and very significantly Edmund Burke, a Bristol Member of Parliament. In London he befriended William Wilberforce, an MP who became as dedicated to the cause as Clarkson himself and who lost no opportunity to bring the matter of slavery before the House of Commons. In 1787 Clarkson travelled to Liverpool, where the local Society for Abolition was formed the following year with William

Hannah More, painting by Frances Reynolds. Hannah More was born in the schoolhouse at Fishponds. She became a leading figure in Bristol society and moved on to the London social circle in the 1770s. Her poetry and her efforts to abolish the slave trade are remembered in Bristol.

Roscoe and the Rathbones, father and son, as prominent founder members.

It was a long and protracted battle. Wilberforce brought forward bills for abolition in 1787 and again in 1791 but both were defeated in the Commons. His work was ably supported by men like the Rev John Newton, a former slave captain who entered the ministry and who published and made known his first hand experience of the terrible middle passage. The abolitionists fought on after their defeats and eventually public opinion swayed behind the movement. It was not until 1807 that the abolitionists were finally successful and the shipment of slaves was made illegal. The battle was not over; the Negroes on the sugar plantations were still in slavery and another 26 years passed before the ownership of slaves was made illegal in the British Empire.

Whene're to Afric's shores I turn my eyes,
Horrors of deepest, deadliest guilt arise;
I see, by more than Fancy's mirror shown,
The burning village and the blazing town:
See the dire victims torn from social life,
The shrieking babe, the agonising wife;
She, wretch forlorn! is dragg'd by hostile hands,
To distant tyrants sold, in distant lands!

Hannah More

CHAPTER TEN

The Thespians

In the 1730s the brothers S. and N. Buck published a set of engravings covering many important English towns. In the case of Bristol they produced two very accurate and detailed views: one from the north-west, drawn from Brandon Hill; and the other from the opposite side of Bristol, viewed from the Temple Meads area.

The North-West Prospect shows women hanging out the washing on the slopes of Brandon Hill, one of the traditional places used for the purpose of drying the clothes. The view of the city is well chosen, showing the many buildings with towers and spires rising amongst them, with a forest of masts visible among the houses. The shipping identifies the location of the Quays and the Backs where the merchant fleets unloaded their cargoes.

The South-East Prospect shows a group of wealthy citizens in the foreground, expensively attired in the fashion of the times and with a small African page boy. Behind is open pasture with clumps of trees outside the city wall. Bucks' view shows many of the city churches and labels them with a numeric key, but in the Redcliffe area the church spires are outnumbered by the kilns of the glassmaking and pottery industries.

Queen Square is easily identified on Bucks' prospect. This newly built grand square was the most sought after and expensive place to live. The square was previously known by the downbeat name of 'The Marsh', but the land between the quays was ideally situated to the merchants who wanted to live near their businesses. It had been well drained, built up firstly as a recreational area and then developed as a high class residential development. In 1702 Queen Anne visited Bristol on a day trip from Bath. It cost the Corporation £466 to provide a suitable banquet and reception. A deafening salute of a hundred guns was fired from the Marsh, accompanied by the cannons of the many ships in the harbours. It was decided to name the new square after her, but with typical mixed logic the central feature became a bronze statue of her brother-in-law, William of Orange.

More frequent visitors were the travelling preachers which had been a common sight from ancient times. John Wesley travelled more miles on horseback spreading the gospel than any preacher before or after him, but prior to his visit to Bristol in 1739 he had never preached to

Overleaf: The North-West Prospect of the City of Bristol by S. & N. Buck, 1734. This was drawn from the vantage point of Brandon Hill, a piece of common land where we see the washing set out to dry, children playing games, and a shooting party.

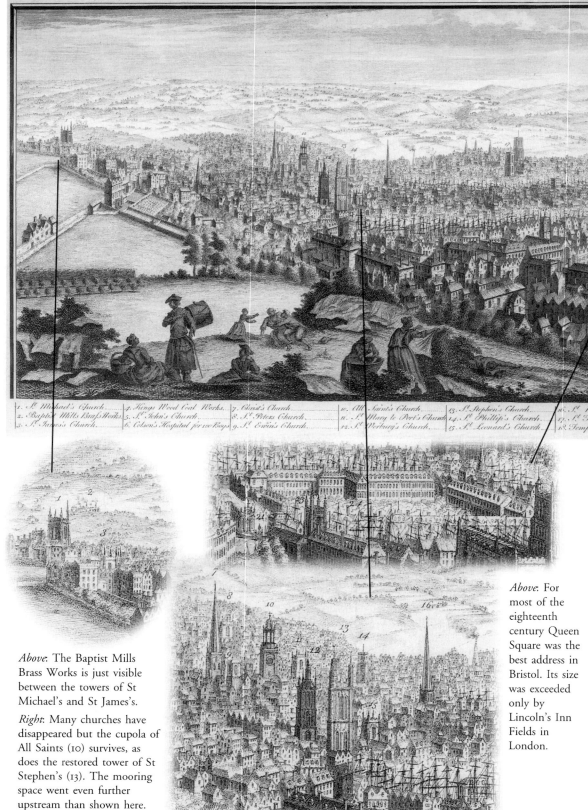

1. St. Michael's Church.   4. Kings Wood Coal Works.   7. Christ's Church.   10. All Saints Church.   13. St. Stephen's Church.
2. Baptist Mills Brass Works. 5. St. John's Church.   8. St. Peters Church.   11. St. Mary le Port's Church. 14. St. Phillip's Church.
3. St. James's Church.   6. Colson's Hospital for 100 Boys. 9. St. Ewin's Church. 12. St. Werburg's Church.   15. St. Leonard's Church.

Above: The Baptist Mills Brass Works is just visible between the towers of St Michael's and St James's.

Right: Many churches have disappeared but the cupola of All Saints (10) survives, as does the restored tower of St Stephen's (13). The mooring space went even further upstream than shown here.

Above: For most of the eighteenth century Queen Square was the best address in Bristol. Its size was exceeded only by Lincoln's Inn Fields in London.

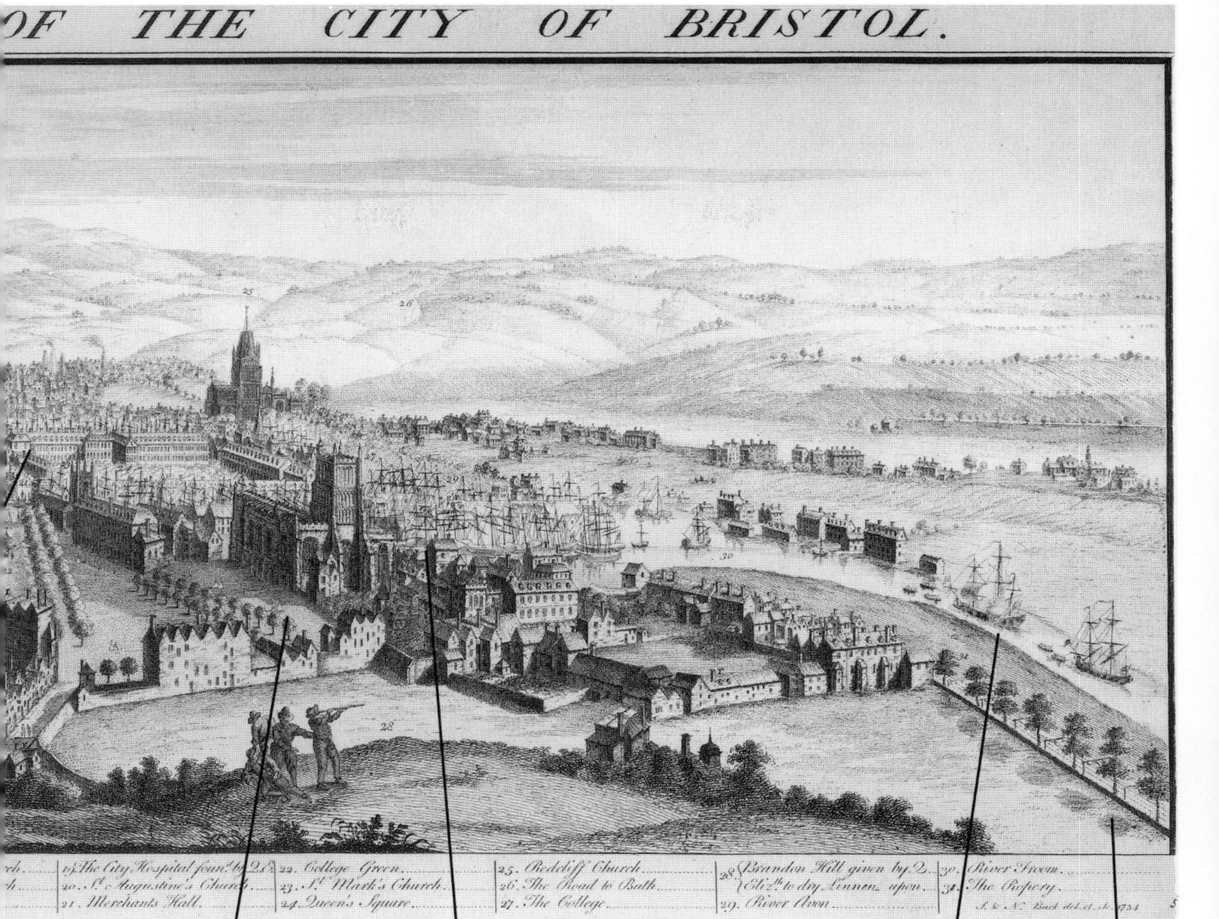

S. & N. Buck del. et Sc. 1734

5

Right: Ships under tow on the Avon. It must have been hard work for the oarsmen!

Right: All of the mooring space is taken in Bucks' depiction of the port.

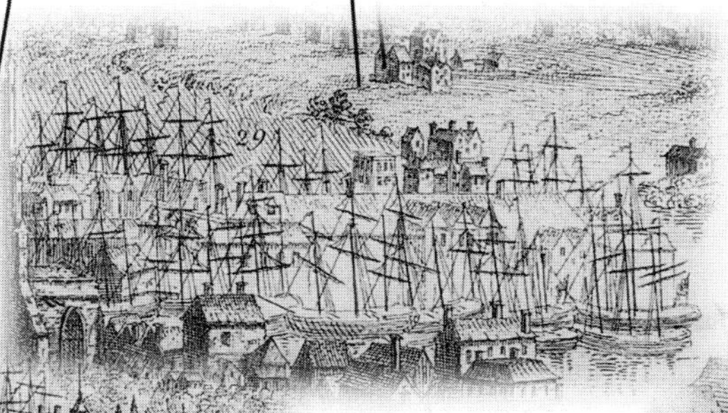

Left: Bristol Cathedral, formerly St Augustine's Abbey, referred to as 'the college'. The absence of the west nave destroyed the beauty of the cathedral. It remained as shown here until the late nineteenth century.

Right: Several maps confirm the existence of the ropewalk in the area near Cannon's Marsh.

Below: The Avon Gorge can be seen, and the Hotwell's 'Long Room' is just visible on the river.

Below right: Early Clifton: the parish church of St Andrews is shown. Goldney House was built at this time, but the major development of Clifton lay in the future.

Above: Prince Rupert's Fort, constructed during the royalist siege of Bristol in 1643.

Below: The river approach to Bristol, an area often used for ship building and repairs at this time. The river never meandered to the extent shown here.

Above: St Mary Redcliffe was the dominant church in south Bristol.

THE SOUTH EAST PROSPECT

Left: Every fashionable household had a black servant, a reminder of Bristol's dominanace in the slave trade.

Below: The city centre churches.

Above: The glass industry was prominent at this time. The number of smoking glass kilns grew to exceed the number of spires and church towers.

1. The Horse Ferry
2. The Hot Wells
3. The Long Room
4. Clifton
5. Brandon Hill
6. The College
7. Padmoor near Frome
8. St Augustine's Church
9. St Marks Church
10. Redcliff Church

11. Prince Rupert's Fort
12. St Stephen's Church
13. St Leonard's Church
14. St Michael Church
15. St Werburge's Church
16. St John's Church
17. St Nicholas Church
18. St Ewin's Church
19. All Saints Church
20. Christs Church

21. St Thomas's Church
22. St Mary le Port's Church
23. St James's Church
24. St Peter's Church
25. Temple Church
26. Kingsdown
27. St Phillips Church
28. The Wing Rock to Bath
29. The Road to Bath

an outdoor audience. He was welcomed by a local preacher, Mr George Whitefield, who had already set about the task of spreading the gospel to the Kingswood mining community. Wesley described his first reaction to Whitefield's unorthodox methods:

> [March 31, 1739] In the evening I reached Bristol, and met Mr Whitefield there. I could scarcely reconcile myself at first to this strange way of preaching in the fields, of which he set me an example on Sunday: having been all my life (till very lately) so tenacious of every point relating to decency and order, that I should have thought the saving of souls almost a sin, if it had not been done in a church.[1]

Two days later Wesley had been completely converted to the new style of preaching:

> [April 2, 1739] At four in the afternoon I submitted to be more vile, and proclaimed in the highways the glad tidings of salvation, speaking from a little eminence in a ground adjoining to the city, to about three thousand people.
>   At seven I began expounding the Acts of the Apostles, to a society meeting in Baldwin Street; and the next day the Gospel of St John in the chapel at Newgate; where I also read the Morning Service of the Church.[2]

By the following Sunday he had audiences of a thousand in Bristol and fifteen hundred at Kingswood; he claimed that he had fifteen thousand at Rose Green but he probably got his figures wrong:

> At seven in the morning I preached to about a thousand persons at Bristol, and afterwards to about fifteen hundred on the top of Hannam Mount, in Kingswood. I called to them in the words of the evangelical prophet: 'Ho! Everyone that thirsteth, come ye to the waters; come and buy wine and milk, without money and without price.' About fifteen thousand were in the afternoon at Rose Green (on the other side of Kingswood); among whom I stood and cried in the name of the Lord: 'If any man thirst, let him come unto Me and drink. He that believeth in Me, as the scripture hath said, out of his belly shall flow rivers of living water.'[3]

In this year (1739) John Wesley set up the first Methodist Meeting House in Broad Mead. Wesley's brother Charles came and lived in Bristol for many years, where the Methodist movement gained a lot of support. But John Wesley wanted to spread the gospel as far afield as he could. He used Bristol as a base from which he could travel to the West Country, and had similar bases in London and Newcastle. He and George Whitefield had much in common. They both became totally dedicated to the idea of outdoor preaching and both did much to spread the gospel amongst the underprivileged and the poorer classes. Whitefield preached amongst the Kingswood miners and he became

John Wesley (1703–1791) first came to Bristol in 1739. The New Room in the Horsefair was built soon afterwards and was extended to Broadmead in 1748. Wesley used the rooms as a base for his journeys to the western counties.

very moved by their reactions. 'The first discovery of their being affected', he claimed, 'was by seeing the white gutters made by their tears, which plentifully fell down their black cheeks as they came out of the coal-pits.' In 1748 John Wesley set up a school at Kingswood to educate the sons of his Wesleyan ministers. His regime was strict in the extreme: the boys were up at 4 a.m. even in the winter, there were no playtimes and no holidays, though the regime was broken by meal times and gardening sessions. In later life Wesley found 'all things just according to my desire, and the whole behaviour of the children showing that they were now managed with the wisdom that cometh from above'. Both John Wesley and George Whitefield were very headstrong characters who had much in common, but they ended up going their separate ways, each believing he was the only one to hold the true faith.

The theatre was well established in Bristol by the time John Wesley arrived on the scene. In the 1720s an attempt was made to open a theatre in Tucker Street and later at St Augustine's Back. The respectable citizens petitioned against it 'by regard to the ill-consequences by the introduction of lewdness and debauchery by acting of stage-plays'. The problem was partly overcome by building a theatre at Jacob's Well, just over the Bristol boundary in Lower Clifton. The new theatre was ideally situated for the growing Hotwells clientele, but it could also be patronised by the people of Bristol. Although the building was very primitive, it quickly became a popular venue. The auditorium held about two hundred people and consisted of a large central box and four smaller side boxes, and there were front and side galleries and an upper gallery. The stage was rather basic and an actor making his exit from one side had to brave the elements to re-enter from the other side. One popular feature was a hole or hatch in the wall which communicated with an alehouse called the Malt Shovel next door – drinks were served through the hole on request to privileged customers at all times. The lighting arrangements were equally basic and consisted of four hoops supporting tallow candles. In an early production of Richard III the leading actor flourished his sword to such good effect that 'he cut the rope holding one of the primitive chandeliers, and had to be rescued from the hoop by the laughing spectators'.[4]

Enthusiastic audience participation was expected in the early theatre. It was entertainment rather than culture that most of the audience wanted, which was one of the reasons why the middle classes were very cautious about opening a theatre in their city. In 1763 the playbill announced that 'the night will be illuminated with the Silver Rays of Cynthia', and a packed house expected to see an exotic eastern lady take the stage. But Madame Cynthia had already taken her leave of Bristol and she never appeared. The audience was very put out and

Overleaf
Donne's Map of
Bristol, 1826.

CHURCHES

V	The Cathedral	1
V	St. Augustines	2
Q	All Saints	3
Q	Christ Church and St. Ewens	4
P		
O	Clifton	5
Q	St. James's	6
P	St. Johns	7
T	Mary Port	8
P	St. Michaels	9
U	St. Nicholas	10
Q	St. Pauls	11
Q	St. Peters	12
U	St. Philips	13
U	Redcliff Church	14
U	Temple Church	15
T	St. Thomas's	16
P	St. Werburghs	17
P	St. Stephens	18

CHAPELS &c.

V	Mayors Chapel	19
P	St. Augustines d°.	20
Q	Ebenezer d°.	21
V	French d°.	22
X	Guinea Street d°.	23
S	Hotwells d°.	24
S	Hope d°.	25
P	Lady Huntingdons d°.	26
P	Moravian d°.	27
J	Portland d°.	28
R	St. Philips d°.	29
N	Methodist d°.	30
Q	Welsh d°.	31
Q	Welsh Indepen¹ d°.	32
P	Catholic d°.	33
Q	Pithay d°.	34
P	St. Johns d°.	35
P	Orphan d°.	36
Q	Castle Green d°.	37
U	Bridge Street d°.	38
Q	Broadmead Meet⁹	39
U	Countership d°.	40
Q	Friends d°.	41
U	D°. d°.	42
Q	Kings Street d°.	43
P	Lewins Mead d°.	44
U	Synagogue	45
Q	Tabernacle	46
R	Sion Chapel	47
O	Bethesda d°.	b

ALMS HOUSES.

P	Colstons Alms Ho⁹	48
Q	All Saints & Johns d°.	49
P	Fosters d°.	50
Q	Batchelors d°.	51
V	Merchants d°.	52
V	St. Nicholas d°.	53
R	Alderman Stephens d°.	54
Q	Taylors d°.	55
Q	Hookes d°.	56
U	D'. Whites d°.	57
X	Redcliff d°.	58
R	Trinity d°.	59
R	D°. for Widows	60
R	Friends Alms Ho⁹	a

A PLAN of BRISTOL

Furlongs West from the Exchange

By an Act of 43 Geo. 3ʳᵈ passed in 1803 commonly
called the Bristol Dock Act certain parts of the
Counties of Somerset & Glocester between the old
and new Course of the River Avon were taken into
and made part of the City & County of Bristol, so
far as related to the Ground & Civil Jurisdiction
of the Mayor & Magistrates and other Officers of
Bristol.

SCALE OF CHAINS
SCALE OF FURLONGS

Furlongs West from the Exchange

Published as the Act directs

...fton, THE **HOTWELLS** &c.
from an ACTUAL SURVEY *by* B. DONNE.

Furlongs East from the Exchange

A VIEW or CLIFTON and the HOTWELLS

Furlongs East from the Exchange

when a stand-up comedian tried to pass the whole thing off as a joke the adverse reaction nearly generated a riot in the gallery. Soon afterwards there actually was a riot when the disgruntled customers pelted the stage and stoned the building:

> Notwithstanding that the opening night of the ensuing season had been offered, the malcontents assembled in force, and on the rise of the curtain, to the accompaniment of a storm of boos and hisses, discharges the ammunition, consisting of rotten apples, oranges etc., with which they had come provided. It was necessary for the actors to scale the proscenium and eject the rioters from the building, when, securing a supply of stones from Brandon Hill, they commenced a bombardment of the outer walls.[5]

It was scenes like these which troubled the anti-theatre party. A larger and grander theatre was required to improve the level of the productions and the image of the performers. In 1764 a list of wealthy citizens appeared as subscribers to a new theatre in King Street. This was of great concern to John Wesley and he wrote to the Mayor and Corporation of Bristol:

> Gentlemen, Both my brother and I and all who have any connexion with us are extremely sensible of our obligations to you for the civility which you have shown us on all occasions ...
>
> The endeavours lately used to procure subscriptions for building a new playhouse in Bristol have given us not a little concern; and that on various accounts: not barely as most of the present stage entertainments sap the foundation of all religion, as they naturally tend to efface all traces of piety and seriousness out of the minds of men; but as they are peculiarly hurtful to a trading city, giving a wrong turn to youth especially gay, trifling, and directly opposite to the spirit of industry and close application to business; and, as drinking and debauchery of every kind are constant attendants on these entertainments, with indolence, effeminacy, and idleness, which affect trade in a high degree.[6]

The façade of Cooper's Hall provides the perfect entrance to the Theatre Royal in King Street. The theatre is completely hidden from the road, but the two buildings are almost contemporary.

In spite of the opposition five thousand pounds was raised for the new theatre. The architect, James Paty, based his design on Christopher Wren's theatre in Drury Lane and a large grandiose theatre was built. On the opening night in 1766 the die-hards were still ranting and raving about the evils of the theatre and there was still no licence to perform plays. To get around the licensing problem the first performance had to be billed as 'A Concert of Music and a

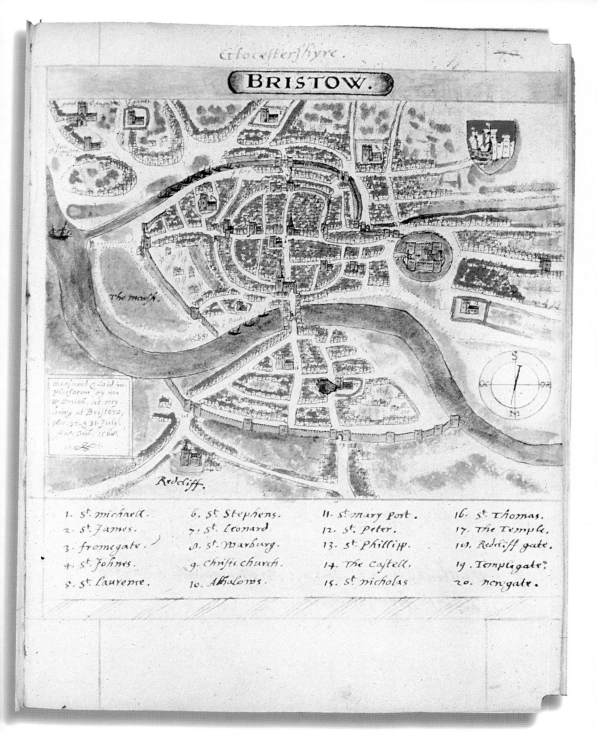

Gloceſterſhyre.

BRISTOW.

The marſh

Reddiff.

1. St. michaell.	6. St. Stephens.	11. St. mary port.	16. St. Thomas.
2. St. James.	7. St. Leonard.	12. St. Peter.	17. The Temple.
3. fromegate.	8. St. warburg.	13. St. Phillipp.	18. Redcliff gate.
4. St. Johns.	9. Chriſts church.	14. The Caſtell.	19. Templegate.
5. St. Laurence.	10. Alhalows.	15. St. nicholas	20. newgate.

William Smith's map of Bristol, 1568.

William Smith's map shows the street plan of Bristol in 1568. Churches are labelled using a numeric key. Only a single stretch of the inner wall survives but several ancient gates are shown, and the southern defences are still complete.

(*British Library, Sloane* MS 2596. *By permission of the British Library*)

The eight gables of St Nicholas's Almshouses on King Street. Dating from 1652–56, these are the oldest surviving almshouses in Bristol.

Merchant Venturer's Almshouses.
This beautiful development dates from 1696 and was originally a full quadrangle, but only half of it survived the Blitz during the Second World War.

Colston's Almshouses, dating from the seventeenth century. They were greatly admired by Celia Fiennes on her visit to Bristol in 1680.

Foster's Almshouses.
Foster's Almshouses are a highly decorative Victorian development dating from 1861, by Foster and Wood. The group includes Trinity Chapel which dates from 1679 but is much altered.

Bristol Docks and Quay, early eighteenth-century by English School.
The view is thought to be painted by Philip Van Dyke who was in Bristol in the 1780s. It is the best depiction we have of the eighteenth-century Bristol quayside and shows a wealth of detail including horse sledges and children at play. The only landmark easily identified is St Michael's church at the highest point of the horizon.
(By permission of Bristol City Museum and Art Gallery, UK/Bridgeman Art Library)

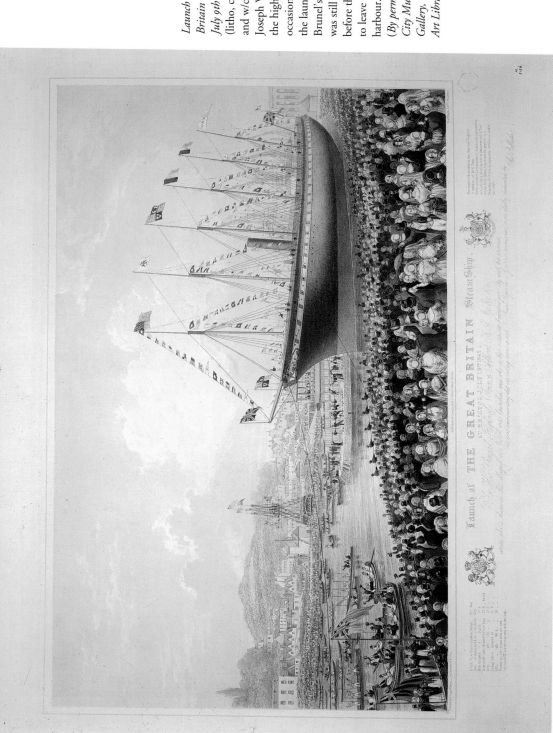

Launch of the Great Britain Steam ship, July 9th 1843, c.1843 (litho, colour printed and w/c). Joseph Walter captures the high sense of occasion generated by the launching of Brunel's great ship. It was still several months before the ship was able to leave the floating harbour. (By permission of Bristol City Museum and Art Gallery, UK/Bridgeman Art Library)

The Stoppage of the Bank, 1831 by Rolinda Sharples (oil). The bank of Browne, Cavanagh and Bayley, known as the Bristol Bullion Bank, stopped payments in 1822. The scene is in Corn Street, showing the Dutch House and All Saints Church. (*Bristol Museums and Art Gallery*)

St James's Fair, Bristol, by Samuel Colman (1780–1845). St James's Fair is mentioned in the thirteenth century and continued until 1838. The painting not only tells a thousand stories, but the costume, merchandise and atmosphere are authentic. (*By permission of Bristol City Museum and Art Gallery, UK/Bridgeman Art Library*)

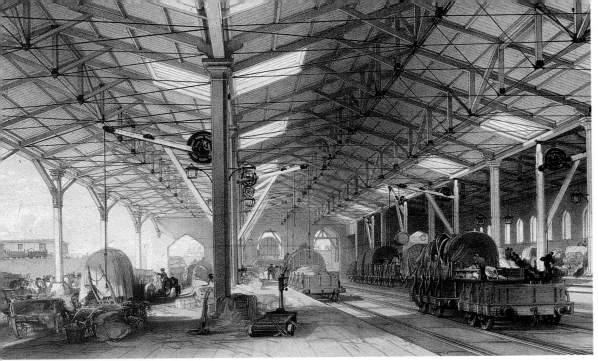

The early days of the Great Western Railway are captured beautifully in J.C. Bourne's lithographs. Here we see the Goods Shed at Bristol in 1846. Note the broad gauge (7 feet) of the tracks. (*GWR Museum, Swindon*)

Bristol Station, 1846. An express locomotive can be seen preparing to leave the station as passengers wait on the platform. Note the exuberant gothic roof. (*GWR Museum, Swindon*)

Specimen of Rhetoric', but the comedy 'The Conscious Lovers' was performed between acts of the concert, and a prologue and epilogue was supplied by David Garrick. An extract from the epilogue describes an actor's view of one of the opponents of the theatre:

> 'Hold!' cries a Prude (thus rising from her stays)
> 'I hate a Playhouse, and their wicked plays;
> O! 'tis a shame to suffer such an evil
> For seeing plays is dealing with the Devil!'

The thespians had a ready answer:

> 'I beg your pardon Madam, 'tis not true;
> We players are moral folks – I'll prove it too.
> Man is a forward child – naughty and cross,
> Without his rattle and his hobby horse;
> We play'rs are little master's bells and coral,
> To keep the child from mischief – a'nt we moral' [7]

The King Street theatre quickly became very popular and it was named the Theatre Royal. In the early years the theatre closed at the end of the summer season, but in autumn 1778 it was decided to put on performances through the winter. *As You Like It* and *The School for Scandal* were performed. In March the Bath Theatre Company took possession under John Palmer, with William Wyatt Dimond. The 22-year-old Sarah Siddons took the leading female parts for the winter season. The company performed alternately at Bristol and Bath for three years and Sarah Siddons proved very popular with both audiences – on one occasion she is even reputed to have taken the part of Hamlet.

The Theatre Royal quickly became a permanent establishment and one of the best-loved places of entertainment in Bristol. William Dimond became Joint Acting Manager with Keasberry and remained with Bristol and Bath Theatre Company until his retirement in 1801. In 1800 Dimond and Palmer were responsible for a major reconstruction to increase the accommodation in the theatre. The roof was raised and an entire new gallery tier was built. The acoustics were greatly improved by the alterations but the gallery was not raked sharply enough for those at the back to see the front of the stage. In the autumn more alterations were made to redress this problem.

One of the best descriptions from behind the scenes of the Bristol theatre comes from the journal of the actress Fanny Kemble, niece of Sarah Siddons, who played the part of Shakespeare's Juliet in July 1831. Fanny was her own harshest critic regarding her performance, but she was not helped by members of the cast who were guilty of improvising on the sacred text:

The play was 'Romeo and Juliet', and the nurse was a perfect farce in herself; she really was worth any money, and her soliloquy when she found me 'up and dressed and down again,' very nearly made me scream with laughter in the middle of my trance. Indeed, the whole play was probably considered an 'improved version' of Shakespeare's Veronese story, both in force and delicacy of the text. Sundry wicked words and coarse appellations were decorously dispensed with; many fine passages received judicious additions; not a few were equally judiciously omitted altogether. What a shocking hash! [8]

The Bristol audiences were more sophisticated than in the early days. Fanny described them as very pleasant and she obviously enjoyed playing to them. The main problem was that the theatre manager Mr Brunton was in difficulties ('a civilised plural for debt', explained Fanny!) and one night his creditors actually stormed the theatre to carry off the night's takings, which included Charles Kemble's benefit (he was Fanny's father). The actors were very depressed and convinced that they would not be paid for their efforts, but the houses were full and eventually the show went on in the best theatrical traditions. The next Friday Fanny broke a mirror. 'Miserrima!', she exclaimed. 'I Have broken a looking-glass! And on a Friday, too! What *do* I think will happen to me!' She was at a very formative part of her career and her feelings were very mixed about carrying on in the theatre. The next week the company acted the play *Venice Preserved*, with Fanny playing Belvidera opposite Charles Mason as Bedamar. Charles did not know

Old Library, King Street. The Bristol Library Society was founded in 1772–73 and housed in this building. Members included Coleridge, Wordsworth, Southey, Pinney, Davy and Beddoes.

his lines but he was such a creative innovator that Fanny could not help but be amused by his performance:

> In the first place C— did not even know his words, and that was bad enough; but when he was out, instead of coming to a stop decently, and finishing at least with his cue, he went on extemporizing line after line, and speech after speech, of his own, by way of mending matters. I think I never saw such a performance. He stamps and bellows low down in this throat like an ill-suppressed bull; he rolls his eyes till I feel as if they were flying out of their sockets at me, and I must try to catch them. He quavers and quivers in his speech, and pulls and *wrenches* me so inhumanely, that what with inward laughter and extreme rage and pain, I was really all but dead in earnest at the end of the play. I acted very ill myself till the last scene, when my Jaffier having been done justice to by the Venetian Government, I was able to do justice to myself, and having gone mad, and no wonder, died rather better than I had lived through the piece.[9]

Fanny described the July 18th performance of the same play, when the theatre was packed. She admitted to being nervous and excited and she nearly went into hysterics over the final incident of the evening. The play was a tragedy which ended with the death of Fanny's character, Belvidera, and when the final curtain fell the actors had successfully managed to get the whole audience into a highly emotional state of sorrow and the sobbing could be heard from all over the house. The sequel may claim to be typically Bristolian, and Fanny described what happened as she heard it from behind the scenes:

> ... the curtain descended slowly amidst sympathetic sobs and silence – the musicians themselves, deeply moved, no doubt, with the sorrows of the scene, mournfully resumed their fiddles, and struck up 'ti *ti* tum ti *tiddle* un *ti* tum ti' – the jolliest jig you ever heard. The bathos was irresistible; we behind the scenes, the principal sufferers (perhaps) in the night's performance, were instantly comforted, and all but shouted with laughter. I hope the audience were equally revived by this grotesque sudden cheering of their spirits. After the tragedy a Bristolian Paganini performed a concerto on one string. Dall declares that the whole orchestra played the whole time – but some sounds reached me in my dressing room that were decidedly unique more ways than one, not at all unlike our favourite French fantasia – 'Complainte d'un cochon au lait qui reve.' But the audience were transported; they clapped and the fiddle squealed, they hurraed and the fiddle uttered three terrific screams, and it was over and Paganini is done for – here, at any rate. He need never show his face or fiddle here, he hasn't a string (even one) left to his bow in Bristol.[10]

CHAPTER ELEVEN

The Marvellous Boy

In a dark bottom sunk, O Bristol now
With native malice lift thy lowering brow!

. . .

Boast thy base Tolsey, and thy turn-spit dogs,
Thy halliers' horses and thy human hogs.
Upstarts and mushrooms, proud, relentless hearts,
Thou blank of sciences, thou dearth of arts.
Such foes as learning once was doomed to see,
Huns, Goths, and Vandals were but types of thee.*
Richard Savage

In the eighteenth century much of old Bristol was lost in the name of progress. The picturesque gates and the bridge were much too narrow and restricting for the volume of everyday traffic in England's second city. The High Cross at the central crossroads of the town was seen as another restriction to trade and traffic. John Vaughan, a goldsmith and banker who lived on the corner of Wine Street and High Street, was prepared to swear that the High Cross outside his door swayed in a high wind. The residents brought a petition before the council, cleverly insinuating to the Protestant community that the cross was a Papal relic:

> It hath been insinuated by some that this cross, on account of its antiquity ought to be lookt upon as something sacred. But when we consider that we are Protestants, and that Popery ought effectually to be guarded against in this nation, we make this our request to you to consider. If the opening of a passage to four of the principal streets in this city ought not to outweigh anything that can be said for the keeping up of a ruinous and superstitious Relick which is at present a public nuisance.[1]

The cross was taken down. In 1736 it was repainted, gilded, and re-erected on College Green. This would seem to be a sensible and

---

* In 1739 the poet Richard Savage arrived in Bristol and he touted around the merchants for sponsorship. Savage was successful at raising money, but he was dishonest in his methods. He promised to supply new editions of his work in exchange for subscriptions but the promised works were never forthcoming. His sponsorship fell away and he became very bitter with the merchants of Bristol

convenient arrangement, but some Bristolians had little affection for their ancient cross – promenaders came forward with the pathetic excuse that it prevented them from walking abreast across the green and that it was 'often defiled by nuisances'. To appease them it was taken down again and stored in the cathedral. In 1764 Mr Henry Hoare (obviously a forerunner of Lord Elgin!) quite legally purchased the stones, loaded them into six wagons and carted them off to his estate at Stourhead. He probably saved the Bristol High Cross from total oblivion:

> Ye people of Bristol, deplore the sad loss
> Of the kings and the queens that once reigned in your Cross;
> Your great men's wisdom you surely must pity,
> Who've banished what all men admired from the city.[2]

Much more of Old Bristol was scheduled for demolition. St Nicholas' Gate was taken down in the year that the High Cross left for Wiltshire. Pithay Gate was removed the following year, Newgate was demolished three years later – the carved figures from the portals were

The gateway to Arnos Court was moved to its present location in 1912. The niches contained figures saved from Lawford's Gate and Newgate – two of Bristol's medieval gates. The original statues are now located in St Nicholas' Museum; those seen here are replicas.

installed on the gateway to Arnos Court at Arnos Vale. Small Street
Gate was pulled down in 1774. An even more significant loss was Old
Bristol Bridge, which for five hundred years had been the busiest
thoroughfare in the West of England. Although the Chapel of the
Assumption had long since gone and nearly all the houses had been
rebuilt several times the bridge still retained its medieval character. But
ancient character was not admired in the modern Bristol. The new
bridge, a very practical but more boring replacement, took more than
four years to build and was opened with great ceremony in 1768. Two
weeks later *Felix Farley's Journal* published a remarkable report; it was
an account of the mayor crossing the Old Bristol Bridge at its opening
more than five hundred years earlier:

> On Fridaie was the Time fixed for passing the new Brydge: Aboute the
> Time of the Tollynge the tenth Clock ... a mickle stong Manne, in
> Armour, carried a hugh Anlance; after whom came six Claryons and six
> Minstrels, who sang the song of Saincte Warburgh; then came Master
> Maior, mounted on a white Horse, dight with sable Trappynges, wrought
> by the Nunnes of Sainte Kenna, with Gould and Sliver; his Hayr brayded
> with Ribbons, and a Chaperon, with the auntient arms of Brystowe
> fasteende on his Forehead ...3

The song of Saint Werburg, which the newspaper did not publish,

The birthplace of
Thomas
Chatterton survives
precariously on the
Bristol inner ring
road. Chatterton's
father was the
schoolmaster and
lived in the house
behind the façade.

had been discovered by the same contributor. It was written in a marvellous old English rhyme with a powerful rhythm and beautiful style. The fourth verse referred to the Bridge at Bristol:

> Now agayne with bremie Force,
> Severn in his auntient Course,
> Rolls his rappyd streeme alonge,
> With a Sable, swift and stronge
> Movynge manie a okie wode –
> We, the Menne of Brystowe towne,
> Have yreed this Brydge of Stone;
> Wyshynge echome it maie last,
> Till the date of daies be past
> Standynge where the other stode.

With so much of Bristol's heritage disappearing for good, the conservationist antiquarians were delighted and fascinated to find such a valuable surviving relic of its past. The poetry must be older than Chaucer, more than a century earlier than Langland and a truly remarkable discovery of English verse from the thirteenth century. The author hid under the pseudonym of 'Dunhelmus Bristoliensuis' but the public clamoured to know more about the antiquarian who had found this remarkable work.

It was quite amazing. The manuscript was submitted by a young boy of sixteen, an apprentice to John Lambert, a lawyer. He had been educated at Colston's School, his deceased father had been sexton at St Mary Redcliffe and the boy had been given access to ancient manuscripts in the parish chest where he had discovered this medieval gem. The boy's name was Thomas Chatterton. Nobody doubted the authenticity of the account. Had they known the truth, that Chatterton had actually written the account and the poetry himself, they would have been speechless with disbelief!

To the delight of the antiquarians Chatterton produced more fascinating manuscripts relating to old Bristol. Two pewter merchants, George Catcott and Henry Burgum, befriended the boy. Catcott was something of an eccentric – he climbed a church steeple for a bet and kept a box with a label 'My teeth to be put in the coffin when I die'. His partner Burgum was very anxious to prove his family pedigree and he was delighted when the adolescent Chatterton produced a coat of arms for the de Burgum family – the honest pewterer suspected nothing when he found that his coat of arms contained three golden hippopotami! Chatterton's forgeries were very convincing and he went on to produce some wonderful medieval poetry which he claimed was written by a fifteenth-century monk called Thomas Rowley.

The deception could not last. Young Chatterton desperately needed a wealthy patron to publish his work. He wrote to Horace Walpole, a patron of the arts, hoping to obtain some sponsorship. The Bristol people were getting suspicions, they asked him too many questions, and in the spring of 1770 he terminated his apprenticeship to John Lambert and left home to try his fortune in London. His letters home were happy and cheerful and he found that he loved the freedom of the metropolis after his provincial life. One of his letters shows that his adolescent interest in the fair sex was roused before he left Bristol:

> My sister will remember me to Miss Sandford. I have not quite forgot her; though there are so many pretty milliners &c. that I have quite forgot myself – Miss Rumsey, if she comes to London, would do well as an old acquaintance to send me her address. London is not Bristol – we may patrol the town for a day, without raising one whisper or nod of scandal. If she refuses may the curse of all antiquated virgins fall on her . . .[4]

Chatterton tried his hand at political satire and at first he seemed to make good contacts. He was unlucky, however, when his contacts ran into business problems and his income suffered accordingly. Horace Walpole replied to his request for sponsorship but he did not offer any money. Chatterton's income began to dry up and his mood swung between optimism and depression. His poetic temperament was extremely sensitive and this, coupled with the strong emotions of puberty, accounted for his very drastic swings of mood. On 25th August 1770 Thomas Chatterton's mood reached rock bottom. He took arsenic and committed suicide. He died in his attic room at Holborn.

At first his death caused little concern in Bristol where he was seen as a forger of manuscripts. The official view was given by an extract from *The New Review* in the 'Trial of Thomas Chatterton':

> . . . Thomas Chatterton, is indicted for the uttering of certain poems composed by himself, purporting them to be the poems of one Thomas Rowley, a priest of the XVth century, against the so frequently disturbed peace of Parnassus, to the great disturbance and confusion of the antiquary society and likewise notoriously to the prejudice of the literary fame of the said Thomas Chatterton. The fact is stated to have been committed by the prisoner between the ages of fifteen and seventeen [and the poems are admitted to be excellent].

Chatterton's view is given in his last verses, written a few days before he took his own life:

> Farewell, Bristolia's dingy piles of brick,
> Lovers of Mammon, worshippers of trick!
> Ye spurned the boy who gave you ancient lays,
> And paid for learning all your empty praise.
> Farewell ye guzzling aldermanic fools,
> By nature fitted for Corruption's tools!

I go to where celestial anthem's swell;
But you, when you depart, will sink to hell.
Farewell, my mother! – cease my anguished soul,
Nor let distraction's billows o'er me roll! –
Have mercy heaven! When here I cease to live,
And this last act of wretchedness forgive.

Thomas Chatterton

To the end of his life Chatterton continued to claim that his 'Rowley Poems' were genuine medieval works. Had he lived longer he could have admitted the truth without losing face, for the poems were accepted to be a work of art in themselves, regardless of their lack of antiquity. His friend George Catcott continued to believe Chatterton's claims and a few years later (1776) a distinguished visitor came to St Mary Redcliffe to try to settle the controversy. Catcott was convinced that if the sceptical Doctor Samuel Johnson could but see the chest where Chatterton found his manuscripts then the learned doctor would become a convert. James Boswell described the incident in graphic detail:

George Catcot, the pewterer, who was as zealous for Rowley, as Dr Hugh Blair was for Ossian (I trust my Reverend friend will excuse the comparison), attended us at our inn, and with a triumphant air of lively simplicity called out, 'I'll make Dr. Johnson a convert.' Dr. Johnson, at his desire, read aloud some of Chatterton's fabricated verses, while Catcot stood at the back of his chair, moving himself like a pendulum, and beating time with his feet, and now and then looking into Dr. Johnson's face, wondering that he was not yet convinced. We called on Mr. Barret, the surgeon, and saw some of the *originals* as they were called, which were executed very artificially; but from a careful inspection of them, and a consideration of the circumstances with which they were attended we were quite satisfied of the imposture, which, indeed, has been clearly demonstrated from internal evidence, by several able cricks.

Honest Catcot seemed to pay no attention what ever to any objections, but insisted, as an end to all controversy, that we should go with him to the tower of the church of St Mary, Redcliffe, and *view with our own eyes* the ancient chest in which the manuscripts were found. To this, Dr. Johnson good-naturedly agreed; and though troubled with a shortness of breathing, laboured up a long flight of steps, till we came to the place where the wonderous chest stood. '*There*, (said Catcut with a bouncing confident credulity), *there* is the very chest itself.' After this *ocular demonstration*, there was no more to be said. He brought to my recollection a Scotch Highlander, a man of learning too, and who had seen the world, attesting, and at the same time giving his reasons for the authenticity of Fingal:– 'I have heard all that poem when I was young.' – 'Have you, Sir? Pray what have you heard?' – 'I have heard Ossian, Oscar, and *every one of them*.'

Johnson said of Chatterton, 'This is the most extraordinary young man that has encountered my knowledge. It is wonderful how the whelp has written such things'.

We were by no means pleased with our inn at Bristol. 'Let us see now (said I), how we should describe it.' Johnson was ready with his raillery. 'Describe it, Sir? – Why, it was so bad that Boswell wished to be in Scotland!' [5]

Thus did the learned doctor not only manage to dispose of poor Chatterton but also to offend Bristol, Scotland and his loyal biographer Boswell all in one sentence.

It was unforgivable for Chatterton to forge documents and to pass them on as authentic and historians have never forgotten these misdemeanours. But Chatterton was not an historian, he was a genuine poet and a mere adolescent boy; this allowed him the liberty of some degree of poetic licence. Perhaps it would be fairer to judge him by the values of his own fraternity, the romantic poets of the eighteenth century.

William Wordsworth was born at Grasmere in the year that Chatterton died. Coleridge was born two year later and Robert Southey was born in Bristol two years later than Coleridge. These three became great friends, and in the 1780s they roamed the streets of the city together and explored the surrounding countryside. They had all read Chatterton's work and it was obvious to all three that his poetry was the work of a genius. They were all greatly influenced by the boy poet who, if only he had lived, they felt could have been a mentor to all of them. 'Poor Chatterton', wrote Southey after musing in the church of St Mary Redcliffe, 'Oft do I think upon him and sometimes indulge in the thought that had he been living he might have been my friend.'

> O Chatterton! That thou wert yet alive!
> Sure thou woulds't spread the canvass to the gale,
> And love with us the tinkling team to drive
> O'er peaceful Freedom's undivided dale.
>
> *Robert Southey*

Coleridge was in complete agreement:

> Flower that must perish shall I liken thee
> To some sweet girl of too too rapid growth
> Nipped by consumption mid untimely charms?
> Or to Bristowa's bard, the wondrous boy
> An amaranth which earth scarce seemed to own
> Till disappointment came as pelting wrong
> Beat it to earth ...
>
> *Samuel T. Coleridge*

Wordsworth too was very impressed. He felt that Chatterton had a claim to be the first of the romantic poets. The marvellous natural grasp of words and meter coming from so young a person was quite amazing – none of the later poets had achieved the same degree of maturity at so young an age. Wordsworth himself used his poetic licence when he had Chatterton following the plough on the mountain side – how he would have loved to have shown the boy his Lakeland scenery. His sentiments echo those of his two friends:

> I thought of Chatterton, the marvellous Boy,
> The sleepless Soul that perished with his pride;
> Of him who walked in glory and in joy
> Following his plough, along the mountain-side:
> By our own spirits we are deified:
> We Poets in our youth begin in gladness;
> But there of come in the end despondency and madness.
> *William Wordsworth*

The story of Chatterton's suicide did not end with the romantic poets. As his work became better known his suicide became an ideal subject for the early Pre-Raphaelite movement. In 1790 John Flaxman painted the spirit of despair giving the cup of poison to Chatterton; in 1794 Edward Orme painted his famous picture of the death scene; the Frenchman Foreau's picture appeared in 1842; and Henry Wallis' picture was painted in 1856. The playwrights were as fascinated by the tragedy as were the poets. Alfred de Vigny's play 'Chatterton' opened at the Theatre Francais in 1835, and later in the century Leoncavallo wrote an opera dedicated to the boy poet.

From the last decades of the eighteenth century and up to Regency times a flourishing school of local literature grew up in Bristol. Southey, unlike Chatterton and Savage, was not disillusioned with his native city. 'I know of no mercantile place so literary', he claimed, and later in life he wrote, 'Landour ... agrees with me that no city in England is to be compared with Bristol for singularity and beauty ... no one ever more dearly loved his native place than I do.'

Hannah More was a prominent member of the Bristol literary circle. She was born at the old schoolhouse in Fishponds and moved to Clifton as a young woman in the 1760s. Her elder sisters founded a school in Park Street and for several years Hannah worked for them as a teacher. She knew the Bristol social scene very well and had many male admirers. Mary Ann Hopkins described her:

There was something of the china shepherdess in her appearance; an innocent naughtiness lit up her countenance, quiet fun twinkled in her large dark eyes and a slight quirk twisted the corners of her mouth. In figure she was on the small side with just the right amount of plumpness. She dressed with marked simplicity, though sometimes in bright colours.

Once she went to a party in a scarlet dress to find the other guests in court mourning . . .[6]

At the age of 28 Hannah was left jilted at the altar of Clifton Parish Church by a man twenty years her senior. It is inconceivable that Edward Turner did not marry her after six years of courtship, but Hannah was a very forgiving person and in later life they remained great friends. Hannah's reaction to her lost marriage was to move to London where her beauty, charm and intelligence very easily gained her access to the highest literary and social circles. She got to know Wilberforce, Macaulay, Joshua Reynolds, Sheriden, David Garrick, Horace Walpole, Fanny Burney and Samuel Johnson. David Garrick labelled her as a 'Sunday Woman' when he discovered that she disapproved of music on the Sabbath, even if it was church music. He also dubbed her a 'blue stocking', but this appellation cannot be taken in the modern context; it was quite literally true because she belonged to the literary group of that name. Sarah More described her sister Hannah flirting with Doctor Johnson:

> Tuesday evening we drank tea at Sir Joshua's with Doctor Johnson. Hannah is certainly a great favourite. She was placed next to him, and they had the entire conversation to themselves. They were both in remarkably high spirits; it was certainly her lucky night! I never heard her say so many good things. The old genius was extremely jocular, and the young one very pleasant. You would have imagined we had been at some comedy had you heard our peals of laughter. They, indeed, tried

Hannah More was born in the schoolhouse at Fishponds in 1745 where her father was the village schoolmaster. She became a philanthropist and she actively opposed the slave trade. She was also a great socialite and a favourite of Doctor Johnson.

which could 'pepper the highest,' and it is not clear to me that the lexicographer was really the highest seasoner.[7]

Samuel Johnson came to see Hannah More on his visit to Bristol, but Boswell did not record the meeting in his journal. James Boswell was not one of Hannah's admirers for it seems that she did not approve of the Scotsman's drinking habits. Boswell's writings do not ignore her completely, however, and he tells an amusing anecdote from another social gathering. The conversation turned to a respectable author who had married a 'printer's devil' (a printer's assistant who had to handle the black inks which stained the hands, face and clothes).

'A printer's devil, sir!' said Joshua Reynolds. 'Why I thought a printer's devil was a creature with a black face and in rags.'

'Yes, Sir', replied Johnson looking very serious and earnest. 'But I suppose, he had her face washed, and put clean clothes on her. And she did not disgrace him. The woman had a bottom of good sense.'

Johnson meant to say 'good sense at bottom' but the word 'bottom' sounded so ludicrous when expressed with such gravity that the polite company could not help tittering and smirking.

'I recollect that the Bishop of Killaloe kept his countenance with perfect steadiness', said Boswell. 'While Miss Hannah More slyly hid her face behind a lady's back who sat on the same settee with her.'[8]

Hannah More may have been prudish but she was very supportive of the poorer classes. She was an active opponent of the slave trade and she was one of the few people prepared to mix with the Kingswood miners, to preach to them and to teach their children. She sponsored Ann Yearsley, a Clifton milk-woman, by tutoring her for over a year and by paying for a volume of her poems to be published. She lived to a ripe old age. It is surprising that in the provincial circle of Bristol she didn't see more of Southey and Coleridge, but when it is realised that the latter were friendly with the Pinney family in Great George Street, only a stone's throw from the school run by the Misses More in Park Street, we are perhaps witnessing the great divide which the slave trade created in Bristol. Hannah More met Samuel Taylor Coleridge for the first time in 1814 when she was nearly seventy. After two hours' conversation Hannah left him with her sisters to speak to a 'titled lady' but later in the evening she fell into conversation with William Wordsworth. According to a witness present at the time, Wordsworth 'made a conquest of the holy Hannah'.

Clifton on the Hill

The decline of Lower Clifton was paradoxically accompanied by the rise of Upper Clifton. The ancient parish of Clifton contained two manors and until the last decades of the eighteenth century it was still a rural parish. Thus, like the great majority of English parishes, Clifton originally earned a living from the soil, but it had the fortunate advantage of a ready market for its agricultural products practically on the doorstep in Bristol.

The high plateau of Durdham Down lay to the north of Clifton village and was much frequented by the gentry as a place to walk and ride. It was a pleasant and healthy spot, sufficiently distant from the smoke of the town, and early in the eighteenth century wealthy merchants decided to build their country retreats there. Thomas Goldney built a house in 1692 which was rebuilt in the classical style by George Tully in the 1720s. Clifton Court was built *circa* 1742 for the

Clifton Court, the house built for Martha Goldney and Nehemiah Champion II who married in 1742. Nehemiah was a founder of the Bristol Brass & Wire Company (1702). His nephew Nehemiah III was a financier to Abraham Darby of Coalbrookdale.

Windsor Terrace. The architect of Windsor Terrace was John Eveleigh, the designer of Camden Crescent in Bath. The builder was William Watts, who had made his fortune in the manufacture of lead shot. The site, overhanging the gorge, was magnificently spectacular, but the immense cost of underpinning the foundations caused Watts to go bankrupt. The terrace was completed in 1796.

merchant Nehemiah Champion who married Martha Goldney. The Champions were a prominent Quaker family who were very involved with manufacture and commerce in Bristol. Clifton Hill House, built for Paul Fisher and designed by Isaac Ware, was the grandest house in Clifton and carried the date 1747 over the doorway. By the middle of the eighteenth century some of the wealthiest of the Bristol merchants were already established at Clifton-on-the-Hill, but Wilstar's map of 1746 shows the area to be still predominantly rural with a field plan very typical of the agricultural parishes of the times.

In 1780 came a very significant development. An enterprising plumber called William Watts had perfected a method of making perfectly spherical lead shot by dropping spheres of molten lead in a cooling tower. Watts made a fortune from his invention and he obtained a lease to build a grand terrace, called Windsor Terrace, on a part of Rownham Woods. The choice of the site, right on the edge of the cliff with views across Bristol to the country beyond, was superb in respect of the panorama but disastrous when it came to building houses. The site was not level and Watts lost his fortune in building a huge retaining wall and expensive vaulting to secure the foundations. After William Watts became bankrupt the terrace was completed by another speculator called John Drew. Drew went on to build the Paragon, a very impressive curved terrace standing above Windsor Terrace. He built ten houses and laid the foundations for three more

before he in turn became bankrupt in 1813. The Paragon was completed by the builder Stephen Hunter.

In 1791 building began on an even more ambitious terrace which became known as Royal York Crescent. Once again the site was on a steep hillside and a fortune had to be spent on foundations. Once again the builders went bankrupt. Once again the project was rescued, but it took nearly thirty years to complete the terrace. The final result, however, was immensely spectacular; it was the longest crescent in Europe and deserved the praises lavished upon it. Immediately below Royal York Crescent came another development almost as spectacular. Originally known as Lower Crescent it was renamed as Cornwallis Crescent and it was not completed until 1837, seemingly without any major bankruptcies.

Not everybody approved of the urbanisation of rural Clifton. In 1793, for example, when Royal York Crescent was a building site, Lady Hesketh wrote that 'The Bristol people have done all in their power to ruin the rural beauties of Clifton Hill by the number of abominable buildings they have erected all over it'. But even she had to admit that 'it is always preferable to any other place'. Maria Edgeworth, the novelist, stayed with her father at Clifton in the same year. He was able to obtain books from the Bristol Library in King Street and she described her situation with enthusiasm:

The Paragon. One of the earliest and most distinctive Clifton Crescents, the Paragon stands high on a rock above Windsor Terrace. It was started by John Drew in 1809, and was completed by Stephen Hunter.

Royal York Crescent. William Paty was the architect of Royal York Crescent, the longest crescent in Europe. Building commenced in 1791 but it took nearly thirty years to complete.

We live very near the downs, where we have almost every day charming walks, and all the children go bounding about over hill and dale along with us ...

My father has got a ticket for the Bristol Library, which is an extremely fine one, and what makes it appear ten times finer is that it is very difficult for strangers to get into. From thence he can get almost any book for us when he pleases, except a few of the most scarce, which are, by the laws of the library, immovable. No ladies go to the library; but Mr Johnes, the librarian, is very civil, and my mother went to his rooms and saw the beautiful prints in Boydell's Shakespeare.[1]

Maria was the sister-in-law of Dr Thomas Beddoes, a scientist who was experimenting with the effect of inhaling nitrous oxide, better known to the layman as 'laughing gas'. His premises were known as the 'Pneumatic Institution' in Hope Square, later moving to Dowry Square in lower Clifton. In 1798 he was joined by the scientist Humphry Davy. One suspects that Davy did not know the Bristol Avon from the Stratford Avon, but his comments on Clifton are worth recording:

Clifton is situated on the top of a hill, commanding a view of Bristol and its neighbourhood, conveniently elevated above the dirt and noise of the city. Here are houses, rocks, woods, town and country in one small spot; and beneath us the sweetly flowing Avon, so celebrated by the poets. Indeed there can hardly be a more beautiful spot; it almost rivals Penzance and the beauties of Mount's Bay.

Our house is capacious and handsome, my rooms are very large, nice, and convenient; and, above all, I have an excellent laboratory ...[2]

The literary circle was fascinated by the doings of the eccentric scientific fraternity. 'A young man, a Mr Davy ... expects wonders will be performed by the use of certain gases', wrote Maria Edgeworth. 'Which will inebriate in the most delightful manner, having the oblivious effects of Lethe, and at the same time giving rapturous sensations on the Nectar of the Gods!' Coleridge and Southey also inhaled the laughing gas. 'Davy has actually invented a new pleasure, for which language has no name', said Southey.

The romantic setting of Clifton with its deep gorge, its lush vegetation, the attraction of Durdham Downs and the marvellous views across Bristol and beyond, attracted compliments from nearly every visitor. The poet George Crabbe described the Avon Gorge as he saw it in 1831:

I look from my window upon the Avon and its wooded and rocky bounds the trees yet green. A vessel is sailing down, and here comes a steamer (Irish, I suppose). I have in view the end of the Cliff to the right, and on my left a wide and varied prospect over Bristol, as far as the eye can reach, and at present the novelty makes it very interesting. Cifton was always a favourite place with me.[3]

This was the same year as the appearance of Fanny Kemble at the Theatre Royal in Bristol. Travelling players did not normally aspire to lodgings as posh as Clifton, but on the long evening of 6 July 1831 Fanny went riding with her father, the actor Charles Kemble, across the Downs and on to the Blaise estate. She saw the setting sun reflected in the waters of the Severn and she described the scenery and the views with great enthusiasm.

The horses having come to the door, we set off for our ride; our steeds were but indifferent hacks, but the road was charming, and the evening serene and pure, and I was with my father, a circumstance of enjoyment to me always. The characteristic feature of the scenery of this region, is the vivid, deep-toned foliage of the hanging woods, through whose dense tufts of green, masses of grey rock and long scars of warm-coloured red-brown earth appear now and then with the most striking effect. The deep-sunk river wound itself drowsily to a silver thread at the base of steep cliffs, to the summit of which we climbed, reaching a fine level land of open downs carpeted with elastic turf. On we rode, up hill and down dale, through shady lanes full of the smell of lime-blossom, skirting meadows fragrant with the ripe mellow hay and honey-sweet clover, and then between plantations of aromatic, spicy fir and pine, all exhaling their perfumes under the influence of the warm sunset. At last we made a halt where the road, winding through Lord Clifford's property, commanded an enchanting view. On our right, rolling ground rising gradually into hills, clothed to their summits with flourishing evergreens, firs, larches, laurel, arbutus – a charming variety in the monotony of green. On the farthest of these heights Blaise Castle, with two grey towers, well defined against the sky, looked from its bosky eminence over the whole domain, which spread on our left in sloping lawns, where single oaks and elms of noble size threw their shadows on the sunlit sward, which looked as if none but fairies feet had ever pressed it. Beyond this, through breaks and frames, and arches made byres, the broad Severn glittered in the wavy light. It was a beautiful landscape in every direction. We returned home by sea wall and the shore of the Severn, which seemed rather bare and bleak after the soft loveliness we had just left ...[4]

More down to earth but just as charming, was Fanny's description of the Bristol market and the country people selling their produce:

After breakfast we sallied forth to the market, to my infinite delight and amusement. It is most beautifully clean; the fruit and the vegetables look so pretty, and smell so sweet, and give such an idea of plentiful abundance, that it is delightful to walk about among them. Even the meat, which I am generally exceedingly averse to go near, was so beautifully and nicely arranged that it had none of its usual repulsiveness; and the sight of the whole place, and the quaint-looking rustic people, was so pleasantly envious. We stopped to gossip with a bewitching old country dame, whose market stock might have sat, with she in the middle of it, for its picture; the veal and the poultry so white and delicate-looking, the bacon striped like pink and white ribbons, the butter so golden, fresh, and sweet, in a great basket trimmed round with bunches of white jasmine, the leaves green and starry blossoms and exquisite perfume making one believe that butter ought always to be served, not in a 'lordly dish', but in a bower of jasmine. The good lady told us she had just come up from 'the farm,' and that the next time she came she would bring us some home-made bread, and that she was going back to brew and to bake. She looked so tidy and rural, and her various avocations sounded so pleasant as she spoke them, that I felt greatly tempted to beg her to let me go with her ...[5]

On July the 16th Fanny left Bristol on the Exeter coach. If she had stayed on a few more days she could have witnessed a premature ceremony which took place of the Clifton side of the Avon – the laying of a foundation stone for a new bridge. It was inevitable that sooner or later the idea would be put forward for a bridge to span the gorge from Clifton to Leigh Woods. It was difficult to justify a bridge on a strictly commercial basis, since both sides of the gorge were thinly populated and the crossings at Bristol were not very far away. But the gorge seemed to be put there to be bridged and the idea of spanning it was a romantic notion. As early as 1753 a Bristol merchant called William Vick left a thousand pounds in his will to be invested for the purpose of building such a bridge. The new expanding population of

Clifton was very wealthy and the residents could easily afford a high toll just to shorten the crossing to Leigh Woods. The idea was bandied around in the eighteenth century when the only technology available was a stone bridge and it was just as well that no attempt to build such a monstrosity was made at that time.

In 1824 Telford's suspension bridge was completed over the Menai Straits. The Menai Bridge was the wonder of the age, and was an engineering work of such striking beauty that the Clifton residents longed to have such a bridge of their own. By 1829 Vick's legacy had reached eight thousand pounds and a subscription fund was started to raise more money, a committee was formed and engineers were invited to submit their designs for a Clifton bridge. Thomas Telford was invited to act as consultant.

Twenty-two designs were submitted. Most of these were of the suspension bridge design with various spans and designs for the supporting towers. Thomas Telford rejected the lot. He then produced his own design which involved building two huge gothic piers rising from the bottom of the gorge. One of the engineers, who had submitted no fewer than four different designs of his own, including one with a span of 916 feet, wrote critically to the Bridge Committee:

> As the distance between the opposite rocks was considerably less than what had always been considered as within the limits to which Suspension Bridges might be carried, the idea of going to the bottom of such a valley for the purpose of raising at a great expense two intermediate supporters hardly occurred to me.[6]

The man's name was Brunel. But he was not Marc Isambard Brunel, the famous engineer of the Thames Tunnel; it transpired that the bridge designer was his son, Isambard Kingdom Brunel. Young Isambard was a tearaway who had nearly killed himself performing heroics beneath the Thames when the water broke into his father's tunnel, and he already knew something of Clifton for he had spent time there recovering after his ordeal. Isambard Brunel proved that he had done his homework; he knew that Telford thought the lateral wind pressure limited the maximum span of the suspension bridge to 600 feet and he had therefore allowed for wind pressure by using very short suspension rods. He had attended to all the minor details of the design.

The Bridge Committee had second thoughts. A second competition was held and Brunel reduced his span to 630 feet by proposing an abutment built out from the Somerset side of the gorge. Brunel produced drawings and lithographs of an elegant Egyptian design with reclining sphinxes guarding the tops of the piers, and was delighted when the committee warmed to his design:

> The Egyptian thing I brought down as quite extravagantly admired by

Brunel's Egyptian bridge design. This was the design with which Brunel won the competition. The towers were to be decorated in the Egyptian style with sphinxes presiding over the top of the chains.

all and unanimously adopted: and I am directed to make such drawings, lithographs etc., as I, in my supreme judgement, may deem fit; indeed, they were not only very liberal with their money, but inclined to save themselves much trouble by placing very complete reliance on me. They seem warm on the subject, and if the confounded election doesn't come, I anticipate a pleasant job, for the expense seems no object provided it is made *grand*.[7]

If the Clifton people wanted grandeur they could not have chosen a better man.

It was high summer in 1831 when an odd little ceremony took place on Clifton Down. A public breakfast was held at the Bath Hotel, after which the participants strolled to a site which had specially cleared to begin the great work. They formed a circle around a pile of stones. Brunel entered the circle, picked up a stone from the heap and handed it to Lady Elton who made a short speech with the stone in her hand. There followed a deafening discharge of cannon from the rocks below and when the echoes died away the faint strains of the National Anthem could be heard from the band of the Dragoon Guards who had been stationed at the bottom of the gorge. A flagpole had been erected and the Union flag was hoisted whilst Sir Abraham Elton delivered a speech. 'The time will come', he said of Brunel, 'When, as that gentleman walks along the streets or as he passes from city to city, the cry would be raised "there goes the man who reared that stupendous work, the ornament of Bristol and the wonder of the age".' The champagne corks popped and a barrel of beer was tapped for the workmen.

It was a necessary and moving ceremony but it was all very premature. The work had progressed for only three months before it had to be suspended following the Bristol riots and it did not restart for four years. In 1836 a second ceremony was performed, on the Leigh Woods side of the gorge, when the foundation stone of the Leigh abutment was laid by the Marquis of Northampton in his capacity as President of the British Association. Crowds gathered on both sides of the gorge and the river was full of ships with flags flying from every mast. When the stone was laid a trumpet fanfare sounded across the gorge and there was a storm of cheering from both sides of the river.

Brunel had slung a wrought iron bar across the gorge, it was an inch and a half wide and constructed in sections totalling a thousand feet in length. The purpose of the bar was to pull materials across in a basket from one side of the gorge to the other, but the workmen could not resist the temptation to cross in the basket themselves. Unfortunately the bar developed a kink and a man got stuck in the middle. Brunel was furious with his workman but he could not resist the temptation to try out the crossing himself. Mary (née Horsley), his wife of two months standing, was present with him but she wisely declined his offer to accompany him in the basket.

Off went the engineer accompanied by a boy called Claxton, probably a young relative of Brunel's friend Christopher Claxton. All went well until the basket reached the lowest point of the journey, then the pulley jammed and the basket could not be moved in either direction! Brunel was something of a showman, and in a feat which equalled those of the great Houdini, and watched by an alarmed new wife, his workmen and the gazing public, he climbed the suspension rope two hundred feet above the river and freed the jammed roller. According to Latimer a similar accident occurred a few weeks later when a bride and bridegroom decided to take the journey on their wedding day. The workmen managed to get the hauling rope tangled just as the happy couple reached the middle of the journey and the newlyweds were left in isolation to admire the scenery for several hours. It seemed that they would be obliged to celebrate the first night of their honeymoon two hundred feet above the gorge, but the ropes were eventually freed and they were hauled to safety.

The bridge piers were completed to a simplified design by 1840, but by then the whole of the fund of £40,000, including William Vick's legacy, had been spent. In the best Clifton tradition, like Windsor Terrace, The Paragon and Royal York Crescent, the Clifton Suspension

'Clifton Folly'. The eerie loneliness of a bridge to nowhere. The Suspension Bridge Trust ran out of money and the piers lay abandoned for many years, until after the death of Isambard Brunel. This photograph was taken in about 1850.

Bridge went bankrupt. In the 1850s when the American writer Mary Russel Mitford came to Bristol the public were still crossing the gorge in the basket in what was a token effort to raise a bit more cash:

> ... the Avon flowing between those two exquisite boundaries, the richly tufted Leigh Woods clothing the steep hill side, and the grand and lofty St Vincent's Rocks, with houses perched upon the summits that looked ready to fall upon our heads; the airy line of the chain that swung from tower to tower of the intended suspension bridge, with its basket hanging in mid air like the car of a balloon, making one dizzy to look at it; formed an enchanting picture. I know nothing in English landscape so

lovely or so striking as that bit of the Avon beyond the Hot Wells, especially when the tide is in, the ferry boat crossing, and some fine American ship steaming up the river.[8]

The trustees collected £125 from the intrepid travellers, but it was a paltry sum compared to the thirty thousand which they still needed to complete the bridge.

It was quite impossible to raise the money. Brunel's career had taken off in a spectacular fashion and he was far too busy planning railways and steamships to organise any fund raising. The Clifton residents were fed up with finding money for high-faluting schemes which invariably went bankrupt. The twin towers of the hopeful bridge remained as a monument to man's folly, standing lonely, gaunt and helpless facing each other across the gorge. After a few years the towers were weathered like ruined castles and defiled by white seagull droppings and petitions were raised to have the eyesores removed. A small boy with courage enough to venture beyond the Clifton tower to the edge of the rocks could lie on his belly and peer over. Far below the ships were pulled along at high tide by fussy black steam tugs, but otherwise the view was little different from that seen by his ancestor a thousand years before. The great chasm between the cliffs still belonged to the realm of the swallow and the skylark.

The Other Half

Living standards in Clifton became the equal of any suburb in England. But there were few places in England where there was a sharper contrast between the uphill and downhill quarters than in Bristol. Early in the nineteenth century the only literate amongst the poor were the fallen middle classes who had acquired the elements of reading and writing when they lived in more favourable circumstances. The written records of the poor are therefore very few and to discover anything at all about their lives and their poverty we have to rely on accounts by well meaning outsiders.

The worst places were the prisons. Few people in the eighteenth century had any sympathy for felons but many of the debtors were thrown into Newgate through no other reason than sheer bad fortune. Nobody in the capital could believe that a fouler place than London's Newgate gaol existed, but John Wesley claimed Bristol Newgate was even worse than its namesake:

> Of all the seat of woe on this side of hell, few, I suppose, exceed or even equal [London's] Newgate. If any region of horror could exceed it a few years ago, Newgate in Bristol did; so great was the filth, the stench, the misery, and wickedness which shocked all who had a spark of humanity left.[1]

The prison was little more than a sewer. In the centre was a dark pit over eight feet deep and about fourteen feet square where seventeen people slept at night; the stench from this dungeon even turned the stomachs of the wardens. There was no bedding, not even straw for the prisoners, and their only light was from one small window high in the wall above. When the prison reformer John Howard first saw Newgate he found it offensive, close and overcrowded, but the one positive thing he did note was that a lot of care was taken to keep the prisoners healthy. Many local people were sympathetic to the debtors, often bringing their surplus food to the jail, and a box was fixed to the door to receive donations. There were also a few philanthropists who raised subscriptions to pay off the debts of poor labourers in order to obtain their release. Newgate was closed and demolished in 1820 when the new jail was built on the New Cut in Bedminster parish, but the depravities in the new jail were almost as bad as the old. There was also the Bridewell. When it came to star ratings this establishment was in much the same category as Newgate, although it had one advantage in that every room had its own cat to prevent the army of rats from gnawing at the feet of the prisoners.

More important than the jails was the condition of the honest poor. It was virtually impossible before the nineteenth century for any member of the lower classes to rise to a position of wealth. The few exceptions were those fortunate enough to be noticed and sponsored by the middle or upper classes and given an education. The great majority of people lived a day-to-day, hand-to-mouth existence and the struggle for survival took priority over everything. In 1793 the masses were pleased to hear that the tolls on Bristol Bridge were to cease, as sufficient money had been raised to put out at interest and maintain the bridge without further charges. Unfortunately the trustees had made an error in their accounts, they changed their mind and tried to charge the tolls for another year.

The dispute over the tolls grew to become a great issue. On the 19th of September the toll gates were thrown open and all traffic passed over the bridge free, and the populace gleefully made a bonfire of the gates and the toll boards. The exasperated trustees then tried to erect a new set of toll-gates, but this angered the masses and they gathered in great numbers, tore down the new gates and made a second bonfire. The magistrates appeared on the scene and read the riot act. The Herefordshire militia was sent for but the crowd was growing all the time and when the soldiers arrived they were greeted with a volley of stones. Tension mounted, the militia had orders to fire and one rioter was killed and three wounded. The tolls were declared legal and on the Sunday they were collected again with the support of the militiamen. On the Monday morning, however, there was renewed violence as a large threatening mob descended on the bridge shouting yells of defiance. Stones and oyster shells were thrown and the soldiers formed rank on the bridge to confront their assailants. The riot act was read out three times. Musket volleys were fired and this was followed by a bayonet charge. There was a very ugly scene, much worse than on the Saturday, and this time eleven people were killed and 45 injured. In the evening a large mob assembled in Queen Square and stoned the windows of the Council House and Guildhall. Eventually a group of private citizens got together and raised the sum of £2,230 so that the liabilities of the bridge trustees could be discharged and there would be no need for the tolls. The outcome was thus seen as a victory for the rioters; the tolls were abolished but the number of dead was a terrible price to pay for what amounted to only a few months of bridge tolls.

The first decade of the nineteenth century was notable for the completion of Bristol's Floating Harbour. The new harbour was long overdue and it was a great asset to the shipping of Bristol, but there was one important factor for which the contractors did not allow. For centuries the Frome had been the main receptacle for much of Bristol's sewage and, although a flow of water had been allowed to prevent the Float from silting up, the flow was nothing like as effective as the river and the tide for taking refuse and sewage out to sea.

In 1817 Queen Charlotte, the wife of George III, paid a royal visit. It was a great embarrassment for the city and the organisers when her carriage reached the drawbridge over the Frome and the bridge became tangled up with the rigging of one of the ships in the harbour. This delay was bad enough but a much greater problem was that the queen was stuck for what seemed an age in her carriage with the stench of an open sewer assailing her royal nostrils.

In 1825 the Commissioners for Paving, Cleansing and Lighting took the Dock Company to court. They claimed that 'a very disagreeable and unwholesome effluvia has arisen from the Frome part of the Floating Harbour'. The appearance of the Frome was 'particularly offensive to the eye, and the stench emitted therefrom was disgusting to the smell and nauseous to the stomach'. The bishop moved out to more pleasant pastures, but the poor had no such option. It seems hard to believe but men and boys frequently used the polluted water of the Float for swimming. The dock company, anxious to prevent 'indecent and improper bathing', sought powers to prevent anyone from 'exposing his naked Body to public view'. The ban became law but it was only effective during daylight hours!

In the Lewin's Mead area the houses near the harbour were built on the steep river bank, typically in blocks of about twelve around a narrow courtyard. A single tap provided water for all the houses in the court. The general plan was for three privies to serve a court and the effluent was discharged directly into the river. 'It is too loathsome to describe', reads a contemporary report. 'When the tide comes up, matters are, for a time, still worse; for it comes loaded with the filth discharged from the sewers that open further down. The stench then becomes almost intolerable.'

In the winter of 1831–32 there was a terrible cholera epidemic in the overcrowded poor house at St Peter's Hospital. Many bodies were taken out for burial and a rumour spread around that the paupers were being buried alive. A mob broke into the burial ground at St Philip's and dug up the bodies, and a similar incident occurred at Temple churchyard. A plot of land was purchased for burials near the cattle market and the bodies, were taken at night by water to escape public notice. The cholera epidemic was comparable to the terrible plagues of the Middle Ages and by the end of October 1,521 had contracted

the disease and 584 of these had died. In the 1840s reliable statistics
were collected by the Goldney report and it was found that in one
year nearly 15,000 children were treated for fever and diarrhoea. Of
these 789 were found to be suffering from cholera and 445 of them
died.

The council posted bills giving advice on the prevention of the
disease. The poor were told to guard against sudden changes of weather
by wearing flannel next to the skin, more especially round the bowels,
they were advised to protect their feet and legs by woollen stockings,
and to bathe their feet frequently in warm water. They were told to
abstain from drink and to keep 'regular hours'. The council was very
badly run at this time. It was always short of cash and had to rely on
wealthy citizens to provide money; typhoid sufferers were given very
patronising advice:

> ... preserve a cheerful contented disposition free from fear, to receive
> with grateful hearts the aid offered by the benevolent sympathy of their
> wealthy citizens, who are now anxiously pressing forward to relieve the
> wants of the indulgent, and so rely with confidence that such measures
> will be taken by the Government and the local Authorities as are best
> calculated, with Divine assistance, to meet the danger.

For those children of the poor who did survive life had little to offer.
Slavery may have been a thing of the past but agricultural wages were
between 8s. and 12s. a week. In the mines at Kingswood boys of ten
or eleven earned 4d. to 6d. a day working underground, their sisters
above ground earned 6d. to 8d. per day. At Bedminster it was found
that colliery children as young as eight were working underground for
twelve hours a day.

These were the conditions of the poor at the time of the great
Reform Bill in 1831. The main issue of the bill was the question of
representation in parliament. Bristol returned two members, industrial
towns like Birmingham and Manchester had no representation at all,
and the old established pocket boroughs and rotten boroughs had
members who were elected by a handful of people. On the surface
Bristol had little to gain by the reform, but the poor knew that the
bill meant more people would have the vote and there would be better
representation for the underprivileged classes. The wealthy had little
idea of the depth of the discontent which was simmering beneath the
surface of the working classes.

Sir Charles Wetherell held the office of Bristol recorder in 1831. He
was a character straight out of Dickens, becoming very unpopular in
Bristol, but he was well liked by the political satirists as is shown by
a passage from Latimer:

> In spite of the coarseness of his invective, his speeches were often amusing,

whilst his extraordinary display of 'gymnastics' in delivery, forgetful of the downward shrinking of his unbraced nether garments, wrought effects on his costume which caricaturists were delighted to reproduce. 'He had no interval of lucidity,' said a witty senator after one of his exhibitions, 'save the interval between his waistcoat and his breeches.' [2]

Charles Wetherell badly misjudged public opinion. He was a staunch opponent of the Reform Bill and he claimed that he spoke for the people of Bristol when he assured the Commons that 'the Reform fever had a good deal abated'. He planned a visit to Bristol on the 29th of October to open the assizes. He was well aware of his unpopularity; he knew there would be trouble and he tried to arrange a bodyguard of sailors, but they refused the job on the grounds that they were not in sympathy with his views. The Corporation then decided to appoint 300 special constables to keep order but they had major problems in finding men willing to do the job. With great difficulty they managed to recruit two hundred men. Soldiers were also held in readiness, one troop of the 3rd Dragoon Guards and two of the 14th Hussars under the command of Colonel Brereton, a retired officer from the Napoleonic wars.

When Sir Charles entered the city at Totterdown he was hissed by a crowd of two thousand; it was a warning of what was to come. In Temple Street the crowd pressed closer and mud was thrown at his carriage. At Bristol Bridge the angry mob had grown larger and the mud was replaced by stones. The constables fought to clear a way for his coach. He was greeted with catcalls and more stones as he arrived at Queen Square. There were soldiers present but they did nothing to disperse the mob and the situation was held in check by the special constables. The constables were heavy handed, they made sorties into the crowd and dragged a few of the ringleaders off to the Bridewell.

In the afternoon many of the crowd dispersed. It looked as though the worst was over and the special constables were allowed to leave for home with instructions to return in the evening. But the rioters had not gone far away; they returned to the square, saw their opportunity and rushed the remaining constables. They tore down the railings in front of the Mansion House. They threw stones and brickbats until all the ground floor windows were broken. At this point the Riot Act was read out and it was greeted with howls of derision. Using the broken railings and the bricks from a neighbouring wall the rioters stormed the Mansion House. Doors and window frames were reduced to splinters. Furniture, mirrors, chandeliers and ornaments were broken and destroyed in minutes. The mob invaded the kitchens where a civic banquet was in preparation and they stole and consumed the food. They piled up straw and other flammable material with a view to setting the building on fire.

Things were getting dangerously out of hand and at this point Sir Charles Wetherell made his escape from the Mansion House by climbing over the roof and changing into the clothes of a postillion. The mob did not know that their quarry had escaped. When Colonel Brereton arrived with his forces the rioters greeted the soldiers with cries of 'God save the king' and some of the tension was released. Brereton did not want any more trouble, so he maintained a presence for some hours in the hope that the rioters would gradually disperse. They were reluctant to go but eventually the 14th Hussars made a charge and cleared the square easily without firing a shot. The rioters dispersed but again they had not gone far away, they simply took refuge in the many narrow alleyways around the square. In Queen Square it was possible to board up the broken windows of the Mansion House. It seemed like the worst of the trouble was over.

On Sunday morning the soldiers guarding the Mansion House were withdrawn. This proved to be a very bad misjudgement on Colonel Brereton's part for the rioters were merely biding their time and they quickly reappeared in Queen Square from the neighbouring alleyways. They broke into the Mansion House a second time, and some were wandering over the roof while others broke into the cellars where they made great inroads into the contents held there:

> Several hundred bottles of port, sherry and Madeira were forthwith stolen and carried into the square, where an astonishing orgie was soon in full swing. A crowd of men, women, and boys were to be seen staggering about, madly intoxicated, yelling, swearing, singing, and vociferating threats against the recorder; whilst scores, too drunk to stand, were rolling on the ground, where those not already insensible from their excesses were re-echoing the maledictions and menaces of their companions. Intelligence of the debauch spread with remarkable quickness into all the low-class quarters of the city, and the concourse in the square was rapidly reinforced by those eager to share in the saturnalia.[3]

The hussars, who had charged the crowd the day before, re-entered the square but this time they were hissed and booed. Brereton ordered them to retreat to Keynsham thinking that he could keep order with his other troops and without bloodshed. Bills were printed and posted with the news that Charles Wetherell had left the Mansion House, but the mob continued to swell and more rioters arrived from other parts of the city. They attacked the Bridewell where a few of their number had been imprisoned. The mob lifted the heavy gates right off their hinges and threw them into the Frome, then they were then able to set all the prisoners free. In a scene reminiscent of the storming of the Bastille the rioters, armed with sledgehammers, next attacked the New Gaol and in a short space of time the massive gates had been broken from their hinges and all the prisoners had been released. A body of

Bristol Riots. The burning of the Mansion House by W. J. Muller. The Mansion House in Queen Square was just one of several historical building lost during the Bristol Riots.

twenty dragoons arrived at the jail led by a young cornet called Kelson, but the soldiers were too few in number to stop the rioters. A hurried meeting was held in the prison yard whilst the rioters planned their next move. They crossed the city to Lawford's Gate where they burnt down the County Prison and the toll houses. With their numbers swollen by the prisoners from three jails they descended on the cathedral. The constables and soldiers tried in vain to hold them off but the Bishop's Palace was attacked and set on fire. It was said that the Bishop's wine was later being sold at a penny a bottle on College Green. The cathedral library was gutted and precious documents were thrown onto a bonfire in the Norman Chapter House. The Bishop's Palace was in flames at the same time as the undefended Mansion House, where many looters were burnt to death as they plundered the cellars.

Things went from bad to worse. The arsonists broke into the houses in Queen Square, systematically setting them ablaze. Soon the Custom House was on fire with the looters busy drinking their spoils on the upper floors. A terrible scene followed with flames lapping all around the building which was still full of looters and rioters. Some looters reached the balcony and managed to escape the conflagration, some jumped desperately from the upper windows and were killed on the pavement below, while others perished in the flames. The magistrates were helpless. There were drunken rioters everywhere and the pile of plunder in the centre of the square grew steadily larger. The looters turned on the neighbouring warehouses. By midnight fifty houses were burning in Queen Square. Chaos reigned everywhere. Charles Kingsley, then a boy of thirteen, remembered the scene which he witnessed from Brandon Hill:

> One seemed to look down upon Dante's Inferno, and to hear the multitudinous moan and wail of the lost spirits surging to and fro amid that sea of fire ... Higher and higher the fog was scorched and shrivelled by the fierce heat below, glowing through and through with red reflected glare till it arched itself into one vast dome of red-hot iron – fit roof for all the madness down below; and beneath it, miles away, I could see the lovely tower of Dundry, shining red.[4]

On Monday morning news of the looting had reached the surrounding countryside. A lawless multitude was descending on Bristol to share in the spoils. Colonel Brereton was roused from his bed and urged to bring his troops. Order was finally restored, but only due to the initiative of Major Digby Mackworth with troops from Keynsham and Major Beckwith arriving from Gloucester. Once the military went into action it took only about two hours to quell the rioters, but it was at great cost and Mackworth estimated that 250 of them were killed or wounded. The aftermath was that 81 rioters were convicted at the inquest but only four ringleaders were hanged. A major casualty was Colonel Brereton, who had done so little to keep order. He faced a court-martial and his conviction was a foregone conclusion. Brereton anticipated the verdict and committed suicide before it was announced.

The flames of the Mansion House, the bonfire in the Cathedral, fifty houses burning and plundered through the night, stolen drink consumed with drunken furore, three jails thrown open and all the jailbirds running free with the looters. Law and order broke down completely and mob rule held for three days and two nights. The riots were perhaps the lowest point in Bristol's long history.

ꝃ CHAPTER FOURTEEN

The Atlantic Challenge

Slowly thy flowing tide
Come in, old Avon! Scarcely did mine eyes,
As watchfully I roam'd thy green-wood side,
Perceive its gentle rise.
With many a stroke and strong
The labouring boatmen upward plied their oars,
Yet little way they made, though labouring long
Between the winding shores

Robert Southey 1799

It was in about the year 1700 that Liverpool first began to be noticed as a rival to Bristol for the transatlantic trade. Celia Fiennes was in Liverpool in 1698 and described the town in glowing colours:

> ... there are abundance of persons well dress'd and very handsome, the streets are fair and long, its London in miniature as much as I saw anything; there is a very pretty Exchange ... which is very handsome town hall; all over is a tower and a cuppilow that's so high that from thence one has the whole view of the town and the country round: in a clear day you may see the Isle of Man.[1]

Liverpool, before the great expansion of her trade, was a seaside town with golden sandy beaches, grand vistas of the mountains of Snowdonia and beautiful sand-hills encroaching against the northern boundary of the town. The Bristol merchants were not concerned. An upstart seaside fishing village, in a county as rural as Lancashire with a population of a mere 6,000 against Bristol's 20,000, was not seen as a serious rival. Liverpool was simply not mucky enough to be a great port.

In the 1750s, therefore, it came as a surprise that Liverpool was carrying as many slaves across the Atlantic as Bristol and two decades later Liverpool was dominating the African trade. This was still not a major concern to Bristol; she was the second city in the kingdom, her trade was expanding at a greater rate than ever before, local industry was also expanding rapidly and by the end of the century her population had risen to over sixty thousand. What was amazing was that the northern seaport had expanded even more rapidly and by 1800 Liverpool was boasting a population of eighty thousand.

155

Some Bristolians claimed that the Liverpool slaving practices were sharper and less honest than their own. This is hard to credit but if it were true it was only a minor factor in the overall picture. Bristol was very good at creating middlemen, the port dues were very high and this was one reason why many London merchants preferred to trade with America through Liverpool. A second reason was that the Atlantic was full of privateers preying on merchant vessels, but the Liverpool ships could avoid the worst of these dangers by sailing to north of Ireland and consequently their insurance rates were lower. The industrial revolution was another major factor. Bristol was well situated with regard to Birmingham and the Black Country and was a major manufacturing centre in her own right, but the opening of the Trent and Mersey Canal gave Liverpool equally good connections to the West Midlands and a distinct advantage with respect to the pottery towns. In the nineteenth century the Lancashire cotton industry accounted for the greatest single element of the Liverpool trade but cotton was hardly significant in Bristol. There was yet another important factor. Liverpool had pioneered the use of wet docks for handling the shipping and by the end of the eighteenth century her dock system was so well developed that it had become a tourist attraction. It was obvious that the medieval quays, which had served Bristol so well for five centuries and a half, were outmoded and something much better was required to compete in the nineteenth century.[2]

The Avon Gorge at Sunset by Nicholas Pocock, 1785. A romantic view of a handsome 34 making her way into the sunset at high tide on the Avon. The five boats contain no fewer than forty oarsmen, showing the increasing difficulties faced by large ships in navigating the Avon into Bristol.

Necessity is the mother of invention. The saying 'Ship shape and Bristol fashion' creates an image of neat and tidy practice, but the saying actually resulted from the chaos in the Bristol harbour when the tide went out. When the ships bottomed on the mud and heeled over masts were pointing in every direction except the vertical, everything on board had to be carefully packed or when the tide went out chaos would ensue both above and below decks. The solution was the wet floating dock but expensive large-scale investment was needed to implement docks on the Bristol waterside.

A wet dock was built at Sea Mills as early as 1712, one of the first in England and a pioneering venture. The dock provided a tide-free berth but it was not a commercial success because of the distance from the city centre. Goods still had to be carried by lighters through the gorge and the unloading was therefore still dependent on the tides. The Sea Mills Dock was abandoned soon after 1770 and by that time William Champion, brother of Richard the porcelain manufacturer, had built a very successful dock at Rownham Meads which became known as Merchant's Dock. The venture was typical of the straight-thinking Quakers and it was surprising that no further development of any note took place before the Floating Harbour was constructed.

Various projects were forwarded for a lock gate on the Avon but they were all rejected on the grounds of cost. The idea was never abandoned for it was obvious that the only long-term solution to Bristol's problem was to make the tidal harbour into a dock with permanent high water. In 1801 the engineer William Jessop was called in to make a survey. His plan was accepted and construction of the new docks began in 1804.

The works were very complex. Essentially the river was to be diverted into a new channel so that the old course could be used as a large dock, to be known as the permanent 'Floating Harbour', the name referring to the fact that the ships were afloat and no longer resting on the river bottom at low tide. The 'New Cut' for the River Avon ran from Totterdown to Rownham Ferry, and was a great engineering feat; in parts it had to be cut deep into the solid rock to accommodate the volume of river water. A smaller cut, called the 'Feeder Canal', was constructed for inland navigational purposes and it connected the new Floating Harbour with the Avon at Crew's Hole. Two great locks were constructed near Rownham ferry and a large basin, called the Cumberland Basin, was built to accommodate the vessels inside the lock, where they could wait for the tide to carry them out to the Severn. It was necessary to allow a controlled flow of water through the floating harbour to prevent it from silting up, so an overflow dam near the locks carried this flow and dredging apparatus was used to help clear the silt. Bathurst Basin was also constructed at the point where the

New Cut and the Floating Harbour came close to each other. Swing bridges were needed at the Cumberland Basin and to enable dock and other traffic to cross the water.

The new harbour took five years to build and it was opened with great ceremony in 1809. There were teething troubles with Jessop's design, the worst of which was the inadequate sewage disposal, which should have been anticipated and did much to tarnish the image of Bristol for a generation. Another serious problem was the silting up of the Float and consequently it was not until 1823 that the company was able to pay the shareholders a dividend. In the long term, however, the work was a great success; it improved the docking arrangements immensely and added about six miles of wharf space where there had previously been only tidal river water. It made the loading and un-loading of cargoes far more efficient and it brought the port of Bristol into the nineteenth century.

Isambard Brunel first appeared on the Bristol scene as an invalid. In 1828 he spent a few months at Clifton convalescing after his accident at the Thames Tunnel. When the competition for the Clifton Suspension Bridge was held he already knew some of the Bristol people and he had acquired some local knowledge. His talents were quickly recognised in Bristol and his opinion was greatly valued, he was brought in as a consultant to advise on the problems with the Floating Harbour.

A detail from Donne's plan of 1826 showing the 'Floating Bason' and the 'New River'. When the tide came in the lock gates were opened at the 'Cumberland Bason', departing ships sailed out, and arrivals came in. Several miles of safe docking was created by the new scheme. Note the docks off the Float, the timber yards and the rope walk at Cannon's Marsh.

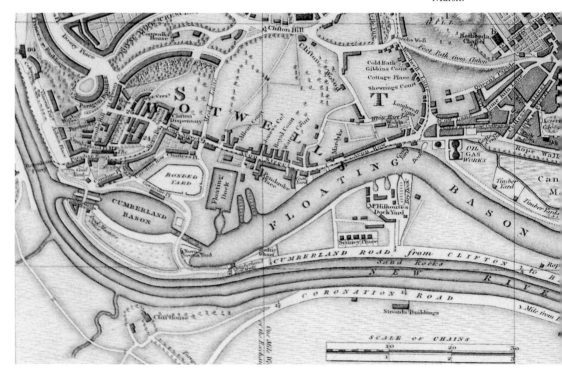

He reconstructed the overflow dam at the Cumberland Basin to an underflow dam as this gave a better and faster flow of water. He also raised the height of the Netham Dam at the inland end to increase the flow of water through the Float and to keep the tidal waters of the Avon from overflowing into the Float at the Totterdown end. He designed a simple but effective dredging arrangement for scouring the Floating Harbour and he designed an improved lock at the Cumberland Basin to replace Jessop's South Entrance Lock.

When the bill for the Great Western Railway was passed Brunel's thoughts turned to the passenger traffic across the Atlantic. He planned to build a steamship which could cross the Atlantic under its own power, an idea which was revolutionary at the time. The early steam engine was a ponderous and heavy machine and for this reason it was adapted for shipping before it was applied to locomotives. A steam vessel called the *Charlotte* appeared in Bristol as early as 1813; it was a river craft rather than a seagoing craft but it could accommodate twenty passengers and plied between Bristol and Bath for a few months before it was withdrawn, probably because of technical problems. In 1817 a sea going craft, the steam packet *Brittania,* arrived from Swansea having made the passage in twelve hours against the ebb tide. Steam tugs were introduced in 1836 to tow the shipping up the Avon, greatly to the consternation of the Pill boatmen who predictably saw the tugs as

The 'Floating Harbour' created wharf space beyond Bristol Bridge as far as Temple Meads, where the Great Western Railway terminus opened in 1841. The old and new Avon were joined at Bathurst Basin. Dry docks are shown at St Augustine's Back and near Prince Street Bridge.

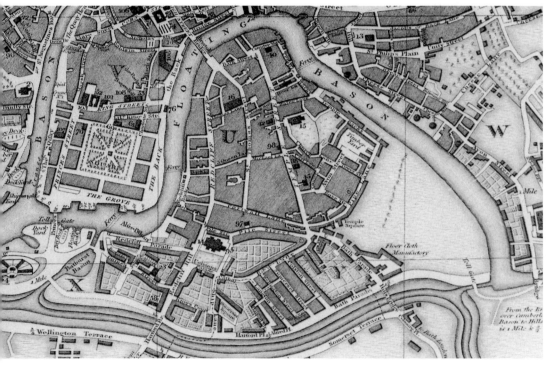

depriving them of their living, and they promptly set the aptly named steam tug *Fury* adrift in the Severn.

The early steamships were small vessels with ironwork for the engine but with hulls of traditional wooden design. The idea of using steam to cross the Atlantic was seen as absurd because it was obvious to all that no vessel could carry sufficient fuel for the journey, and the larger the ship the more fuel it needed (Q.E.D.!). Brunel knew the answer to this problem. The water resistance was proportional to the wetted area of the ship – basically the square of the length – but the carrying capacity was in proportion to the cube of the length. This meant that the larger and longer the ship the more efficient it was in fuel consumption and he calculated that a vessel of 1340 tons displacement could carry sufficient coal for the journey to New York.

Brunel's connections in Bristol at this time were excellent. When the Great Western Steamship Company was floated in 1836 it found many backers, including Brunel's friend Thomas Guppy and the shipbuilder William Patterson. The stern was laid in July 1836 and in just under a year the hull was floated out into the harbour, from where it sailed for London to be fitted out with engines.

The news that Brunel was planning to build a transatlantic steamship quickly spread, and the rival ports of London and Liverpool decided to try to beat Bristol to the honour of being the first to cross the Atlantic under steam. The Londoners started to build the *British Queen*, a ship slightly larger than the *Great Western*, and the Liverpool merchants bought a ship called the *Liverpool*, of 1150 tons. Neither London nor Liverpool could get a ship ready before Bristol, however, so the Londoners purchased a smaller ship called the *Sirius* and the Liverpolitans bought the *Royal William* from Dublin. The honour of three great ports was at stake and in the undignified rush to be the first across the Atlantic corners were cut and safety procedures ignored. To Brunel's dismay the *Sirius* left London on March 28th with nearly three days start over the *Great Western,*. He knew that his rival had to stop and refuel at Cork but the *Great Western* had to call in at Bristol and that gave the *Sirius* a lead of two days. On the last day of March the *Great Western* left her mooring on the Thames, but after only two hours of steaming clouds of black smoke suddenly belched out from the forward boiler room. George Pearne, the chief engineer, described what happened next:

> The fore stoke-hole and engine room soon became enveloped in dense smoke, and the upper part in flames. Thinking it possible the ship might be saved, and that it was important to save the boilers, I crawled down, after a strong inhalation of fresh air, and succeeded in putting on a plunger and opening all the boiler feed cocks, suffering the engines to

work to pump them up, as the steam was generating fast from the flames round the upper part of the boilers.³

The lagging around the boiler had caught fire and was burning fiercely, although the damage was not serious, looking far worse than it actually was. Captain Claxton was below deck playing a hose on the flames when a heavy object fell on him from above. The object was a body and Claxton saw a man lying on the boiler room floor. The man was Isambard Brunel who had fallen 18 feet when a rung had collapsed under his feet. Claxton had fortuitously saved his friend's life by breaking his fall. Brunel was laid on a sail and taken by boat to Canvey Island where he took several weeks to recover. The accident wasted about twelve hours, but the *Great Western* was quickly underway again and she arrived at Kingroad two days later to a surprised and delighted reception in Bristol – the rumour that the *Great Western* had been destroyed by fire had travelled faster than the ship. Apart from the disaster with the boiler lagging the ship behaved impeccably, but coaling and re-victualling took several days and it was not until the 8th of April that the ship left Bristol for New York. The *Sirius* left Cork on the 4th so there was little hope of catching her.

To overpraise the *Great Western* may be to detract from the achievement of the *Sirius*. At 703 tons the latter was little over half the size of the *Great Western*, but on April 22nd she docked in New York and made the historic crossing with only fifteen tons of coal to spare. She had been nineteen days at sea, and four barrels of resin had been taken from the cargo to fuel the boilers. The Americans gave the gallant little ship a richly deserved reception. The day was not over for the New Yorkers, and if there had been a Blue Riband to present then the *Sirius* held it for only a few hours. In the afternoon a second plume of smoke appeared in the distance and soon the superstructure of Brunel's new ship became visible on the horizon. The *Great Western* glided in and docked in the harbour after only fifteen and a half days at sea. The New York *Morning Herald* described the event in graphic detail:

> The approach of the *Great Western* to the harbour, and in front of the Battery, was most magnificent. It was about four o'clock yesterday afternoon. The sky was clear – the crowds immense. The Battery was filled with the human multitude, one half of whom were females, their faces covered with smiles, and their delicate persons with the gayest attire. Below, on the broad blue water, appeared this huge thing of life, with four masts, and emitting volumes of smoke. She looked black and blackguard ... rakish, cool, reckless, fierce, and forbidding in sombre colours to an extreme. As she neared the *Sirius*, she slackened her movements, and took a sweep round, forming a sort of half circle. At this moment the whole battery set forth a tumultuous shout of delight, at the revelation of her magnificent proportions. After making another

turn towards Staten Island, she made another sweep, and swept towards
East River with extraordinary speed. The vast multitude rent the air with
their shouts again, waving handkerchiefs, hats, hurrahing![4]

It was a famous day and very significant event, yet the result was
full of paradoxes. The Liverpool entry, the *Royal William*, did not
arrive until July after a crossing of just under nineteen days. All three
ports were the losers and all three ports were the winners. The
Londoners had won the race, Bristol had the best ship but it was
Liverpool which was destined to carry the bulk of the North Atlantic
passenger trade. The race across the Atlantic was another of Bristol's
magnificent defeats.

Brunel had learned a great deal from the *Great Western* and it was
not long before he was planning another vessel so large that it would
put the *Great Western* into the shade. Brunel proposed a vessel of 3,270
tons gross – by far the largest ship the world had ever seen. The new
ship was to be called the *Great Britain*, and the hull would be
constructed entirely of iron. As usual, Isambard was pushing at the
leading edge of technology, but his enthusiasm and charisma enabled
him to raise the money. An iron foundry was built on the dockside
at Patterson's yard so that parts could be made in situ. Francis
Humphrys, the engineer responsible for the huge paddle shaft, was at
his wit's end in trying to keep up with Brunel. 'There is not a forge
hammer in England or Scotland powerful enough to forge the inter-

The Royal
Western Hotel,
now known as
Brunel House,
dates from 1837/8.
The design was
shared with R. S.
Pope. The hotel
was part of
Brunel's grand
scheme to extend
the Greet Western
Railway across the
Atlantic.

Brunel's *Great Britain* was the greatest and most advanced ship in the world. She left Bristol in 1844, and she returned as a rusting hulk in 1970. The preservation society has been able to restore the ship to her original condition and the ship is now a major tourist attraction.

mediate paddle shaft of the *Great Britain*,' he wrote to an old acquaintance. 'What am I to do? Do you think I might dare to use cast iron?' The acquaintance was the engineer James Nasmyth who immediately rose to the challenge. Within half an hour, it is said, he had designed the Nasmyth steam hammer with all the necessary details for its construction, on a page of his scheme book. Brunel's problem was solved.

Construction of the *Great Britain* was pushing ahead with great speed when a very unusual vessel arrived in Bristol harbour. She was a three-masted schooner powered by a set of steam engines built by the Rennie brothers. The *Archimedes* could make headway without sails but she had no paddles to thrash the water into foam. She glided along driven by a revolutionary and invisible screw propeller located beneath the water. Brunel was so taken by the *Archimedes* that he managed to charter her for six months so that he could study the new mode of propulsion. In fact he was so impressed that he decided his new ship would be driven by a screw propeller instead of paddle wheels.

The shareholders were not happy. Many Bristolians believed that Brunel's decision to build a 3,000 ton ship was wrong in the first place, and that the money should have been used to build three or four sister ships for the successful *Great Western* so that Bristol could offer a weekly steamer service to New York. It was obvious that such a radical change in design was going to cost them a lot more money and the money already spent on paddle wheels was completely wasted and could not be recovered. The comments of his workforce, when they were told to change horses in mid-stream, were not recorded but poor Francis Humphrys, who had worked so hard on the paddle engine, contracted a brain fever which carried him off to higher realms.

Brunel made many other innovations. The hull was of iron and it was divided into six compartments by watertight bulkheads. The engine was of a striking design with four great cylinders in the bowels of the ship, each with a stroke of six feet, driving a massive overhead crankshaft which in turn drove a huge drum. Four sets of chains drove the propeller shaft from the drum. Brunel designed the screw propeller of six blades with a carefully calculated pitch and geometry. Above deck the smokestack of the *Great Britain* stood in line with no fewer than six conventional masts – the days when the steamship could dispense with emergency wind power were still in the future even for Brunel. The hull was 289 feet long and 51 feet wide. The whole of Bristol watched the great ship under construction before their eyes and they admired the work of their great engineer. To have the world's greatest ship taking shape in Patterson's yard on the Floating Harbour was an event of immense local pride.

In July 1843 the great ship was ready to be floated. Prince Albert travelled down from London to launch the ship, which was crewed by Daniel Gooch and Isambard Brunel who broke all the records with a journey time of 190 minutes from Paddington to Temple Meads. Six hundred guests sat down to a banquet and speeches in the dining room of the *Great Britain*. Then they had to be prised out of their seats whilst the sluice gates were opened at Patterson's yard and the dock filled with water to float the iron ship. Prince Albert smashed a bottle of champagne against her bows. As the tugs towed her through the lock gates into the floating harbour flags flew from all six masts and from everywhere else around the harbour. There was the thunder of a gun salute and when the echoes died away the church bells could be heard sounding out across Bristol. Military bands struck up with patriotic tunes. The greatest gathering ever seen in the ancient city packed every vantage point and cheered until they were hoarse. Brunel, Patterson and Guppy held their breath. The greatest ship in the world was afloat and the day was an unqualified success. The enthusiastic engine drivers lost no time in getting Victoria's beloved Albert back home to his wife:

> The greatest speed which I have personally witnessed, occurred on the return of a train from Bristol, on the occasion of the floating of the 'Great Britain.' I was in a compartment, in conversation with three eminent engineers, when one of them remarked the unusual speed of the train: my neighbour on my left took out his watch, and noted the time of passage of the distance posts, when it appeared that we were then travelling at the rate of seventy-eight miles an hour. The train was evidently on an incline, and we did not long sustain that dangerous velocity . . .[5]

There were still trials to be done on the new ship and more fitments to be added. The ship had only got as far as the floating harbour and she remained there until December when the very tricky operation of getting her out to the Avon began. The *Great Britain* was both too long and too wide for the tidal lock at the Cumberland Basin. To accommodate the length the operation had to be timed so that the height of the tide was exactly the same as that in the Float, so that both the lock gates could be opened together. The width of the ship presented an even trickier problem and masonry had to be removed from the side-walls so that the ship could pass through. It was a dangerous and delicate operation and on the first attempt the *Great Britain* stuck in the lock. Luckily Claxton just managed to free her and tow her back into the harbour again. More masonry had to be removed so that another attempt could be made on the night tide. The second attempt was successful, but it was a close call and took longer than planned to get through the lock, by which time it was too late to make the run out to the Severn. The ship had to be grounded overnight outside the lock and Brunel could not relax until she was re-floated on the next tide. The next day she made it to the open sea at last.

The *Great Britain* sailed first to the Thames to complete her fitting out. London society flocked to see the latest wonder of Victorian engineering with her luxurious saloons, cabins and fittings. Even her gracious majesty Queen Victoria paid a visit with her consort Prince Albert, who enjoyed seeing the ship for the second time. In the summer the ship left the Thames for the Mersey and set out on her maiden

voyage from Liverpool to New York on 24 August 1845. Brunel was
delighted with his new ship, but the problems he had encountered,
coupled with the many concurrent headaches of the Great Western
Railway, left him exhausted and contemplating an early retirement.
The feeling did not last, however, and a few years later, between his
sketches for a new Paddington Station and a broad gauge route to
Birmingham, there appeared a drawing of the 'East India Steamship'
with the incredible dimensions of 600ft by 65 by 30. This was the
birth of the 'Great Leviathan', which in reality became the *Great Eastern*
– at 17,000 tons she was the largest ship afloat for thirty years.

It was ironic for Bristol that Brunel did more than any other engineer
in his time to increase the size of the ocean going ship. It didn't need
the tearing down of the masonry at the Cumberland Basin for Bristol
to know that the ships of the future would find the Avon too narrow
and twisting for their length and bulk. The *Great Eastern* was far too
large for Bristol, so she was built on the Thames and all three of
Brunel's great ships ended up sailing from the Mersey. Liverpool lacked
an engineer with the charisma of Isambard Kingdom Brunel but in
the nineteenth century she had a man-made dock system which was
the best in the world. When Edward Cunard first saw the Liverpool
docks he had no hesitation about choosing Liverpool as the terminus
for the North American Royal Mail Steam Packet Company, better
known as the Cunard Line, which landed the lucrative American mail
contract. Even as the *Great Britain* was under construction in Patterson's yard Cunard's four Clyde-built steamers were providing the first
commercial steam service from England to New York.

There was still a hope that Bristol could regain something of her
former glory when Brunel proposed a floating landing stage at Portis-
head, where the large ships could moor alongside. Compared to the
Floating Harbour and other schemes this required a relatively small
outlay and it had the prospect of capturing some of the glamorous
transatlantic passenger trade which Bristol had tried so hard to attract.
But Brunel was totally absorbed in his latest ship and the expansion
of the Great Western Railway, with the result that he did not press
his idea and by the time it was taken up it was too late for Bristol to
capture the coveted passenger traffic.

CHAPTER FIFTEEN

'Brunel's Billiard Table'

Brunel's contribution to the docks and harbour were immense but they were minimal compared to other plans which were afoot in the 1830s. In 1832 four Bristol merchants met in a small office at Temple Back. They were George Jones, John Harford, William Tothill and Thomas Richard Guppy. Their plan was to build a railway from Bristol to London. Brunel soon got to hear of the new venture. He knew Guppy well and he felt confident that with a little luck he would get the post of engineer. Early in March 1833 Brunel had to attend the annual meeting of the Thames Tunnel Company in London, on the 6th he hurried back to Bristol where a decision was being made which radically effected his future. On his arrival in Bristol he received the welcome news that he had been appointed engineer of the new railway, although it had been a close thing and Brunel was chosen by the narrowest possible margin – one vote.

The Great Western was not the first railway in Bristol, however. As early as 1824 a prospectus appeared for a Bath and Bristol railway to be powered by 'that grand improvement, the locomotive steam engine', but, like most railway proposals of the time, it was a very risky project and proved to be premature. The Bristol and Gloucestershire Railway, however, did become a reality in 1835. The railway did not match up to its grand title, serving only a small corner of Gloucestershire and carrying coal from the Coalpit Heath and Mangotsfield workings to the Bristol dockside. It was standard gauge and the reason it did not achieve any fame was that it used horse traction.

Brunel's railway, by complete contrast, was planned on a magnificent scale. In fact the engineer was determined to create the finest railway ever built. The Bristol terminus at Temple Meads was to be a Tudor-style temple in itself. The Paddington terminus was planned to be even grander with a huge single-span arched roof. Isambard Brunel was a great experimenter and innovator. The stations at Reading and Slough were 'one sided', with both platforms on the same side of the running track. The signals were distinctive perforated discs, or in some cases a fantail design. The tracks were to be laid on longitudinal timber supports instead of the stone blocks pioneered by George Stephenson. But the most radical experiment was the distance between the rails – Brunel's grand scheme was to build the railway to a gauge of seven feet!

Brunel's radical ideas were not accepted without opposition. Many of the shareholders were investors with interests in other railway companies and it was increasingly obvious that a national rail network would soon be completed. The Bristol Chamber of Commerce knew that trade with the Midlands, the North and other areas of England would be detrimentally affected by using a non-standard gauge. Brunel's innovation also meant that the Great Western would be unable to use locomotives and rolling stock from existing companies. But Isambard Brunel was a persuasive and a convincing figure. He was sure that his broad gauge was superior to the narrow; in fact he was so confident that he predicted the other railways would change over to the broad gauge when they saw the advantages of his system. After a stormy shareholder's meeting at the London Tavern on 9th January 1839 his enthusiasm carried the day and the broad gauge was approved by the narrow margin of 7792 votes against 6145. Too many Great Western histories depict the 'standard gauge' supporters as fanatic 'narrow gauge' luddites, but in fact the gauge issue only really affected the western counties. Northern proprietors holding thousands of proxies came down from Liverpool. They did not vote against Brunel as Rolt and others have suggested, they arrived with an open mind, listened to the arguments, and voted in favour of the broad gauge.[1]

Brunel always enjoyed the best of relationships with the Stephensons, and when the broad gauge was finally adopted the Northeners kept out of the controversy and let the Great Western Railway get on with its own business. Contrary to popular belief, the strongest objections to the broad gauge came from within Bristol itself when it became obvious that trade was detrimentally affected by a gauge which differed from the rest of the country. John Latimer's Geordie accent can be heard when he gives his opinions on the broad gauge but his views were shared by many of the Bristol merchants:

> The time has long passed away since there was any difference of opinion as to the deplorable error of the original board in neglecting the sober-minded, practical, and economical engineers of the North, already deservedly famous, and in preferring to them an inexperienced theorist, enamoured of novelty, prone to seek for difficulties rather than to evade them, and utterly indifferent as to the outlay which his recklessness entailed upon his employers. The evil consequences of his pet crotchet, the 'broad gauge' system, on the commerce of Bristol will have to be noticed hereafter.[2]

In the early days Brunel was beset with problems of locomotives and rolling stock but these were largely solved by the time the railway became fully operational. As predicted, the worst of the problems was at Gloucester where the broad gauge met the standard gauge line from Birmingham. People and goods were delayed and lost in the chaos

Firefly class locomotive at tunnel portal. The portal is thought to be the Foxhill tunnel near Brislington. The locomotive is one of Gooch's *Firefly* class, the type which hauled the first train from Temple Meads to Bath in 1840.

during the transfer of the gauges. Brunel stood faithfully by his broad gauge system but he knew it could not last for ever. He had the good fortune to appoint as his locomotive designer Daniel Gooch, who had worked for Robert Stephenson & Company at Newcastle, the company which supplied the first successful broad gauge locomotive, the *North Star*. Gooch developed the *North Star* into his own *Firefly* class of locomotive. These had the same chassis and the same 2–2–2 wheel arrangement with a single seven-foot driving wheel, but the firebox was redesigned with a polished metal dome and Gooch experimented with the cylinder sizes and other technical details. The width and space of the broad gauge put the GWR engines in a class of their own and ensured a dedicated following amongst the railway partisans. The locomotives became known as 'Broad Gauge Flyers', originally with

an open cab, painted in the bright company livery, with timber clad boilers and tall chimney stacks, a polished brass dome and bright metal fittings. Brunel paid great attention to the details of the rolling stock and the stations and the railway soon became a source of great pride to Bristol and all the places it served. The seven-foot gauge made it unique among railways and the patrons had every right to sing its praises as the finest railway in the world.

Brunel was very anxious to provide a smooth ride at a high speed and he employed Charles Babbage, the inventor of the difference engine, to experiment with the rolling stock in an attempt to reduce some of the jolting and vibration which was very common in early railway travel. The two men met in Bristol at the British Association meeting and they were good friends. On this occasion Babbage's son Herschel met a Clifton girl called Laura Jones to whom he became engaged, but young Herschel did not have his parental approval for the lady of his choice.

Babbage turned up on a Sunday to take out his experimental train of three wagons with thirty tons of iron as ballast, but the engine was about fifteen minutes late in arriving. There was only a single line open but he was assured by the station officer that the only Sunday train had departed and that there was no other train on the line that day. Babbage described what happened next:

Whilst we were conversing together, my ear, which had become peculiarly

Locomotives at the Swindon works The shed at Swindon where the first locomotives were built and serviced for the Great Western Railway.

sensitive to the distant sound of an engine, told me that one was approaching. I mentioned it to my railway official: he did not hear it and said, 'Sir, it is impossible' – 'Whether it is possible or impossible,' I said, 'an engine *is* coming, and in a few minutes we shall see its steam.' The sound soon became evident to both, and our eyes were anxiously directed to the expected quarter. The white cloud of steam now faintly appeared in the distance; I soon perceived the line it occupied, and then turned to watch my companion's countenance. In a few moments more I saw it slightly change, and he said. 'It *is*, indeed, on the north line.'

Knowing that it would stop at the engine-house, I ran as fast as I could to that spot. I found a single engine, from which Brunel, covered with smoke and blacks, had just descended. We shook hands, and I enquired what brought my friend here in such a plight. Brunel told me that he had posted from Bristol, to meet the only train at the furthest point of the rail then open, but had missed it. 'Fortunately,' he said, 'I found this engine with its fire lit up, so I ordered it out, and have driven it the whole way up at the rate of fifty miles an hour.'

I then told him that but for the merest accident I should have met him on the *same* line at the rate of forty miles and that I had attached to my engine my experimental carriage, and three wagons with thirty tons of iron. I then enquired what course he would have pursued if he had perceived another engine meeting him upon his own line.

Brunel said, in such a case he should have put on all the speed he could command, with a view to driving off the opposite engine by the superior velocity of his own.[3]

The anecdote shows something of Brunel's sense of humour, although nobody was more conscious of safety than Brunel. But nobody had been hurt, the incident was over and, in any event, it was not a regular operating situation. Brunel had travelled through the night and he was much too busy to lose any more sleep over his near miss. Charles Babbage was not at fault over the incident, but for a man with such an outstanding logical mind he does not come out of it with any credit. The fault was clearly that of Brunel, yet Babbage was not prepared to challenge Brunel; he seems to have put the blame on an innocent railway official who was obviously not responsible for Brunel's actions and who was, of course, his social inferior.

Two short sections of the Great Western Railway were already opened by the time the seven-foot gauge was agreed, but at the Bristol end the line to Bath was one of the most difficult sections to build. No fewer than seven tunnels were required to get the rails beyond Brislington, and one of these was 1,017 yards long. On the approach to Twerton a viaduct of 28 arches carried the rails alongside the Avon and the entry into Bath was elevated on a viaduct with 73 arches. Beyond Bath was the controversial Box Tunnel, and on to Chippenham, Swindon, the Vale of the White Horse, and from thence along the Thames Valley to the distant great smoke of London.

The first train ran from Bristol to Bath on 31 August 1840. The passengers gathered at Temple Meads at 7 a.m. on a Monday morning, where Gooch's *Fire-Ball* locomotive was steamed up, ready and panting to haul out the first railway travellers ever to leave Bristol. As the first passengers boarded the train there was frantic activity in Bath where the last rail of the permanent way was being still being driven into place. The train consisted of five second-class carriages with three first-class in the rear. Other locomotives were waiting in steam ready to follow the *Fire-Ball* with their own train of coaches.

Temple Meads Station. Much of Brunel's original façade survives from 1840–41. The station complex was soon redesigned to accommodate through trains from London to Exeter and the West, so that Brunel's magnificent terminus eventually became a goods shed! It may, however, have been the saving of the station for posterity.

> Gaily decked with flags, at a few minutes after eight, the ponderous machine was attached to the first carriage, and its shrill whistle announced that the start was about to take place. The departure of the train was accompanied by loud cheering and waving of hats and handkerchiefs by the passengers, and by the thousands who at this time had congregated in every direction around the terminus and works, every window being filled and the tops of the houses being covered with wonder-struck spectators. All the other locomotives with flags flying, followed the train and added greatly to the interest of the spirit-raising scene. With most commendable caution on the part of the directors, the engineers had received instructions not to attempt any great speed but to proceed with the utmost care; and scrupulously following their directions, they scarcely exceeded the speed of twenty miles per hour, accomplishing the distance, including a stay of two minutes and a half at Keynsham, in thirty-six minutes.[4]

Brunel's terminus at Temple Meads, looking outwards. The view looking inwards can be seen in the colour section. In the foreground is a mechanism for the transfer of rolling stock between rails.

The other trips in the course of the day were performed in periods varying from an impossible claim of nineteen minutes to thirty-two minutes, inclusive of stoppages. As the trains passed through the longer tunnels the passengers were thrown into a state of panic when they found themselves in complete darkness. When the train puffed out into the fields it 'excited no small consternation among the cattle, whose attention was of a sudden distracted from their morning meal'. The sheep fled in amazement, the cows ran off with tails erect and the horses either 'pricked up their ears and stared in astonishment at this symptom of their occupation being all but gone', or else took to their heels and galloped off in utter dismay. A solitary donkey was alone unperturbed, and he continued his feed confident in the assurance that his lot would neither be bettered nor lowered by the new intruder. Thousands of spectators gathered on every spot which commanded a view of the line, and as the train approached the station at Keynsham the bridge was completely covered with people, whilst the church bells were ringing out a 'merry peal'. The journey to Keynsham took fourteen minutes. Passing through Saltford the line came within a few yards of the road, and for a short distance railway and road ran parallel. The passengers enjoyed the 'extremely varied scenery at this part of our environs'. The laying of the tracks into Bath had been finished amid great panic, partly because of unusually high flood water which had delayed the completion of the bridge over the Avon. In the August evenings bonfires and torches lit up the workings so that the navvies could work though the night, and the social life of Bath had moved to the railway to observe its progress. Brunel decided to build a timber bridge over the Avon with a view to getting it finished on time, and according to the local paper he had money staked on its completion. Brunel decided to work on the Sabbath, which generated much disapproval and staring through monocles and *pince-nezs* amongst the Bath purists:

> Approaching Bath, the scene, which towards the centre of the journey had become less animated, began to assume a more lively appearance. Thus at Twerton the number of spectator rapidly increased; and the entrance into the city was witnessed and hailed by many thousands from windows and roofs, from walls and hills, and any elevation which commanded a view of the train. The passage across the Avon over the extraordinary timber bridge near the entrance into Bath was made with the greatest caution. Confident assertions had been made that it would not be in a fit state to permit the passage of the train by the day fixed for the opening of the line; but the unremitting exertions of Mr Brunel and those immediately under him so hastening the work that it was completed on time, though we understand that the last rail was not laid until seven o'clock on Monday morning. It is said that Mr Brunel and Mr Wilcox, the contractor for the bridge, who had betted largely that the structure would be in readiness, won considerable sums of money on the occasion. Arrived in safety at the Bath station, the passengers gave expression of their joy by the utterance of a loud cheer, which was warmly and cordially responded to by those on the platform and the surrounding multitudes ...[5]

Brunel's station at Bath, where the first train arrived from Bristol in 1840. The picture shows the construction of the broad gauge track and the spacious rolling stock.

Bristol and Exeter
Railway. The
Bristol and Exeter
Railway Offices,
designed by
S. C. Fripp in 1852.
The arch of
Temple Meads
station is just
visible on the
extreme left.

The first through train to London was almost another year in coming. It had to wait for the completion of the Box Tunnel which was nearly two miles long and built on a gradient of one in a hundred. By this time the Bristol and Exeter Railway was open as far as Bridgwater and the newspapers announced that 'by the opening of this unrivalled line, London is brought (if the term may be used) within about four hours of Bristol and by the continuation line within five and a half of Bridgwater'. There does not seem to have been a formal opening ceremony and the railway generally made little of what should have been a great occasion. The journey through Box Tunnel was made with no lighting except for the ventilation shafts which were open to the sky. In the early days there was only a single track through the tunnel and the workmen were still laying the second track as the first passenger trains steamed through. The experience of passing through the tunnel for the first time, hauled by a fire-breathing monster which hissed and thundered in the darkness, was likened to a voyage through hell by the reporter of the *Bath and Cheltenham Gazette*:

> On nearing Box, a ridge of hills, towering far up in the sky, and bestriding the country as far as the eye can reach, seems to bar all further progression to 'the levels', but at the next mount appears in the distance the dark and dismal entrance to the subterranean passage and you begin to fancy yourself about to enter the region of perpetual night. You now think of

Aeneas and his sybillic companion. Already goes before you the 'spelunca alta, vastoque immanis hiatu scrupea' and nothing but the 'tenebrae nemorum' is wanting to make the object before you a genuine 'decensus Averni'.* But you have no time for the indulgence of fancy. You have passed the gloomy portal, and now you begin to experience a set of feelings to which you have hitherto been a stranger. You feel an undefined feeling of awe, but yet that feeling partakes more of sublimity than of terror. You thunder on, the atmosphere every moment more tenebrose than before, till presently you are involved in utter darkness. It is now you are fairly in the tunnel; hurried at a fearful rate though the bowels of the everlasting hills. It is now, if possible, darker than ever. The air is chill and sepulchral. You are no longer a passenger in a railway. You have left the earth and all its concerns far behind, and are now being hurried through the regions of perpetual night by the fiery demon who cleaves the murky air with a speed belonging to nought but creation of darkness! Hark! How he screams with savage delight, as though in the very wantonness of fiendish exultation, and how the cry is taken up and re-echoed through the gloomy cavern. To cry – to shriek for help – is useless. Those who could help are far behind, and you are every moment plunging deeper into those fearful regions. See how the baleful gleams from the eyes of the monster light the damp sides of his dreary abode. Suddenly a ray of light shoots through the gloom. You look up there, far up – appear the deep blue of the summer sky you are never doomed never again to behold. One moment – (one single glance is all you can catch of it) – it is gone, and the darkness is tenfold darker than before! How the monster rushes on. How his caverns reverberate in thunder to his mighty progress. The living rock shakes and trembles to its founda- tions. That dreadful scream of savage delight again thrills through your frame, and now a roar still more appalling follows. The foetal breath of the fiend-like being fills the cavern. Sparks fly from his flaming jaws. Alas they do but lend a momentary light to shew the outline of the fearful abode to which you are being buried, still onwards, shrieking, bellowing, gasping and belching fire, plunges the monster.

You sink back in despair. All is over. Sight in such Egyptian darkness is useless. You can hear no noise around but what dismays you. Your voice is drowned in the thunder of its bellows through these doleful, these dismal, regions. But see, in the distant gloom, what unearthly forms appear? See them as they stand half revealed by the feeble lights around! Ah these are the gnomes who inhabit these sepulchral caves! No! They are men – at lest they once were – carried away, perhaps, as we now are: and we – dreadful thought! – we are about to share their lot – to toil amidst darkness and cold in these sunless regions. But no! The monster does not pause: our fate may be more dreadful. The captives are left behind. We shoot on blindly and fiercely as before. But what gleams in the distance? – surely some star that has lost its way, and wandered into these regions of darkness. But yet it cannot be: each moment it increases

* The Latin quotations allude to Virgil's *Aeneid*, book 6, lines 237–8.

its size. It is – it is – the sign of returning day. Look! There is the blue sky there is the green turf once more; once again the cheerful light of the sun breaks upon us. We look around, and find our dream vanished: the reign of terror is over. Our dragon-like monster is changed into a combination of iron, fire, and water, and the exit of Box Tunnel appears in our rear still vomiting forth from its tremendous jaws the steam which we had left behind in our passage. We lose all fear of danger, are convinced that the passage through the tunnel is fully as safe as that along any other part of the line, and continue our journey with the determination of advising every friend and acquaintance to take an early opportunity of visiting this wonder of the West.[6]

New sections of the railway west of Bristol were opened every year until 1844 when the line was completed as far as Exeter. The Bristol and Exeter was originally a separate railway company from the Great Western and their terminus at Temple Meads lay at right angles to Brunel's station. A set of curves was laid to connect the railways but the new rails bypassed both the stations and most of the through passengers had the annoying problem of changing trains at Temple Meads. It was this factor which eventually made Brunel's original station obsolete, as the obvious place for the platforms was on the curves joining the two railways. This may have turned out to be a stroke of good fortune for posterity because it transpired that the original Temple Meads station was preserved almost in its original condition.

The Great Western Railway expanded very rapidly, with tentacles reaching into Wales and the West Country. It gained a strong hold on the midland counties and pushed northwards to Shrewsbury and Chester. The line that Brunel had created was quickly recognised as one of the great engineering feats of the times. It became known as 'the finest work in England', 'Brunel's Billiard Table' and 'God's Wonderful Railway'. It needed an open mind to grasp the wonder of the railway journey and the sense of speed which was unthinkable to the previous generation. Small boys jumped up and down with glee at the sight of an *Iron Duke* class locomotive entering Temple Meads station. Girls screamed with delight and hugged each other as the train dived into the darkness of the Box Tunnel. Noses were flattened against the carriage windows whenever a train passed slowly over one of Brunel's curving timber viaducts. It was an era when children stood on the fences and waved their handkerchiefs at every passing train. When Robert Louis Stevenson came to Bristol to get some atmosphere for *Treasure Island* he travelled broad gauge on the Great Western. Perhaps it was this journey which inspired him to write of the railway through the eyes of a child:

> Faster than fairies, faster than witches,
> Bridges and houses, hedges and ditches;

And charging along like troops in battle,
All through the meadows and horses and cattle;
All of the sights of the hill and the plain
Fly as thick as driving rain;
And ever again, in the wink of an eye,
Painted stations whistle by.

Robert Louis Stevenson

The Great Western Railway went from strength to strength, but its expansion was limited by standard gauge railways to the north and south. Brunel also had other interests, with the Clifton Suspension Bridge and his iron steamships. He was one of the busiest men in the kingdom, always on the move from one railway construction site to another, to Patterson's yard in Bristol, to director's meetings in London, to Devon for the construction of the atmospheric railway, to Cornwall to advise on the building of the Tamar Bridge. His worries with the *Great Western* and *Great Britain* were as nothing compared to his problems with the *Great Eastern* and he was constantly rushing off to Millwall to try and solve the latest problem. After years of taxing his health with a twenty hour working day the toll of his lifestyle began to tell. The stress and worry of his last great ship told heavily on Brunel, and he became a sick man and a shadow of his former self. He lived just long enough to see his Royal Albert Bridge over the Tamar completed but he did not live to see the completion of the

Clifton Suspension Bridge from the Clifton side.

Opening of Clifton Bridge. A badly touched-up postcard shows the opening of the Clifton Suspension Bridge, 6 December 1864.

Great Eastern. Saddest of all he did not live to see the completion of his first and favourite child, the Clifton Suspension Bridge. On 15 September 1859 Brunel died of heart failure. He was only 53 years old. His hectic way of life had finally caught up with him.

The nation mourned the death of a great man. The Institute of Civil Engineers wanted to raise a monument to Brunel. In Bristol and elsewhere all was forgiven when his monumental achievements were seen in perspective. It happened at the time of his death that his footbridge over the Thames at Hungerford was due to be demolished to make way for the Charing Cross Railway Bridge. When any other engineer would have given a king's ransom to throw a bridge across the Thames, Brunel's private comment on Hungerford was: 'I have condescended to be engineer to this but I shan't give myself much trouble about it.' The Clifton Bridge on the other hand, he described as 'my first child, my darling'. It was a bridge much more suited to his romantic taste. It was therefore very appropriate that the new Clifton Bridge company was able to purchase the chains from the Hungerford Bridge. Subscriptions were raised yet again to complete the Clifton Suspension Bridge as a memorial to Isambard Kingdom Brunel. What had started as a local project was now seen as a national project and by December the fund had reached £30,000 of the £45,000 which was required. Modifications were necessary to Brunel's original designs, so the roadway was narrowed by five feet and the Egyptian sphinxes were forgotten – but work began again at last.

It was the 8th of December 1864. At 10am a procession left the city

centre with five army regiments and a Royal Navy band. Six teams of horses hauled six field guns up the hill to Clifton. Every trade, organisation and friendly society joined in the procession to Clifton and sixteen bands accompanied them. Many of the crowd remembered the day twelve years before when they had cheered the launching of the *Great Britain*; some had watched with wonder as the *Fire-Ball* hauled the first train out of Temple Meads in 1840; and a few of the middle-aged remembered the day 28 years before when they had witnessed the laying of the foundation stone of the Clifton Bridge. Never before had the Avon Gorge seen so many faces. Every vantage point was taken. The new bridge was decorated with flowers and greenery. At noon the field guns fired their salute as the first dignitaries crossed to Leigh Woods.

Clifton Suspension Bridge from the South bank of the Avon.

The bridge was breathtaking. It harmonised with the scenery of the gorge and it seemed to belong exactly where it was built. The shallow curves of the suspension chains looked as if they been there from the creation, just waiting for their moment to appear. The span was immense. The drop to the water below was awesome. Was it a work of art or was it a wonder of engineering? From the valley below the chains looked like slender cords and the bridge appeared as a fragile walkway high in the heavens. No city anywhere in the world had an entry to match this symbolic gateway into Bristol. The bridge was so high that the people crossing above appeared like fairies in the sky. The image of Bristol was lifted for ever onto a higher plane. Dull would he be of soul who could pass by a sight so touching in its majesty. It was a fairy tale bridge which joined the ancient kingdom of Mercia to the Wessex of Alfred the Great.

CHAPTER SIXTEEN

The Philanthropists

William Shadwell Mylne was one of the unsung heroes of Bristol. His achievement was to build an underground culvert to carry the polluted water of the Frome into the New Cut, where the river water and tidal action carried it to the sea. There was little for the eye to see, simply a stinking mass of sewage discharging into the New Cut, and the Bedminster residents complained that the smell had simply been removed to another part of the city. Mylne's culvert was not enough on its own to defeat the problems of typhoid and cholera, but for those unfortunate enough to live on the banks of the Frome it represented an immense improvement.

One great advantage of the Reform Act was that local boundaries were expanded to include middle class areas and these were brought under the control of local government. In the case of Bristol it brought the wealth of Clifton into the city and taxes could be raised to improve conditions in the poorer areas. The early decades of the Industrial Revolution seemed to bring only dirt and misery into the manufacturing cities, but by the middle of the nineteenth century the benefits of the technology were being felt; far more wealth was being created and the causes of disease were better understood. In less than a century science and technology achieved more to improve living standards than a millennium of feudal politics.

Amongst the many doctors who dedicated their work to improving the conditions of the poor was William Budd (1811–1880), a physician at the Bristol Royal Infirmary. He studied the causes and spread of cholera and typhoid. He recognised that the key to prevention lay in the improvement of the sanitary conditions. In 1846 the Bristol Waterworks Company began laying pipes from the reservoir at Chew Valley to provide a purer water supply. A Sanitary Committee was formed to improve the drainage and the sewers. The number of cesspools, pigsties, dung heaps and slaughter-houses was progressively reduced. Streets were paved to provide better drainage, and crowded courts and alleys were demolished and progressively replaced with better housing. Bristol's first Medical Officer of Health, Dr David Davies, was appointed in 1864. From 1852 to 1884 a hundred and fifty miles of sewers were constructed. The mortality rate dropped ten points in these 32 years, from 28 to 18 per thousand.

In 1857 the Frome was culverted from St John's bridge to Stone Bridge, thereby creating a new street which became Rupert Street. Ten years later money became available to cover the stretch from Union Street to Merchant Street, and then from St John's Bridge to the Bridewell. Narrow Quay and Broad Quay remained open for shipping and both were as polluted as ever, but higher up the Frome living conditions were improved a little more.

There was a great deal of enterprise from private individuals who wanted to improve the lot of the poor. In the summer of 1846 a meeting took place to instigate a 'ragged school' for the many gutter children and street urchins roaming the city. The leading light in this movement was Mary Carpenter, the daughter of Dr Lant Carpenter, a well respected Unitarian local minister. A room was

St Mary le Port Street, by G. Delamotte, 1824. Mary le Port Street was destroyed in the Blitz. It was so narrow that the houses across the road could support each other. The narrow streets were full of life and small businesses.

Opposite
The view looking up Broad Street towards Christ Church early in the nineteenth century. The picture is a watercolour by the artist Edward Cashin. His work dates from the 1820s, but no details of his life are known.

opened in Lewin's Mead, one of the poorest parts of the town, offering free instruction to any child who wished to attend. On the first Sunday, the second of August, three boys arrived before noon. In the afternoon about ten more turned up. The master in charge was dismayed by their behaviour:

> That afternoon I shall never forget. Only thirteen or fourteen boys present; some swearing, some fighting, some crying. One boy stuck another's head through the window. I tried to offer up a short prayer, but found it was impossible. The boys, instead of kneeling, began to tumble over one another, and to sing 'Jim Crow'.[1]

The task seemed impossible. The street urchins were barefooted. Some had no shirt; many had no home; and they slept in casks on the quayside. They lived by begging, scavenging and petty stealing. They had never been to school and had never been taught anything of the gospels. Mary Carpenter and her colleagues persisted in their efforts and soon the regular attendance grew to thirty boys who behaved in a more orderly fashion. In September the school moved to new premises at St James' Back. Miss Carpenter had ambitious plans and she opened a night school whose roll grew to 200 pupils. She also followed in the footsteps of John Wesley and Hannah More by establishing a reformatory school in the mining district of Kingswood. The school was in the house hired by John Wesley in the previous century. In 1854 she held reformatory classes for girls in one of the grand rooms of the Red Lodge on Park Row, where she was sponsored by Lord Byron's widow.

At the same time as Mary Carpenter was starting her ragged schools there was a significant development on the other side of the Atlantic. In Philadelphia Elizabeth Blackwell, the world's first woman doctor, graduated from medical college. Elizabeth was born in Bristol, her father, Samuel Blackwell, was a sugar merchant and she was one of eight children. Samuel Blackwell, knew as well as anybody that his product was grown and harvested by slave labour, but he was an active member of the anti-slavery society. In 1821, when his daughter Elizabeth was born, the family lived at Counterslip, just south of the Avon and opposite the remains of Bristol Castle. About three years later they moved to more pleasant premises at Wilson Street, on the rural outskirts of the city and close to the church of St Paul's.

In 1832 there was a fire at the sugar warehouse and Samuel Blackwell became bankrupt. The Blackwells decided to leave Bristol to make a new start in America and it was the subsequent career of his daughter Elizabeth which made the family notable. As a child Elizabeth Blackwell had little idea what to choose for a vocation, until in New York a family friend who was dying of cancer told her 'You are fond of study,

Elizabeth Blackwell's House. Elizabeth Blackwell was born in Bristol in 1821 and became the first woman doctor. She lived for a time in Wilson Street before her family emigrated to America where she qualified at Geneva College in Philadelphia.

and have health and leisure; why not study medicine?' It was a ridiculous and impossible idea. No woman had ever graduated from medical college either in England or in America and at first Elizabeth recoiled from the suggestion. Then she found herself unable to remove the idea from her mind and for the next two years she worked and saved hard towards her ambition. A friendly physician taught her anatomy and physiology in her spare time.

Sixteen colleges turned down Elizabeth's application. She felt totally rejected. Then the small Geneva College in Philadelphia offered her a place. The offer was an administrative blunder but the faculty had no problem in finding a way of wriggling out of their mistake. They decided to let the students cast a vote on whether or not a woman should become one of their number, knowing that it was a foregone conclusion she would be rejected. However, the elders misjudged their students. At a meeting on 20 October 1847 the students resolved that:

> ... one of the radical principles of a Republican Government is the universal education of both sexes; that to every branch of scientific education the door should be equally open to all; that the application of Elizabeth Blackwell to become a member of our class meets our entire approbation; and in extending our unanimous invitation we pledge ourselves that no conduct of ours shall cause her to regret her attendance at this institution.[2]

The jaws dropped amongst the dons of Geneva College. Elizabeth quickly became the best student at the college and she graduated with honours in all subjects. Miss Blackwell became known as the 'American

The Dutch House and High Cross re-united. The Dutch house and the High Cross were neighbours for a century, but Fred Little's picture is a fantasy; the High Cross was moved from this location long before the camera was invented.

Host Street, by Fred Little. This narrow city-centre thoroughfare was destroyed by enemy action in 1940. Before the war it was a lively residential street with shop frontages and small businesses.

Redcliffe Parade and dockside. The *Viganelle* of Hamburg anchors beneath Redcliffe Parade in about 1910. The houses and church have hardly changed in nearly a century.

Bristol, St. Mary Redcliffe & Docks.

lady doctor' even though she lived over half of her life in England, and she returned several times to the city of her birth. She was buried, at her own request, at Kilmun churchyard in Scotland.

By sheer coincidence the Blackwells' house at number one Wilson Street figures again in this period of history. When Elizabeth Blackwell was working at her anatomy and physiology in New York her father's old house was being used by George Muller as a home for orphaned children. Muller was born in the year 1805 at Kroppenstaedt in Prussia

Tramways Centre *c.*1910, showing trams of Bristol Tramways & Carriage Co. The large co-op building on the left has long disappeared but the Watershed

and he was educated at the University of Halle. After graduation he was still undecided about his future, but he had faith enough to allow the decision to be taken by God:

> ... he first drew a lot in private, and then bought a ticket in a royal lottery, expecting his steps to be guided in a matter so solemn as the choice of a field for the service of God, by the turn of the 'wheel of fortune'! Should his ticket draw a prize he should *go*; if not *stay* at home.[3]

Divine guidance told him to leave home and at the age of 24 he became

on the right-hand page is clearly recognisable. On the right is the approach to College Green and Park Street. On the left is Broad Quay.

a minister at Teignmouth in Devon. It was there that he met and married Mary Groves. In 1832 he arrived in Bristol where he preached in the Gideon Independent Chapel and at the Bethseda Chapel near Brandon Hill. Like Mary Carpenter, he too set up a school for the children of the poor. One day an orphan boy had to leave the school and was removed to the poor house on account of his poverty. The moral injustice of the situation made a deep impression on George Muller and he wondered if there was anything which could be done about it. The incident made him decide that his true calling was to help the orphaned children.

Muller's first orphanage was in rented premises at 6 Wilson Street. Within 18 months his orphanage had expanded to three houses and it was housing 75 children. When he expanded to a fourth house in Wilson Street the neighbours were beginning to complain. It became obvious that he needed larger accommodation, ideally with its own grounds and purpose-built for his requirements.

He purchased a site at Ashley Down and began to raise funds for a huge orphan house large enough to house several hundred children. He had divine faith that the money would be forthcoming, and he was proved to be right when two gifts of a thousand pounds were made towards his efforts. The purpose-built orphanage provided homes

St Augustine's Bridge and Harbour. A view from the Co-op building (see illustration on previous page) looking in the opposite direction.

Victoria Street, Bristol. 1731.

The George Hotel with Dock Railway Bridge. The railway carried goods traffic from Temple Meads to the docks at Wapping. The bridge remained for many years after the closure of the line.

for four hundred orphans – but Muller went from strength to strength and he eventually built five great orphan houses and by 1870 he was caring for more than two thousand children!

It was an amazing achievement. Many people wondered how George Muller obtained all the money, it seemed as though he must have inherited a large fortune from somewhere, but this was not the case and in his early years he was frequently poverty-stricken. He was a deeply religious man and he always claimed that his success was due to divine providence, but much credit must be given to the people of Bristol, they obviously recognised his work and his organisational skills and when they saw how successful he was they gave willingly and generously. He tells a story of a widow who sold her house, her only asset, for ninety pounds and gave the whole sum to the orphanage. George Muller, knowing the circumstances, did not want to accept the money. He persuaded the widow, with some difficulty, to keep five pounds for herself but she insisted that the rest must go to the orphans.

There were many Victorians who wanted to improve the lot of the poor and in 1873 there was great excitement amongst the sailors of Bristol when a Member of Parliament spoke from the deck of a gaily

Park Street, Bristol

decorated steamer called the *Great Western* which was moored at Mardyke Quay on the Floating Harbour. This was not Brunel's ship but a successor of the same name:

> I am thankful to God for this meeting; for these meetings are evidence of the determination of the people of this country to put an end to a system of manslaughter. 1872 was so stormy that it is officially described as 'That extremely disastrous year'. The number of ships listed at Lloyds as 'Missing' in that year, is infinitely less than in the present year ...[4]

The speaker was Samuel Plimsoll, member for Derby, he had been conducting a campaign against the 'coffin ships'. He quoted fifty grain ships, forty coal ships and nineteen timber ships which had perished on the high seas through deliberate overloading – in many cases so that the owners could claim the insurance money and regardless of the loss of sailors' lives:

> The country will be horrified to hear that in the first six months of the year 1,747 men have been sacrificed, the major part of them to the accursed greed for gain. They can call me an agitator or what they please; wherever I can get a crowd of men to hear me, I will tell the story of the sailors bitter wrongs and how wholesale murder is done, and how it is sending woe and anguish into the humble homes of the poor.[5]

Plimsoll was born in Colston's Parade at Redcliffe, the eighth of thirteen children born to Thomas and Priscilla Plimsoll. He hardly remembered his birthplace for the family moved north to Penrith when

The housing on Park Street looks very familiar but George Oatley's university tower at the top of the hill has not yet been built.

Samuel Plimsoll was born in Redcliffe, the eighth of thirteen children. He left Bristol at a young age but his subsequent work on the plight of sailors gained him great recognition in his birthplace.

Samuel was four years old. Plimsoll became a great campaigner for improving the conditions of the poor. His early work was with the miners but he later put his efforts into the plight of the sailors. He only visited Bristol a few times in his life but his efforts were greatly appreciated by the seagoing community. The *Western Daily Press* described his visit in 1880:

> At the height of this campaign on behalf of sailors' conditions and the Loadline in particular, Samuel Plimsoll came to Bristol. He was received at the station by a great number of his admirers; his carriage was drawn by willing hands through cheering crowds to the 'White Lion' in Broad Street. Then in response to clamours for a speech, he stepped out onto the balcony and opened his address with the words: I was born in Bristol and today I feel like coming home.
>
> Shortly after this spectacular event, the 'White Lion' hotel changed its name. It was called 'The Grand Hotel' on June 1 1880, when Samuel Plimsoll wrote to Joseph Chamberlain. A 'Plimsoll Bar' in 'The Grand Hotel' recalls this historic association with the Sailor's friend.[6]

Plimsoll's greatest contribution was the Plimsoll Loadline which became known in every port throughout the world when every British merchant ship was obliged to carry the markings on her hull. The owners complained bitterly when foreign vessels were leaving British ports heavily overloaded, but by 1906, when the British ports refused to trade with any ship which did not have the official marking, nearly every ship in the world carried the Plimsoll Line.

Where Samuel Plimsoll was known as the 'sailor's friend', Emma Saunders became known as 'the railwaymen's friend'. Born in 1841 at Sion Hill in Clifton, she recognised the long hours, the low pay and the dangers faced by the employees of the railways. She was not an exceptionally wealthy benefactor, but she produced an abundant supply of flowers which she carried around in a wicker basket, and she moved amongst the workers giving out bunches of posies and daffodils for the workers to take home to their wives and loved ones. For fifty years Emma Saunders was a common sight at Temple Meads and other local railway stations, until the sight of the frail octogenarian hobbling round with her flower basket became part of the railway folklore. When she died, her funeral was attended by hundreds of railway workers, all of whom wore her favourite flower, the daffodil, which she had given away by the million. As a mark of respect the GWR mounted a marble plaque to commemorate her near the entrance to Temple Meads Station.

When the thirteenth annual congress of the National Association for the Promotion of Social Science was held in 1869 it was Bristol's turn to be the host. The congress was held in the meeting rooms at the top of Park Street. It was to be expected that the speakers would

have a local bias, but the quality was exceptionally high and the event turned out to be quite an historic occasion. Among the speakers were the writer Charles Kingsley, who had been to school in Bristol and who did so much to bring the plight of the boy chimney sweeps to the public notice; William Budd the Bristol Medical Officer of Health; Mary Carpenter, and Elizabeth Blackwell who was lodging with her in Great George Street. Charles Kingsley asked to be properly introduced to Elizabeth Blackwell and he told her how much he admired her work. Elizabeth felt flattered and embarrassed but when they discovered that they were both Bristol born they enjoyed exchanging childhood memories of Old Bristol, and they both had stories to tell of the Bristol riots. The *Times* reporter felt that Doctor was a masculine title and he therefore invented a feminine for Ms Blackwell. No males were allowed to attend the women's proceedings, not even reporters, and the account is therefore second hand:

> The ladies' conference held its first meeting yesterday, and about 150 ladies were present. Reporters were not admitted, but a lady has communicated to the press that Miss Carpenter took the chair, that a letter of sympathy and encouragement from Miss Nightingale was read, that Doctrix Elizabeth Blackwell, from New York, spoke upon the education of women in the medical profession, that Miss Twining brought forward the subject of workhouse visiting, and Miss Duck that of training nurses. A few observations on intemperance and secret drinking were then made by Miss Carpenter and Mrs Nash, and the meeting was adjourned after a session of three hours duration.[7]

Action on the question of women's education was taken by the government soon afterwards. In the 1870s the Winkworth sisters, Catherine and Susannah, arrived in Bristol from Manchester and they immediately became involved with social work. Catherine was concerned with improving the housing standards of the poor and she

Above left: Designed by Ponton and Gough in 1869, the Granary on Welsh Back is the finest example of a unique Bristol style which flourished in the nineteenth century.

Above right: The Bush Warehouse by R. S. Pope dating from 1832 is one of the best industrial buildings in Bristol. It now houses the Arnolfini Arts complex.

Bathurst Basin provided an alternative route from the Floating Harbour to the New Cut, but this could only be used by small craft. The basin was a hive of activity from its completion until well into the present century. It now provides quality housing close to the city centre.

The original Bristol Museum building in Queen's Road, based on the Doge's Palace in Venice, was a very controversial design in its time. The building served as a university refectory and a restaurant, and is now highly valued as a piece of architecture.

was the prime mover behind the Jacob's Wells Industrial Dwellings project of 1875. She became a governor of Red Maid's School and a founder of Clifton Girls High School. Education for middle class girls was further advanced by the foundation of Redland High School in 1882. The latter was so successful that within two years the school was able to move to the spacious premises of Redland Court, an eighteenth-century Palladian mansion in the heart of the expanding suburb of Redland.

Very radical changes were afoot in education. In the year following the Social Science conference the Elementary Education Act of 1870 brought free education to all children for the first time. Thousands of

Royal West of England Academy. An impressive mid-Victorian building combining both Greek and Italian influences. Charles Underwood and J. H. Hirst were the architects in 1854–57, with alterations by H. D. Bryan and S. S. Reay in 1909–12.

Pevsner described the Victoria Rooms, dating from 1838, as a first-class example of the turn from the neo-classical to a more modern style. He compared is to the École de Belle Arts' in Paris. The fountains in the forecourt have helped to make it a popular rendezvous on New Year's Eve.

Redland Court Mansion, built by John Cossins in 1735 in the Palladian style of the period. It was originally a country estate but the countryside was swallowed up by Victorian housing developments. In the 1880s the building became the home of Redland High School for Girls.

new elementary schools were created throughout the country. In Bristol there were more than 23,000 new scholars to be catered for and this meant that 236 new schools were required. Existing schools were expanded, many church halls and other buildings were converted into schools and eleven new purpose-built schools were under construction.

The contribution of the Victorian women was not confined to social work and education. One of the most interesting and lively people of the Victorian scene was Amelia Edwards, who was living in Bristol from 1861 until her death in 1892. Where Elizabeth Blackwell was born in Bristol but made her career elsewhere, Amelia Edwards was born in Islington but made her name when living in Bristol, where she chose to settle after the death of her mother. She did not choose to live in either the bustling city centre or in Clifton but made her home at a retreat called 'The Larches' in the quiet suburb of Westbury-on-Trym. Amelia was a musician and an accomplished artist but she was also a gifted writer and in the 1860s she was already making a living as a novelist. In 1871, when in her early forties, she took a holiday in Italy with a friend called Lucy Renshawe. They dismissed their inadequate English guide in the best no-nonsense tradition, and spent several months exploring the uncharted Dolomites on their own. Amelia described a person she met in the yard of their inn:

It wears highlows, a battered straw hat, and a brown garment which may be described either as a long kilt or the briefest of petticoats. Its hair is

Redland Chapel. The chapel was originally the place of worship for Redland Court Mansion and is therefore thought to be by John Strahan. Building work commenced in 1740.

sandy; its complexion crimson; its age anything between forty-five and sixty. It carries a knapsack on its back and an alpenstock in its hand. The voice is that of a man; the face, tanned and travel-stained as it is, is the face of a woman.[8]

The phenomenon was presented as a female German tourist, but it would not be beyond Amelia's sense of humour to be describing herself.

In 1873 Amelia and Lucy were off again, this time to France, but the weather was so bad they decided to travel further south to find some sunshine. They made an arbitrary decision to go to Cairo and to travel by boat up the Nile. It would be wrong to imply that Amelia Edwards knew nothing of Egypt before she arrived there, but it is true that her expedition up the Nile was totally unplanned. Amelia was thrilled and totally fascinated by the ancient civilisation of Egypt. She wrote up her experiences in her book *A Thousand Miles up the Nile*, which became a best seller and was remembered long after her novels. Her description of how to mount a camel has never been equalled:

> The camel has his virtues – so much at least must be admitted; but they do not lie upon the surface. My Buffon tells me, for instance, that he carries fresh-water cistern in his stomach; which is meritorious. But the cistern ameliorates neither his gait nor his temper – which are abominable. Irreproachable as a beast of burden, he is open to many objections as a steed. It is unpleasant, in the first place, to ride an animal which not only objects to being ridden, but cherishes a strong personal antipathy to his rider. Such, however, is his amiable peculiarity. You know that he hates you, from the moment you first walk round him, wondering where and how to begin the ascent of his hump. He does not, in fact, hesitate to tell you so in the roundest terms. He swears freely while you are taking your seat; snarls if you but move in the saddle; and stares you angrily in the face, if you attempt to turn his head in any direction save that which he himself prefers. Should you persevere, he tries to bite your feet. If biting your feet does not answer, he lies down.
>
> Now the lying-down and getting-up of a camel are performances designed for the express purpose of inflicting grievous bodily harm upon his rider. Thrown twice forward and twice backwards, punched in his 'wind' and damaged in his spine, the luckless novice receives four distinct shocks, each more violent and unexpected than the last. For this 'execrable hunchback' is fearlessly and wonderfully made. He has a superfluous joint somewhere in his legs, and uses it to revenge himself upon mankind.
>
> His paces, however, are more complicated than his joints and more trying than his temper. He has four: – a short walk, like the rolling of a small boat in a chopping sea; a long walk that dislocates every bone in your body; a trot that reduces you to imbecility; and a gallop that is sudden death. One tries in vain to imagine a crime for which the *peine forte et dure* of sixteen hours on camel-back would not be a full and sufficient expiation. It is a punishment to which one would not willingly be the means of condeming any human being – not even a reviewer.[9]

On her way back through Nubia, Amelia made her last sketch of Philae from the South. She was left alone with her thoughts as she sketched the perfect reflection of the temple in the still waters of the Nile. Amelia knew that she would never return to her beloved Egypt and she wanted to savour the moment and hold it as a memory when she returned to England:

> I peep once again into the mystic chamber of Osiris. I see the sun set for the last time from the roof of the Temple of Isis. Then, when all that wondrous flush of rose and gold has died away, comes the warm afterglow. No words can paint the melancholy beauty of Philae at this

hour. The surrounding mountains stand out jagged and purple against a pale amber sky. The Nile is glassy. Not a breath, not a bubble, troubles the inverted landscape. Every palm is twofold; every stone is doubled. The big boulders in mid-stream are reflected so perfectly that it is impossible to tell where the rock ends and the water begins. The Temples, meanwhile, have turned to a subdued bronze; and the pylons are peopled with shapes that glow with fantastic life, and look ready to step down from their places.

The solitude is perfect, and there is a magic stillness in the air. I hear a mother crooning to her baby on the neighbouring island – a sparrow twittering in its little nest in the capital of a column below my feet – a vulture screaming plaintively among the rocks in the far distance.

I Look; I listen; I promise myself that I will remember it all in years to come – all the solemn hills, these silent colonnades, these deep, quiet spaces of shadow, these sleeping palms. Lingering till it is all but dark, I at last bid them farewell, fearing lest I may behold them no more.[10]

Amelia Edwards spent the last twenty years of her life working on the Egyptian civilisations. She became the first president of the Egyptology Society and endowed the first chair of Egyptology at London University. She was buried in Henbury churchyard, a few yards away from the negro boy Scipio Africanis.

CHAPTER SEVENTEEN

The Bells of Abbot's Leigh

An all too common tragedy in the bend of the Avon. The *Demerara* was launched in 1851 and she struck on the horseshoe bend. All the shipping in and out of Bristol was held up for several days.

The *Demerara* was a paddle steamer of 3,000 tons, comparable in size to the *Great Britain* and built in the same Patterson's shipyard. She was launched in 1851 and it was intended that she should carry mail to the West Indies. Unlike the *Great Britain* her engines were to be fitted on the Clyde. The new ship was manoeuvred through the lock at the Cumberland Basin and a steam tug was attached to tow her down-river to the sea. Unfortunately the operation had taken longer than planned and the tide was on the ebb before she got underway on the Avon. The tug steamed up to maximum power and reached a speed of 7 or 8 knots but Patterson, who was on board the new ship, saw danger ahead and he shouted out to reduce the speed. It was too late. The tug lost control and as the new ship passed Round Point her bows struck hard against the north bank of the bend. The ebb tide carried the stern of the ship round in a great arc across the river. There

was no way to move the *Demerara* and as the tide ebbed out further she lay straddled across the muddy banks of the Avon.

The ship presented a sad sight when the tide went out, her deck was twisted and some of her iron seams split under the strain. A great effort was made to re-float the *Demerara* on the night tide. Every available hand was called to help and in the light of the blazing torches they re-floated her and managed to moor her to the bank near Eglestaff's quarry. But the nocturnal efforts proved to be of no avail, and an hour later she broke her moorings and swung back again across the river. The whole of the shipping in and out of the Port of Bristol was blockaded and it was another two weeks before she could be towed back into the floating harbour. Everybody thought the *Demerara* was a total wreck. She never got her engines but she eventually made it to the high seas as a sailing ship called the *British Empire*.

The disaster showed, more obviously than any previous incident, how dangerous it was to risk ships of over a thousand tons on the Avon. There was talk of converting the whole of the river into a floating dock. There was talk of straightening out the horseshoe bend to allow longer ships to navigate the river. The plans were far too costly for the returns they would bring. The final outcome was inevitable: the only way to handle larger ships was to abandon the Floating Harbour and to build docking facilities at the mouth of the Avon.

A plan was put forward in 1852, the year after the *Demerara* disaster, for a large non-tidal basin on the site of Avonmouth. The cost of £1.5

Horse Fair and Bond Street. A peaceful view of Bond Street early in the century, long before the major redevelopments at St James' Barton.

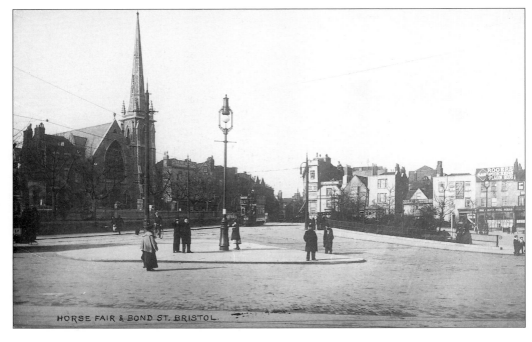

HORSE FAIR & BOND ST. BRISTOL.

The Royal Edward, entering Avonmouth Dock, April 29th 1910.

The liner *Royal Edward* enters the dock of the same name at Avonmouth.

Royal Visit 1908. Children welcome Edward VII and his queen on the royal visit of 1910.

million was too high to consider but the proposal generated other less ambitious ideas. In the 1860s a pier was built at Avonmouth and a railway called the 'Port and Pier Railway' was built along the Gloucestershire bank of the Avon to bring the cargoes into Bristol. A few years later a rival railway was built on the Somerset side to connect the Bristol Docks with a second pier at Portbury. Avonmouth was the more favourable site but it suffered a disadvantage in that the Port and Pier Railway was isolated from the main rail network, whereas the Portbury line connected directly with the Great Western.

Port and Pier Railway tunnel. The remains of the South Portal are still just visible off the Portway. It was used as an air-raid shelter during the war.

It was not until 1875 that the Port and Pier Railway got a connection to the main network by a mile-long tunnel driven beneath the downs. If the Clifton Down Tunnel had been on a main line as opposed to a branch line it would have achieved much more recognition as a major engineering work, but what actually happened was a bureaucratic battle more akin to a comic opera. The tunnel was completed but the trains ran no further than Clifton Down Station because the government inspectors insisted on a station at Sneyd Park near the junction between new railway and the Port and Pier line. The dispute dragged on for ten years before passengers were allowed through the tunnel, by which time the Severn Tunnel was almost completed and Avonmouth had a connection to the main rail network at Pilning.

The first of the large wet docks was completed at Avonmouth in the 1870s. Bristol still managed to retain the bulk of the Avon shipping trade until the end of the nineteenth century but after 1900 the advantage swung rapidly to Avonmouth. For a time there were three ports competing for custom, but common sense eventually prevailed and in 1884 all three came under the control of the Port of Bristol Authority. In spite of other incidents similar to the *Demerara* disaster

King sr.

The Llandoger Trow still survives (see the photograph on page 79), but the two extra gables shown here on the left were lost during the war.

Bristol retained an active shipbuilding industry at the Albion Yard, Patterson's Yard and at Clift House on the New Cut. A steam navigation company ran eight small steamers to Ireland and a few emigrant ships plied to the USA and Canada.

Other developments, notably the Clifton Suspension Bridge, helped Bristol to improve its image in the latter half of the nineteenth century, but in the 1860s the cathedral could not be counted amongst these improvements. After the Bristol Riots the bramble-covered ruins of the Bishop's Palace did nothing to enhance its image and the accommodation for worshippers was cramped and uncomfortable:

Up to this time [1859] the internal arrangements of Bristol cathedral, adopted in the reign of Charles II, were such as to prevent more than a handful of persons from attending divine service. There being no nave, the appearance of one was produced by cutting off a large portion of the space originally included within the choir. The transepts and aisles were also shut off, and formed mere ambulatories for strollers. The area actually available was thus reduced to the proportions of a small college chapel, and was chiefly occupied by stalls and pews; the only accommodation offered to persons who did not purchase the favour of the beadles consisted of the narrow, unfurnished, unbacked benches – to one of

College Green.

Bristol.

which, as has been noticed, the Prince of Wales was relegated on his visit to the building.[1]

Sir Giles Gilbert Scott was consulted and he recommended a new nave which would increase the accommodation from three hundred to a thousand. The architect George Edmund Street was subsequently appointed to design the new nave, work began in 1868 and was completed in 1877. Restoration work continued on the west towers until 1888. George Street's work was sympathetic, so although the new nave was Victorian the style was in harmony with the older parts of the building. During the alterations the ground plan of Abbot Knowle's Norman nave was discovered, dating from 1298. For the first time Bristol had a cathedral to be proud of. Although its anqituity (evident in the Norman Chapter House, the Cloister Court and the thirteenth-century Elder Lady Chapel) had never been in question, the whole was at last complete with a cathedral-sized nave to seat the congregation.

It was not only Bristol Cathedral but also St Mary Redcliffe which was greatly in need of restoration. Much of Canynge's medieval stonework was badly decayed and over forty thousand pounds was needed for repairs. The most significant part of the restoration was the

A view of College Green before the building of the Council House and showing the replica of the High Cross. The Cabot Tower is just visible through the trees.

rebuilding of the spire more than four hundred years after it had been struck by lightning. The rebuilt spire had been a long time coming, it was not rebuilt in 1446 because there was no way of knowing if the spire would fall again, it was not until Victorian times that the architects had the engineering knowledge to calculate the stresses with any confidence. On 9 May 1872 the capstone of the spire, a piece of Portland stone weighing about one ton and measuring four feet in diameter, was put into place. The Mayor of Bristol, Alderman W. P. Baker, performed the heady ceremony 276 feet above the ground accompanied by his wife and other dignitaries. St Mary's could at last stand by her claim to be the fairest parish church in all England.

Wills Tower,
George Oatley's
masterpiece.

In the same decade there was a movement to upgrade the University College to full university status. The plan was given some impetus by the meeting of the British Association at Bristol in 1875. Amongst the prime movers were Bishop Percival and Catherine Winkworth, both of whom were very involved with founding new schools in the same era. It was not until 1908 that the college became a fully chartered university, but Catherine Winkworth's wishes were upheld and women students were admitted from its foundation. The university made a slow start but then it quickly gained momentum and credibility to become one of the countries leading centres of learning. George Oatley's mock castle, built on the site of the Royal Fort, housed the Physics Department from 1921, and his great gothic tower standing prominently at the top of Park Street became a reality in 1925.

In its early years the university relied greatly on the financial backing of local industry, mainly from the Fry and Wills families. The sugar industry had declined from its peak in the eighteenth century but it was replaced by a thriving chocolate industry. Fry's chocolate factory employed 350 workers in 1866 and this number grew to 4,600 by 1904. The Wills family made a fortune from tobacco and became easily the largest local manufacturer: in the 1880s the industry employed about 500 workers but within a few years this number had grown to over a thousand and continued to grow through the first half of the twentieth century.

An interesting nineteenth-century development was the Great Western Cotton Works, a company formed in 1836, and which built a large cotton mill at Barton. Skilled workers were imported from Lancashire and within a few years the mill was employing 1,500 workers. In spite of the Cotton Famine produced by the American Civil War the number of workers remained steady for many decades and the mill was still producing cotton and calico goods after the First World War.

At the turn of the century John Latimer gave a summary of progress in the previous hundred years, seen through the eyes of a visitor transported from the Bristol of 1801 to that of 1901:

> The tiny weekly newspaper of 1801 cost sixpence, and the average workman was too illiterate to read it. The halfpenny daily paper of 1901 is twice the size of the sixpenny sheet; over 60,000 children are in free public schools; and free libraries are open to all. The artificial light of 1801 was limited to smoky lamps and dismal tallow candles. Our imaginary visitor would behold the street illuminated with lamps of 1,000 candle power. He had left the world when travelling was not merely tedious but perilous. He would now see luxurious carriages speeding along at the rate of fifty miles per hour, at one third of the former charge, and conveying more passengers every day than an old mail coach could convey in a year; sedan chairs displaced by tramcars, motor carriages and

The Great Western Cotton Factory in Barton Hill, seen here in an illustration from 1838, employed 1500 workers. It manufactured cottons from 1838 to 1925, an island of Lancashire within the city boundaries.

bicycles; postboys superseded by electric messengers; and, most astonishing of all, merchants transacting business with London and other great centres by telephonic conversations.[2]

Glass and soap manufacture had many ups and downs but managed to survive until the twentieth century. The coal industry shifted its centre of gravity from Kingswood to South Gloucestershire and the winding gear came within the Bristol boundary at Bedminster. Handel Cossham, the son of a staunch Congregationalist minister, made a scientific study of the geology of the area. He purchased the mining rights in St George and Stapleton and became the largest coal magnate in the area. In 1887 only seventeen pits were working on the Bristol coal-field and they were employing about a thousand miners. By the end of the century the number had grown to three thousand miners with four hundred in Bedminster alone. Coal production grew steadily and reached its peak at one and a half million tons in the 1920s. Most of the coal was consumed locally; it was good-quality household coal, but it was seldom exported outside the region.

Engineering manufacture expanded rapidly in the early years of the new century. Trams were assembled at the Brislington works and the Douglas motor cycle factory was established at Kingswood. Bristol's first tramway was laid in 1874 along Queen's Road and Whiteladies Road, but the contractors were unable to purchase enough iron rails to complete the route and for six months the residents grumbled about the state of the road whilst the works remained unfinished. Once opened, however, the tramways proved very popular, using small horse-drawn vehicles until electric traction became available. When the Kingswood tramline opened in 1895 the motor car had made an appearance and eight cars joined in the ceremonial opening procession. The foremost entrepreneur in tramway development was Sir George White, who became chairman of the Bristol Tramway & Carriage Company. In 1907 he extended the Horfield tramline right out to a new tramway terminus at Filton, but his new line was not profitable. He began to think of a means to persuade the public to travel on his tramway. He formulated the idea of holding a flying display on the meadows at Filton, using the new heavier-than-air flying machines which were making an impact in France and America.

Easton Colliery (Hanham), *c.* 1900. Coal was mined in Bristol until after the war, yet very few pictures of collieries survive. The picture shows wooden pit-head gear and other details of the colliery workings at the turn of the century.

Old Market St Bristol. 53.

Above: Old Market Street was a major tramway terminus. The 'Fox and Hounds' is just visible on the right in the middle distance, showing that the view is located where the Old Market underpass now stands.

Below: The Hotwells tram stops at the Clifton Rocks to drop passengers for the Clifton Rocks Railway. The majestic span of the Suspension Bridge is high above.

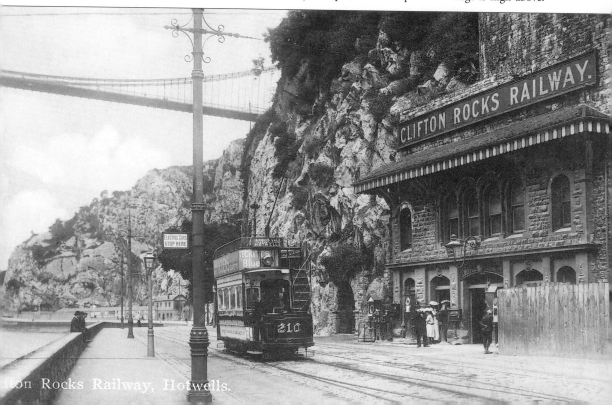

...fton Rocks Railway, Hotwells.

M. Tetard. Starting a Flight with Passenger

Bristol Biplane on Durdham Down (*above*) and Farman Flyer (*below*). The biplane became known as the Bristol Boxkite. In 1910 it was the first aircraft to enter manufacture at the Filton factory. This first Bristol aircraft was well known to be an exact copy of the Farman Flyer, one of which is shown above on Southport sands. It requires an expert to spot the difference.

The Boxkite is
prepared for a
flight at the old
tramshed in Filton,
12 November 1910.

Everard's Printing
Works. A striking
façade in Broad
Street dating from
1900. The architect
was Henry
Williams and the
faience decoration
is by W. J. Neatby.

VICTORIA ST.
and NEPTUNE STATUE, BRISTOL.

The British and Colonial Aeroplane Company was registered in 1910. The Company began to assemble five Zodiac biplanes in the tram repair shop, but they were abandoned in favour of the Farman biplane design. The Farman brothers complained that the new company had infringed their patents and when the first Bristol Biplane, nicknamed the 'Boxkite', appeared in public it was impossible to deny the pedigree. The Boxkite was an excellent name for the aeroplane. It had a box frame of wooden stays braced with steel cables, two pairs of wings of taut canvas, an elevator mounted on a triangular frame at the front and a tail-plane behind. The power unit was a 50hp petrol engine driving a rear-facing propeller mounted behind the pilot. The undercarriage was a pair of bicycle wheels with wooden skids. When Maurice Edmond made the first flight in July 1910 the spectators lay flat on the ground hoping to see a few inches of air between the flying machine and the ground. It rose to 150 feet! The Bristol Aeroplane Company was in business in what was to become one of the major local industries for the rest of the century.

The string and ceiling wax image of the aeroplane was replaced by more robust constructions and the company soon became sufficiently experienced to produce its own original designs. In 1911 the Bristol Racing Biplane was built and in the same year came the Bristol Monoplane, a single-seater aircraft with an air speed of 50 mph. The company went from strength to strength and training schools for pilots were established at Larkhill and Brooklands. At the outbreak of the

Neptune's statue is shown at the junction of Victoria Street and St Thomas Street. The statue by Joseph Rendall dates from 1723 and has graced several locations. In 1949 it was moved to face the Floating Harbour on St Augustine's Bridge. In 1999 it was moved 100 yards to form part of the new Millennium Centre.

The height of Edwardian fashion, Bristol Stock Exchange, which was designed in 1903 by Henry Williams, is described by some purists as a 'shockingly late …debased Italian-ate classicism'.

First World War the Filton works was supplying biplanes for military use. The number of workers grew to four hundred and a new aircraft left the assembly line every day. Aircraft design moved on rapidly, and the Bristol Scout, for example, was a small but powerful biplane capable of nearly 100 mph. The most famous of the early aircraft was the Bristol Fighter of which nearly five thousand were built in several variants and which achieved a reputation in the First World War comparable to the Spitfire at the Battle of Britain. The fighter had a lewis gun mounted at the rear and a 120 hp Beardmore engine. In all, 4,717 Bristol Fighters were built.[3]

Aircraft were also built at Park Row in the centre of Bristol by Parnell and Sons. Here the Short Seaplane, the 250 hp Short Bomber and the 130 hp Scout Seaplane were manufactured. In terms of supplies aircraft manufacture was the main contribution made by Bristol to the First World War, but almost as important were the 25,000 motorcycles supplied by the Douglas Motor Cycle Company. The Douglas WD 2.75 hp 2-speed model served the armed forces in weather conditions from the frozen winters of northern Russia to the deserts of Persia. There were many other Bristol manufactures including explosives, spelter, clothing and footwear.

In 1916 stories of the grim reality of the western front became known nearer home as hundreds of soldiers, followed by thousands of sick and wounded, returned home. Many new hospitals were created. Red Maid's School in Westbury-on-Trym was converted to a hospital with 200 beds, while Southmead Hospital expanded from 260 beds to 1,300. In Sneyd Park Bishop's Knowle House, with its panorama over the Avon Gorge, was converted to a convalescent home. The barrack room story of two Australian soldiers is told by Stone and Wells:

> They both found they had been in hospital and commenced comparing notes, each claiming his hospital to be the finest in the world. So keen did the discussion grow that words came to blows, until the better boxer gave his opponent one straight from the shoulder saying, 'Now will you own Bishop's Knoll is the finest hospital in the world?' The other exclaimed, 'You silly fool! Why didn't you say what the name of your hospital was? Why that's where I was!' The result was a hearty laugh, and the two became the best of friends.[4]

Sixty thousand soldiers and sailors left the city to fight in the trenches on the Western Front and to serve their country on the high seas. Four thousand never returned. Hardly a family in Britain did not lose a relative in the great conflict. Some died in action at Ypres and others were ordered over the top into the teeth of the German guns at the Battle of the Somme. Sailors who fought for their country at Jutland, Dogger Bank and the Dardanelles were buried at sea. Many of those who returned from the trenches were maimed for life. Some lost their limbs; others suffered permanent injuries from gas poisoning; some died of disease in the trenches; and others perished from sheer exhaustion. Many suffered psychological damage from the horrors of warfare.

On Armistice Day in November 1918 the church bells rang out across the city. There was great rejoicing when the people knew that peace had come after four years of fighting. When Rose Sharland wrote her lines she was well aware of the first sound heard by the servicemen as their ships entered the home waters of the Avon. None but the soldiers and sailors could know the feeling of relief which they felt when the bells of Abbots Leigh rung out on the starboard bow.

> With the thrushes' hush-song throbbing,
> Swelled to joy, or sunk to sobbing,
> Born on purring thymy breezes comes the fairy peal to me;
> Even birds that hymn the mating

Bristol suffered as much as any comparable city during the two world wars. The dead of two world wars are commemorated by the war memorial on Colston Avenue.

Pause to hear the air vibrating
With the humming
Music coming
From the bells of Abbot's Leigh.

Here is tranquil Peace abiding,
Quiet calm in Nature hiding,
For Joy's spirit broods immortal on the hill-tops and the sea.
Nature sings new-crowned and vernal-
'Pain is brief, but joy eternal!'
Mellow laughter
Echoes after
From the bells of Abbot's Leigh.

Rose Sharland

CHAPTER EIGHTEEN

My Edward and My Gilbert Long Ago

The years between the wars began with a growth in prosperity which only lasted for a few years. The roaring twenties were followed by the general strike, the stock market collapse and the great depression of the thirties, all of which were felt in Bristol. The best description from this period is by J. B. Priestley who made a visit in 1933. In contrast to certain of his predecessors Priestley was highly complimentary about the people of Bristol:

> My impression of the folk here – especially the working folk – is that the females are above average in good looks and that the men are above the average in breadth of shoulder and stockiness.[1]

He was familiar with many of the main industrial towns of England. In Bristol he could find nothing as grand as Leeds Town Hall, but as a city he still rated Bristol above Leeds. The comparison would be of

The Council House on College Green was designed by Vincent Harris in 1935 and took until 1952 to complete. It is the largest neo-Georgian building in Bristol, with an impressive curved frontage, but greatly criticised by the architectural purists.

little value if Priestley had been anything other than a Yorkshireman, but in the event his comments are very generous:

> ... I was surprised – and still am surprised – when I find that a provincial city, comparable in size and wealth to the ones I know best, is not a dirty nineteenth-century hotch-potch, not merely an extended factory and warehouse, but a real city with a charm and dignity of its own. I never get over it. I stand gaping, like the barbarian I am. Bristol is not as big as Leeds, for example, but it looks ten times the place that Leeds looks. It is a genuine city, an ancient metropolis. And as you walk about in it, you can wonder and admire. The place has an air.[2]

He knew of the turmoil which Bristol had been through. He knew about the slave trade. He knew of the loss of the shipping. He knew of the Bristol Riots and the history of violence. He saw the blackened faces of the miners working the coal seams in Bedminster. Bristol was not a dormitory town living off the backs of the manufacturing centres, it was a place where wealth was being created. Above all he understood about the industrial revolution and he knew the pains which the industrial city had to endure to make a technological contribution to posterity and to raise the living standards of all mankind.

> ... What is especially admirable about Bristol is that it is both old and alive, and not one of your museum pieces, living on tourists and the sale of bogus antiques. It can show you all the crypts and gables and half-timbering you want to see; offers you fantastic little old thoroughfares like Mary-Le-Port Street and Narrow Wine Street; has a fine display of the antique, the historical, the picturesque; but yet has not gone "quaint" but is a real lively bustling city, earning its living and spending its own money. The Merchant Venturers have vanished; the slave trade, on whose evil proceeds this city flourished once, is now only a reminder of man's cruelty to man; the port, depending on the shallow twisting Avon, is only a shadow of its old self; but Bristol lives on, indeed arrives at a new prosperity, by selling us Gold Flake and Fry's chocolate and soap and clothes and a hundred other things ...[3]

Bristol was an industrial and manufacturing centre, but it was isolated from the industrial conurbations of the Midlands, Lancashire and Yorkshire. It had coal but it was not part of the much larger Welsh coalfield; it stood on its own and had a distinctive West Country accent. One thing which it had in common with the northern industrial towns, however, was a fanatical devotion to football, rugby and cricket. If Priestley had chosen to visit two years later he could have seen the fourth round FA cup tie fought between Bristol City and Portsmouth at Ashton Gate. A crowd of 42,885 paid to see the match and another 8,000 saw it without paying, as the main gates were forced open and a barrier collapsed, pushing a hundred spectators onto the pitch. Many

Copyright.   **BRISTOL RUGBY FOOTBALL TEAM—Season 1904-5.**

BENNETT(*Trnr.*) H. WELLINGTON(*Sec.*) PAUL CHICHESTER VINNICOMBE NEADS DAVIS J. W. JARMAN(*Chairman*) G. E. LOC
WATSON   MOORE   THOMAS   SMITH(*Vice-Capt.*) WEBB(*Capt.*) LAMOND SHEWRING MEYER   (*Tre*
WOOD   OATEN   SPOORS   OATES

climbed to the roof of the stand to get a better view. Play was fast and exciting, but at half time neither side had scored. The Bristol Babes were a third division side taking on first division opponents. The second half still found the teams evenly matched:

Bristol Rugby Football XV 1904-5

> ... following a misunderstanding on the part of the City players Worral broke clean through, but when all seemed lost for the home team, Bridge saved the day by conceding a corner and suffering injury in the process. After seventy-five minutes came the first goal of the game when the Robin's right-wing broke clear and Hodge centred wide of the Pompey backs for Harston to head through a brilliant goal.
>
> This success produced frantic scenes, and Portsmouth attacked with desperation, but within another seven minutes the visitors found themselves two down following a movement on City's left wing. Landells lobbed the ball over to Banfield who headed to Hodge, and the latter player drove the ball smartly inside the post, which produced more cheering and added to the din of rattles and bells.[4]

Bristol City went into the draw for the fifth round where they met Preston North End. The official attendance soared to a record gate of

A local derby between Rovers and City. This is usually a friendly occasion, but the local rivalry is very acute and occasionally breaks out in violence.

43,335. The result was a goal-less draw but the Bristol Babes lost 0–5 in the return match at Deepdale.

The Rugby Union code was well established in Bristol before the spherical ball was being kicked around. Clifton RFC was formed in 1872 and played fixtures against the South Wales clubs. In 1885 a local club called the Arabs drew a crowd of two thousand when they played against Newport on Durdham Downs. In 1881 Clifton RFC travelled to Weston Super Mare where they played a local team under novel electric floodlights. Bristol RFC was founded in 1888 when the Carlton club united with Redland Park, their first games being played at the County Ground of the Gloucestershire County Cricket Club at Ashley Down.

Association football first appeared in the 1880s and several local leagues were created. When the game became professional in 1897–98 four local clubs, namely Bristol South End, Eastville Rovers, St George and Warmley, opted to follow the professional route. However, Bristol was not large enough to support four professional teams. The Warmley side was the most successful club of the 1890s but they suffered badly from injuries and financial problems. Eastville Rovers, formerly known as the 'Black Arabs' changed their name to Bristol Eastville Rovers and (in 1898) to Bristol Rovers. They remained firmly attached to Eastville. Bristol South End changed their name to Bristol City and became established at Ashton Gate in the south of the city.

In the 1900–01 season both Bristol teams competed in division one

COPYRIGHT.   BRISTOL CITY. F.C. 1906.   A.H.WRIGHT.

Bristol City FC 1906, the squad which won the Division Two championship in 1906 under manager Harry Thickett.

of the Southern League. City gained promotion to division two of the Football League. They rose steadily up the table and in 1905–06 they won 14 consecutive league matches and became division two champions, finishing four points ahead of Manchester United. This was a vintage team under manager Harry Thickett, and in their first season in division one they achieved their highest position ever, finishing second to Newcastle and only three points behind the league champions. In the 1908–09 season, still under Thickett as manager, Bristol City reached the final of the FA cup. They made very heavy weather of it with replays against Southampton (first round) Bury (second round), Glossop (fourth round) and Derby County (semi-final). Norwich City (third round) was the only club beaten without a replay. The final was played against Manchester United at the Crystal Palace before a crowd of 71,401

It was a pleasant afternoon, the crowd was good-natured and they obviously enjoyed their day out in London. At first there was little to choose between the two sides, the play was very fast and open, moving rapidly from end to end. Bristol City were noted for their strong tackling but, as they tended to lose possession, they resorted to a policy of heavy charging in a desperate attempt to pull the game round. Manchester United had two excellent wingers in Meredith and Wall, both were great dribblers of the ball and were capable of deep swerving runs into the Bristol defence. Halfway through the first half Manchester's efforts were rewarded when Turnbull put the ball in the back of the net. Bristol continued with their determined efforts and United were frequently put out of their stride by the Bristol defence – the Manchester club tended to play the ball too high when their skills lay with their accurate ground passing. At half time the score remained one-nil and Bristol City had to play into the wind for the second half.

They came out in a confident mood, they kept the ball low and displayed great skill in passing along the ground. Their forwards brought off some of the best combined runs seen during the afternoon, and for long periods they dominated the midfield play and frequently beat the Manchester half backs. But one goal proved sufficient to win the game; the Bristol supporters came home disappointed but well satisfied with their team's performance.

Rovers and City played north and south of the Avon, both were very Bristolian but with a different local character. The old Gloucestershire and Somerset rivalry was bound to come out when the teams played against each other and the results of the local derbys with their partisan supporters bore little relationship to the form and league position of the clubs. The teams frequently found themselves in the same division of the Football League. One of the most important clashes was in 1990 when the third division championship was at stake. Bristol Rovers were the underdogs, having suffered an atrocious misfortune by losing their traditional home at Eastville Stadium and were having to play home matches at Twerton Park in Bath. They were

G. Bradford, a popular Bristol Rovers' regular at their old home in Eastville.

always in financial difficulties but promotion would help their image and bring in more support to the terraces.

Both teams had two league matches left to play when Rovers, under manager Gerry Francis, met City at Twerton Park. It was an evening of high emotion. The local derby was always fiercely contested, even when there was no promotion at stake, but here both promotion and the divisional championship were still there for the taking. It turned out to be Rover's night. Devon White scored two goals and Ian Holloway converted a penalty to give the home side a win by the comfortable margin of three goals to nil. It was too much for the City fans, they invaded the pitch and pelted the police with coins. Play was held up play whilst City manager Joe Jordan appealed to the fans to hold their peace for the good name of the club.

'The Bristol Rovers promotion party ended in highly emotional scenes last night as thousands ran onto the pitch to acclaim their heroes,' said the *Western Daily Press*. 'Jubilant Rovers supporters swarmed from the terraces at the final whistle as the players dashed to the safety of the dressing rooms.' But the players soon came back with champagne corks popping and leading the singing and they celebrated with their fans.

The following Saturday Rovers clinched the title when five thousand fans travelled to Blackpool to see their team win 3–0. On the same night City beat Walsall 4–0 to finish only two points behind their rivals. It was a great season for Bristol with teams finishing both first and second in division three. The fans were convinced that it would only be three years before their teams came first and second in the premier division, but they were deeply divided about the ordering.

Sporting rivalry between Gloucestershire and Somerset surfaces on a wider scale on the cricket field. The origins of cricket in the western counties are lost in antiquity but it was certainly played in Bristol in the eighteenth century and probably earlier. In 1706 William Goldwin, who became Headmaster of Bristol Grammar School, wrote a Latin poem describing a rural cricket match in Kent. Latimer mentions a cricket match in 1752, when an eleven of Bristol took the field against an eleven of London for a stake of twenty guineas. The result was not recorded.

Cricket became very popular in the nineteenth century and there are plenty of records of local matches played in the area. In the 1850s clubs existed at Bedminster, Bitton, Clifton, Frenchay, Knowle, Shirehampton and Westbury-on-Trym. By the 1860s several county cricket clubs had been established and discussions were afoot to create a county club for Gloucestershire. Moves were well underway to create the county club at Cheltenham and this would probably have been the case had it not been for Dr Henry Mills Grace, a fanatical cricketer

W.G. Grace: the greatest cricketer of the nineteenth century, who dominated the game for fifty years.

who lived at Downend. Doctor Grace had eight children, one of whom, Edward Mills Grace, had already established a reputation as the finest batsman in the county. He also had a younger son who in 1866, at the age of eighteen years and a few days, scored 224 not out for an England XI against Surrey.

In 1870, when the Gloucestershire Cricket club was founded, the Grace family had a virtual stranglehold on the county team. It was this factor, as much as any other, which caused the headquarters of the club to be located in Bristol. In the first decade of their existence the Gloucestershire club's success can only be described as legendary. They shared the County Championship with Nottingham in 1873 and went on to win it outright in 1874, 1876 and 1877. Much of their success was due to the 'Three Graces' – the brothers Edward Mills Grace (b. 1841), William Gilbert Grace (b. 1848) and George Frederick Grace (b. 1850). The Graces were so numerous that they had to be differentiated by their initials.

There was an intense sibling rivalry between E.M. and W.G. E.M. was the older brother by seven years and it was not until W.G. was in his late teens that he began to overtake his prolific brother as a run-making machine. In 1877 W.G. stood several inches taller than his elder brother at 6 feet 2 inches, but E.M. still beat his precocious sibling in the batting averages. In 1878, the year frequently quoted as the start of the modern game, the county champions Gloucestershire travelled to Old Trafford to meet Lancashire. The fame of the three Graces was already a legend and the north–south rivalry was accentuated by the fact that Lancashire employed professional players in their team. A crowd of eighteen thousand arrived to see the game. It was estimated that another two thousand climbed over the fences. Francis Thomson described the encounter in what was to become the most famous cricketing poem of all time:

> It is Glos'ter coming North, the irresistible,
> The Shire of the Graces, long ago!
> It is Gloucestershire up North, the irresistible,
> And the new-risen Lancashire the foe!
>
> A shire so young that scarce has impressed its traces,
> Ah, how shall it stand before all resistless Graces?
> O, little red rose, their bats are as maces
> To beat thee down, this summer long ago!
>
> This day of seventy-eight they are come up North against thee,
> This day of seventy-eight long ago!
> The champion of the centuries, he cometh up against thee,
> With his brethren, every one a famous foe!
>
> The long whiskered Doctor, that laugheth rules to scorn,
> While the bowler, pitched against him, bans the day that he was
>   born:
> And G. F. with his science makes the fairest length forlorn;
> They are come from the West to work thee woe!
>
> *Francis Thompson*

The game ended in an honourable draw.

W.G. dominated the Victorian cricket scene. He captained the Gloucestershire county club from its birth in 1870 to the end of the century. He made 54,896 runs and took 2,864 wickets in his first class career – these figures are frequently in dispute as the authorities try to decide which of the nineteenth-century matches count as first-class cricket. At the height of his powers he could bat all day without tiring and without giving away the slightest chance. Bowlers became so disheartened that they asked to be taken off rather than be hit all over the field by him. The piercing eyes, the great black shaggy beard, the huge frame, the attacking stance and his fearsome reputation struck terror into every bowler.

His batting achievements are all the more remarkable when the state of the pitches is taken into consideration and when it is recognised that the number of first class matches was far fewer than in the twentieth century. As a bowler Grace had a fiery round arm action with his hand hardly rising above the shoulder. In later life he was noted for guile rather than speed.

Such became the reputation of the great man, and so many anecdotal stories are told, that it is difficult to sort the facts from the legends. It was said that W. G. hit a six in Gloucester which struck the ground in Bristol. The ball landed in a railway wagon and was carried 36 miles on the broad gauge before it was recovered. A lesser-known record is that in 1895 he became the heaviest person to play for England when he weighed in at eighteen stones. At Sheffield Park in 1896 Earnest Jones (Jonah) nearly lost the ball by firing it through his beard. The young blood was quickly put in his place.

'Whatever ye at, young fellow? Whatever ye at?'

'Sorry Doctor, she slipped,' apologised the bowler.

'In the religion that was cricket W. G. stood next to the Deity,' said Clement Attlee. It was true, but the problem with W. G. was that his will to win was so strong he often acted like a deity and he frequently challenged the decisions of the umpires and of those who played against him.

Nowhere in sporting history is there a greater paradox than W. G. He always claimed to be championing the case for the amateur cricketer, yet he made far more money out of the game than any professional. On his first tour of Australia, for example, he demanded a fee of £1500 and by the time of his second tour he had doubled his fee to three thousand! He was welcomed as a hero at every venue in Australia but, after accusing his opponents of fixing the toss and constantly arguing with the umpires, the Australians were invariably glad to see the back of him. He sometimes appears as the most atrocious snob, such as when he insisted that the 'players' stay in second-class hotels while the 'gentlemen' in the same team lorded it over them in the best hotels on full expenses. In direct contrast, when he qualified as a doctor he chose to treat the poor at the workhouse when he could easily have obtained a lucrative middle class area in which to practice. He was the most accomplished cricketer of all time but it took him eleven years to qualify as a doctor – he finished fifth out of six in an aptly-named 'Class of General Perpetual Students' at the Bristol Medical School. His medical knowledge was very suspect yet his patients thought very highly of him. He walked with kings on at least two occasions, yet he spoke with a Gloucestershire accent and mixed easily with the common people. In 1882 he so upset the Australian team, and especially the demon bowler Frederick Spofforth, that the English team suffered a devastating retribution on the cricket field – but later in life all was forgiven and Spofforth spoke of W.G. with great affection. Beneath the beetling brow and the diamond eye was a warm heart which his competitive edge hid from all except his closest friends.

At Ashley Down and even at Lord's, when it came to cricket the last word must be given to W.G. When he died in 1915 his friend Sir Arthur Conan Doyle described him as having 'a masterful personality and a large direct simplicity and frankness which, combined with his huge frame, swarthy features, bushy beard, and somewhat lumbering carriage ... made an impression which could never be forgotten'. Few men have done more for the generation in which he lived, and his influence was none the less because it was spontaneous and utterly unconscious.

> With the beard of a Goth or a Vandal,
> His bat hanging ready and free,
> His great hairy hands on the handle,
> And his menacing eyes upon me.
> *Sir Arthur Conan Doyle*

There was no way in which the Gloucestershire club could live up to the success of the early years. In the twentieth century they consistently produced great players and great characters but further success eluded them for nearly a hundred years until they won the Gillette Cup in 1973 and the Benson and Hedges Cup in 1977. Gilbert Jessop, known as 'the croucher' because of his aggressive stance, started his county career in the same side as the three Graces. The new century produced the legendary Walter Hammond, and after the war came the Bristol-born Arthur Milton who played both cricket and soccer for England, the stylish Tom Graveney and overseas players like Mike Proctor and Zaheer Abbas. Among the bowlers were Tom Goddard, Sam Cook, Bomber Wells and David Allen.

Gloucestershire proved very successful at limited over cricket and the new knockout competitions. After the successes of the seventies it seemed that nothing more would achieved until the new millennium, but how could the loyal supporters know that their team had saved their finest hour for the very end? In 1999, as the millennium dome approached its final shape at Greenwich, thousands of Gloucestershire supporters converged on Lord's to watch their team play Yorkshire in the final of the Benson and Hedges Super Cup. It was well worth the journey, because the Ashley Down side recorded a memorable victory and returned home with the trophy. The cheers had hardly died away before there was something even more amazing to shout for – in a nail-biting finish at Bristol, Gloucestershire beat Yorkshire a second time to earn a place in the final of the NatWest Trophy – the last such trophy of the century, the last of the summer wine. It was quite unbelievable that their opponents in the final were their old Wessex rivals south of the Avon, the famous cider making county of Somerset!

This was a final for the history books. Lord's was invaded, not only by Bristolians but by both of Bristol's neighbouring counties. Never before had the Great Western Railway and the M4 seen a convoy to match the one which followed the trail to Lord's on August the 29th. The headquarters of the MCC, with its new space-age press box looking like an alien craft, was packed again to capacity with a crowd determined to savour every moment of the day.

The game started well for Gloucestershire with an opening stand of 125 between Kim Barnett and Tim Hancock. Then the Somerset supporters had something to shout about as Gloucestershire suffered a minor collapse to 193 for 6. Some determined batting from the tail end brought the score up to a respectable 230 from the 50 overs, but the Somerset men knew that this total was well within their capabilities. Somerset got off to a dreadful start, however, and after only 16 overs they had lost five wickets for only 52 runs. The Gloucestershire supporters were jubilant, but they were a little premature, for Somerset rallied with a stand of 82 between Keith Parsons and Rob Turner. At this point it looked as though the match might still be just within the reach of Somerset, but when the next wicket fell the result was never really in doubt. Gloucestershire won by the comfortable margin of fifty runs. Wicket keeper Jack Russell was voted man of the match.

For most of the twentieth century the old men at Ashley Down could be heard spinning yarns of the days in their youth when they saw their Edward and their Gilbert long ago. The times have moved on. Well into the new century their great grandchildren will begin their cricketing anecdotes with the words 'When I was at Lord's in ninety-nine ...'.

CHAPTER NINETEEN

Our Darkest Hour

'I was in Trinity Methodist Church, Whiteladies Road, when last night's raid began. We opened the church doors and half of Bristol seemed to be on fire! At that the congregation (except a few who lived 'Just across the way') descended to the shelter of the underground schoolrooms. The air rang with zooming 'planes and the barrage of the guns; the roofs sang with falling shrapnel. Now and then a thud told of a high explosive bomb. You could read by the light of the fires – the nearest one a church not fifty yards away. During the occasional lulls in the devil's symphony outside, odd groups slipped home. The roofs of the burning church fell in, a house across the street caught fire, and southwards over Bristol the flames roared their fury to the sky.

'My pass expired at 10.30. So I borrowed my sister's bike and set off to return to camp – and see what I could of the damage. It took me 25 minutes to reach the *Press* office in Baldwin Street. I used to do it in five minutes. I struck Whiteladies Road just above Clifton Down Station, and from there to the centre, what with hosepipes and fires and endless detours, I pushed and carried the cycle as much as I rode it.

'On either side of my route, most of the streets had a house or two on fire, but they were 'nothing'. Near the Whiteladies Cinema, Week's auction rooms and part of their furniture depository were one high-storied mass of concentrated fire. A hundred yards to the east, St Joseph's Home, in Cotham Hill, was paying the price of a regime which knows not charity.

'Down to the Victoria Rooms, the road was clear, but there I should have stopped in amazement even had not the snaking hosepipes outside the Academy barred my path. Lennard's fine buildings (and the block including the Triangle behind) was one surging wave of fire. Firemen – professional and A.F.S. – were valiant in heart and hands. They stopped that wave from flooding to the buildings neighbouring the pro-cathedral, and they stopped them from lapping and engulfing the eastern end of Queen's Road. When, baulking at the fiery gauntlet of Queen's Road, I turned past the Embassy and went behind along Elmdale Road, the sparks from Lennard's were falling even there, like fiendish snow. Up Eldon Road the handsome 'prep' wing of the

Grammar School was burning out. I intended to turn down University Road to join the main street again, but a policeman said 'No'. For the Museum, that strange incongruous copy of the Doge's Palace in hostile Venice, was well afire. Sharp cracks and crashes told of havoc among those treasured showcases. I turned up towards Royal Fort – and on my right the university was ablaze. Obviously the fire went deep into the heart of the place, but I didn't realise as I actually rode down Woodland Road that the Great Hall was gone.

'Somehow the Prince's Theatre gave me a nasty shock, because it stood for so many peace-time things that I love – the D-Oyly Carte, the Ballet, good plays and cheerful music … No Prince's Panto this year …

'I turned right at the bottom of Woodland Road, intent on going down Park Street. Boot's was ablaze in Queen's Road, but I hardly noticed it. Park Street was ablaze, it seemed, from end to end. The road was covered with glass and stones and steel and hosepipes. Fire engines steadily roared their applause to the heroic efforts of firemen fighting impossible odds. The heat was considerable and I veered from one side to the other, according to the intensity of the flanking fires, to avoid its worst. When I got to the bottom of Park Street and looked back at this mighty torch flaming to the skies, I estimated that every third shop was ablaze.

'At the end of College Green Gane's furniture shop was burning like tinder, but round the corner – surprise and relief – the centre was its accustomed Sunday self – except that it was almost daylight, and odd hosepipes drew their life blood from its unnoticed main water pipes. But along the harbour wall behind me I had a message of the fires of the wharfs and, looking up Clare Street, I was appalled at the view of Wine Street. I could see All Saints Church intact, but beyond the site of the old High Cross all detail was lost in one vast sheet of orange flame. I dropped in at the *Press* office where the tape-machine ticked steadily away in the air-raid shelter. *But what news had England for Bristol that night?*

'Further along Baldwin Street this tremendous story began all over again. The Rowland Adams corner was already a ruin, and I had a vague impression that parts of Charlotte Street and the Welsh Back were burning. On the other side of the Cunard-White Star Offices had taken the blow … at the end, St Nicholas' church shared the proud sacrifice of the secular buildings. On Bristol Bridge I stayed still for a full five minutes. From there I had another impressive view of the Wine Street area. The whole block to St Mary le Port was burning, and I guessed that Union Street and Narrow Wine Street were in very like plight. Straight through what had been the top of Bridge Street I saw the furnace that had been Castle Street – Castle Street, with the

very new hiding the very old, where you could not drive your car on
a Saturday night because of the crowd.

'With a sudden shock I realised that St Peter's Hospital and half of
the church had disappeared, I didn't mind so much the burning of
the Regent next door, nor the carnage among the great stores further
on, because they can, and will be, replaced.

'Behind me the Avon was being pumped on to a great fire on the
Redcliffe waterfront, I turned to the drama nearer at hand – Victoria
Street.

'You know now, of course, that Robinson's on the right and George's
Brewery Offices on the left made a flaming gateway to another trail
of havoc that rivalled and, in parts surpassed the pity of Park Street.
Along most of Victoria Street, and in Temple Street too, when I made
a forced detour, I protected my face with my hands from the sparks
and the heat, and every now and then picked a singeing spark from
my spray-damped clothes. But all around me the A.F.S. fellows noticed
nothing but the unremitting demands of their Herculean jobs. The
worst spot was near Temple Church, where the aisle of the weaver's
chapel was gone, but the solid tower leaned no more than of old.

'From some unexpected stable, carters and a couple of bluejackets
were leading those familiar Bristol draught horses to safety – frightened,
but unflinching, like the thoroughbreds they are. The vast furnace that
had been Mardon's factories was a mighty valediction with a vengeance.
The road I took then led to lesser scenes of destruction – fires and

The Dutch House is thought to have been built in 1676. It stood in a prime position on the corner of High Street and Wine Street. It was a large timber-framed house of five storeys plus attic rooms. It suffered a direct hit in 1940.

Opposite
St Peter's Hospital was the finest of the timber-framed buildings of old Bristol. It was reconstructed in 1612 and served as the Bristol Mint before becoming a hospital. It was totally destroyed in the November blitz of 1940.

bomb craters, and the whole A.R.P. services in gallant action – but always I turned to look at the city itself . . .' [1]

The *Western Daily Press* report by Eric Buston describes the air raid on 24 November 1940. It was the first of nine great air raids by the Luftwaffe over Bristol. The date can be found on a plaque at the site of the parish church of Clifton, one of several churches destroyed in a night of terror; the same date appears in Whatley Road where the church of St Anselm's was bombed.

The centre of old Bristol was an inferno hotter than hell itself. The houses were very old and many were timber framed, burning as readily as dry tinder. Mary le Port Street was a river of fire, Wine Street was like the entrance to Hades. St Nicholas' church was hit by an incendiary and the spire was burning like a like a great orange torch as masonry fell to the pavement below. Fearful screaming thunder sounded as another bomb fell in a neighbouring street, the eerie hiss of another incendiary sounded overhead. The medieval decorated wooden roof of Spycer's Hall in Baldwin Street blazed away like a great bonfire. The Dutch House, a timber-frame structure of four storeys built around a frame of unhewn tree-trunks, was helpless against the flames – the cracking as the plaster ceilings and plate windows gave way to the heat, could be heard above the roar. Dorothy Hazard's nonconformist chapel survived the Cavaliers by three hundred years but it was destroyed in minutes by the inferno. Dolphin Street blazed like a furnace from end to end. St Peter's Hospital, the finest Elizabethan building in Bristol, was a timber-framed mansion with high gables, richly carved barge-boards and decorated arabesque plasterwork. The rooms inside were wainscoted and much of the wooden furniture was of priceless antiquity. The hotel next door caught fire and burning fragments felt onto the inflammable Tudor building – within minutes it was burning like a beacon. Fire fighters braved the inferno of fire but the narrow alleys and the overhanging upper floors hampered what little they could do. Rivers of molten lead flowed from the roof of St Peter's church as the building burnt like a brazier. Sparks flew from roof to roof like a giant firework display and the burning city was reflected golden in the surface of the river. Officials and air-raid wardens moved in with the fire fighters, messengers and ambulance men followed. The police broke open doors and windows to free the terrified residents trapped behind them. Nurses and ancillaries followed to tend the sick. A large part of historic Bristol was destroyed for ever on this terrible night.

Just before the all clear sounded, a little before midnight, E. H. Skeeles was in the Colston Hall where the theatre-goers were waiting until it was safe to make their way home. He realised that the vivid orange glow outside did not flicker – the fire was so intense that the city was illuminated as brightly as if the dawn was breaking:

'I opened the door and looked out, but it is well nigh impossible to find words to describe what followed that night. I had the impression of being in a dream-world – what I saw seemed so terrible that for the first time in my life I was unable to believe my own eyes. When I opened the door, I found myself in Trenchard Street. The air was full of drifting ash and burning particles – some of them almost as large as half a sheet of newspaper. Everywhere I looked I could see fires raging, and the light from them was so brilliant that I could read every word of a scrap of newspaper that caught my eye, as easily as if it had been broad daylight. Here and there the underside of a barrage balloon shone bright with the reflected flames and I could hear a roar which told me that a major part of the conflagration was hidden by the cramped surroundings of Trenchard Street. An army officer came down the street at this moment and his advice was to make a dash for it, so off I went, up Trenchard Street, down Colston Street, and down to Colston Avenue, via a narrow alley and some steps. Somewhere about this time the 'All clear' sounded. I crossed Colston Avenue which was littered with debris, running with water and criss-crossed with dozens of hose-pipes and made my way to St John's Arch, intending to go home via Broad Street, Wine Street and Old Market Street, but one look up Broad Street told me that it would be impossible, for at the top I could see the Dutch House and all the buildings flanking that side of the High Street blazing fiercely from top to bottom. A few steel helmeted firemen were there, but the jets from their hoses looked pitifully inadequate against the inferno. I could feel the heat well over a hundred yards away. I retraced my steps and turned right along Nelson Street. My face was scorched, and the drifting ash and burning particles were thicker than ever. A small group of firemen were directing their hoses toward the blaze, but with little effect. Arriving at Union Street, I saw too, that this thoroughfare was impassable as the whole of the top of the hill was in flames. The fires fanned by a breeze, roared fiercely, huge warehouses were ablaze from top to bottom, their outlines almost hidden by the flames, and smoke that swirled around them. Occasionally there would be a rumbling crash as some huge building collapsed; the whole scene was one of indescribable and awe-inspiring magnitude ...

'... [I entered Old Market Street] ... which was ankle deep in broken glass, and the air so full of hot ash that I had to protect my face with my coat collar. I looked down Old Market Street in the direction of Castle Street beyond, and saw the most amazing spectacle of the whole night. I was looking at a whole city burning. It was obvious that street after street and block after block was one raging furnace ... Acres of roaring flames devouring everything before them, combined with the smoke and the showers of sparks and ash, to form a most dreadful and never-to-be-forgotten spectacle. My position at the end of Carey's Lane was directly down wind from this terrible scene and the heat was tremendous, even at that distance.' 2

When the cost was counted the dead numbered 149, and 133 were seriously injured.

The main targets of the German bombers were the aircraft factories at Filton, the docks at Avonmouth and the city centre, industrial targets, gas-holders, chemical plants and the railway yard complex near Temple Meads Station. The November raid was the first heavy raid to strike at the heart of Bristol, but Avonmouth had already been bombed in the preceding August and Filton was hit in September. The Filton raids took place in broad daylight. The first raid, with a force of a hundred enemy aircraft, came as a complete surprise and caused untold damage on the site. Ninety-one employees were killed and nearly two hundred injured. The raid was repeated two days later but by this time a squadron of Hurricanes had been posted to Filton. In spite of the warnings from air raid wardens, crowds of residents and workers came out to watch in awe at the dog-fights in the sky above Bristol. Ten enemy aircraft were shot down.

When the drone of the enemy bombers was heard overhead the long white beams of the searchlights raked across the sky and tried to lock on to the aircraft. The heartening sound of anti-aircraft fire followed soon afterwards. The shrill wail of the sirens sounded out over the city and the residents left their homes for the air raid shelters or in some cases for the disused railway tunnels in the Avon Gorge.

The tunnels offered more comradeship and seemed to offer better protection, but they suffered from frequent outbreaks of disease because of the pitifully inadequate sanitary conditions. It was a twilight world of shelters and air raids, gas masks and blackouts, shortages and ration books. It was a trying time for young families, as children aged from three to thirteen were taken from their parents and evacuated to safer places, each child carrying a change of clothing, an identity label and a gas mask.

On the night of the 3rd of January 1941 came Bristol's fourth Blitz. It was a twelve hour ordeal, lasting from dusk until dawn, and made even worse by the bitterly cold weather conditions. The water from the fire hoses froze to form sheets of treacherous ice on the roadway, worse still was when the water actually froze inside the hosepipes. The fire-fighters did the best they could in the adverse conditions. Fred Hooper describes the dilemma:

> Water froze in the hose, due to drop in water pressure as often happened then, and escapes and ladders were frozen to buildings. A turn-table ladder was frozen to the roof of the General Hospital, with tons of ice hanging in great icicles from the ladders. It took over a week, using hot water from the hospital, to free it. Hose could not be drained of water and rolled up, but had to be folded (or flaked) and collected by lorries. At Coronation Road Fire Station in Bristol the hose was piled to the roof in a great heap, and coke braziers kept burning day and night, with

In January 1941 it was so cold that the firemen's hoses froze solid. They had to be thawed out before any fires could be tackled.

Winston Churchill
on his visit to
Bristol after the
'Good Friday' raid
in 1941.

men pulling at the hose, trying to disentangle each length, thaw it, and drain it.

The clothing froze hard on the firemen's bodies. They fought on encased in ice. When the sun rose on the morning of January 4th the dead numbered 149. There were 351 people injured of which 133 were considered serious.

In the 'Good Friday Raid' of 1941 Winston Churchill, the Chancellor of the University, was due to arrive by train to confer some honorary degrees. His train pulled into a siding for the night where Churchill witnessed the city of Bristol burning before his eyes. The next morning the Prime Minister went to look at the bomb damage. The air raid services were feverishly at work and people were still being dug out of the ruins of their homes. The casualty figures in this raid were 180 dead and 146 seriously wounded. At one of the rest centres he found a number of old women whose homes had been wrecked and who were sitting shocked and stunned, the very picture of rejection. When Churchill appeared the women wiped away their tears and cheered wildly for king and country. Winston Churchill too was seen to wipe the tears from his eyes. At the university the bright robes of the academics did not conceal the soaked and grimy uniforms of the night's toil. Churchill made one of his famous wartime speeches:

> Many of those here today have been all night at their posts and all have been under the fire of the enemy in heavy and protracted bombardment.

I see side by side with the devastation and amid the ruins, quiet, confident, bright and smiling eyes, beaming with a consciousness of being associated with a cause far higher and wider than any human or personal issue.

I see the spirit of an unconquerable people.

I see a spirit bred in freedom, nursed in a tradition which has come down to us through the centuries, and which will surely at this moment, this turning point in the history of the world, enable us to bear our part in such a way that none of our race who come after us will have any reason to cast reproach upon their sires.[3]

The Filton aircraft factory was again a key factor in the war effort. The Bristol Blenheim was a pre-war aircraft which was immediately brought into service for the RAF. It was a twin-engined bomber with a gun turret and swivel guns and took part in many actions over the Netherlands, Russia, the Mediterranean and even against the Japanese in Malaya. Several variations of the aeroplane were built including the Bolingbroke, assembled in Canada, and the Bisley which had a re-designed nose section. The Bristol Beaufort was also a pre-war aircraft, and it was chosen by the Australian government for manufacture in Sydney and Melbourne. The Beaufort was followed by the Beaufighter, of which nearly six thousand were built including 364 in Australia. This aircraft played a major part in the war effort and was used to carry the first air-born radar. During the French Occupation a Beaufighter flew across Normandy at tree-top height to plant a French Tricolour on the Arc de Triumph.[4]

Hundreds of barrage balloons dotted the sky like great floating elephants. A row of chimneys followed the line of the Portway to make a smoke screen over the Avon. The war dragged on. Then came a new invasion, but this time a friendly one. The Americans arrived and army camps were established at Bedminster, Failand, Flax Bourton, Backwell and Shirehampton. The Americans built army hospitals at Tortworth, Tyntesfield and Frenchay – the latter hospital was left behind with most of its equipment to become an important local hospital after the Americans had gone. Clifton College evacuated to Cornwall and the buildings were used by the Americans for the planning of the D-Day landings. The Muller Road orphanage and the West of England College of Art were also put at the service of the American army. Eleanor Roosevelt, wife of the President, came to visit the troops. General Eisenhower and Omar Bradley were seen frequently in the streets of Bristol but they were seldom recognised out of uniform.

American troops paraded through the streets. An American show was put on at the Victoria Rooms. American bands performed on the football fields. Baseball was played on the cricket fields. American GIs dated the local girls. More and more Americans came to be billeted

The VE day street party in Whitehall for residents of Ivor Road, Ida Road and Herbert Street. The girl at the window is Dorothy Hill who was suffering from the mumps: her house is Number 8 Ivor Road.

in Bristol. The Americans seemed to outnumber the locals. But suddenly the Americans were gone!

> Not long ago some residents on the west side of Bristol were bewailing the fact that they had to have Americans billetees. Now there is real sorrow in many homes. The young men came, they conquered, and they are gone – literally vanished in a single night ...[5]

It was June 1944 and the *Augusta* left Avonmouth accompanied by a large flotilla of warships bound for the South Coast. Their mission was to meet up with the allies for the great effort of the D-Day landings. The landings were a success but the loss of life on the Normandy beaches ran into tens of thousands. The liberation of France had begun and so too had the forcing back of the Nazi war machine. The injured returned home from the Normandy landings. Autumn came, then Christmas arrived followed by another hopeful New Year, but still the war dragged on. The Colston Hall was destroyed by fire. In Bristol alone 9,092 homes had been destroyed or demolished by the blitz and 1,299 civilians had been killed. The bleak winter was followed by another spring and the flowers bloomed to take away some of the harshness from the empty bombsites, but the injured were still returning from the front. The roll of honour, of those who died for their country, continued to grow longer. It was not until May that England heard the news for which she had been waiting so long. Only then did the people know that the last all clear really had sounded. The dreadful years of misery and fighting had come to an end.

The guns were silent.

The war had ended.

CHAPTER TWENTY

Towards 2000

A flotilla of royal barges, rowed by cadets of the National Sea Training School at Sharpness, worked its way slowly up the Avon and under the newly illuminated suspension bridge. An Elizabethan water pageant was staged to welcome in the second Elizabethan age. Mary Steele took the part of Elizabeth the First. When the royal procession arrived at the centre a trumpet fanfare rang out from the same Elizabethan trumpets which had sounded the fanfare for the Good Queen Bess in 1574. The queen, accompanied by her attendants, mace-bearers and officials, alighted from the royal barge and was carried to a royal platform in the gardens where she made a speech to a patriotic multitude.

The centre was more attractive than it had ever been. It was re-laid with lawns and gardens with June flowers forming a kaleidoscope of colours. A large square pedestal about twenty-feet high supported a huge crown in red and gold standing on a blue base with golden tassels. The pillars of the pedestal were entwined with flowers and the decorated pediment was emblazoned with shields and roses. There were union jacks and bunting everywhere and when darkness fell the coloured fairy lights were switched on. In Queen Square the main attraction was the Guinness Clock, every suburb had its patriotic display of flags and the children had local street parties which they would remember all their lives. The whole city was involved with the coronation. A torchlight procession of a thousand people walked from Hanham to Kingswood and a great bonfire was lit on Hanham Mount as part of a national beacon chain. Other bonfires were lit on Brandon Hill, in Victoria Park, Eastville Park, St George Park, Greville Smythe Park, Bedminster Down, Oldbury Court, Blaise Castle, Purdown and Horfield Common. An exceptionally large bonfire was lit near Sea Walls on Durdham Downs.

The weather did not co-operate and the rain, which had been threatening all day, came down in torrents. Blackboy Hill was chaotic with the traffic four abreast and unable to move. But nobody cared, it was Coronation Day and as midnight struck the crowd at the centre sang out 'Land of Hope and Glory' at the top of their voices. Nearly all the crowd had watched the Coronation live, it was the first such national event to be broadcast on the new television sets. The day was a national holiday but schools, cinemas and church halls were opened for communal viewing, so that those who could not afford the new electronic wonder in their homes could still see the crowning of their new queen on the broadcast from Westminster Abbey.

The fifties represented a new era of hope after a great depression and two world wars. When the decade started there was still rationing on many products, prefabs had been built to house the homeless and the scars of the war were still very much in evidence. Broadmead, where the new shopping centre was planned, was an area of bulldozers and rain filled craters. Post-war recovery was much quicker across the Atlantic and American fashions appeared in the shops. Novel supermarkets opened where shoppers helped themselves to the goods on the open shelves, Hollywood blockbusters and jazz musicals were shown in the cinemas. The favourite male film-star was a pre-war actor, for there was nobody to compare with the Bristol born Cary Grant. Dance halls grew in popularity and the disused quarry on the downs became a dance venue. Summer fashions for girls consisted of full skirts with starched underskirts, so wide that they had problems passing each other in a narrow corridor. Formal evening fashions were even more glamorous with full silk gowns, low necklines and high heels. At the university the college scarf was an essential item, at the art college girls dared to wear tight jeans with cardigans worn back to front. The craze was jazz. Louis Armstrong and Duke Ellington played to packed houses at the Colston Hall. The Rock and Roll craze hit the country and the young set were rocking around the clock. Then came the teddy boys with hairy side burns, brylcream, velvet collars, drainpipe trousers and thick crepe soles. National service was abolished. Scooters appeared everywhere, the seaside became the venue for confrontations between the mods and rockers. At first it was Bill Haley and the Comets, then Cliff Richard and Lonnie Donegan became the rage.

The scene was set for the swinging sixties. The waltz and the quickstep were overtaken by the jive, the twist, the shake and the cha-cha-cha. The American artists were elbowed out by the Liverpool sound. Fashions changed again, girls not only showed their calves but their thighs as well as the miniskirt rapidly shrunk to become the micro. The daring high-cut swimming costumes of the fifties were replaced with ever smaller bikinis. Hairstyles became beehives and the short dresses appeared in bright colours and psychedelic patterns. The smarter young male still wore a suit but ties, lapels, turn-ups and flares rang the changes every year. Employment was high, more and more labour saving devices became available, central heating and fitted carpets became the norm. Minis appeared to race up the new motorways and larger cars in bright colours with acres of shining chromium plating created parking problems in the city centre.

In every direction out of Bristol the country was re-enacting the times of Isambard Brunel as armies of navvies cut great swathes through the countryside. North of Bristol the Almondsbury interchange became an important crossroads on the new motorway network, with the M4 leading east to London, the M5 heading north to the Midlands and beyond and south for the main holiday route to Devon and Cornwall. The Severn Road Bridge opened in 1966 as part of the M4 motorway route to South Wales. The motorways were one of the new wonders of the age, they followed the same routes as the railways 150 years earlier and to a lesser extent they followed the waterways built in the early years of the Industrial Revolution. The trade routes, which had caused Bristol to become an important mercantile centre when she was first born, had changed very little after a thousand years.

The Bristol Brabazon, designed in 1949 and first flown in 1951, was in a time capsule of its own. It was a luxury aircraft with sleeping compartments, designed to amble overnight across the Atlantic at a leisurely 250 mph and to arrive in time for breakfast in New York. It was superseded by the Brittania which in turn was made obsolete by the first jet passenger aircraft. Only fifteen years after the Brabazon an

Known as the whispering giant, the Bristol Brabazon is still remembered by many at Filton. It was designed as the most luxurious passenger aircraft of its time, but it was overtaken by technology and it never entered into service.

aircraft was designed to cross the Atlantic at twice the speed of sound and before the end of the sixties the supersonic passenger aircraft had become a reality.

On 9 April 1969 the world was watching as Concorde 002 stood poised at the end of the Filton runway. There was a holiday atmosphere at Filton and Patchway. Workers from the British Aircraft Corporation lined one side of the runway; workers from Rolls Royce, who helped supply the four Bristol Olympus 593 engines, lined the other side. There was a touch of drama as a problem arose with the reheat on engine number four, but it was quickly corrected and test pilot Brian Trubshaw felt confident enough to take the aircraft off the ground. The distinctive Concorde droop-snoot was angled down, the roar of the engines announced to all that the aircraft was in motion, she quickly accelerated to 120mph, the nose wheel left the ground, and seconds later the great white bird was in the air. The maiden flight was a mere 22 miles to the test site at RAF Fairford in Gloucestershire. A few years later Concorde entered commercial service with British Airways and Air France.

Aircraft construction made great strides in the 1960s, as both digital and analogue computers were used extensively for both design and manufacture of the aircraft. The analogue machines could solve the differential equations used to simulate the dynamics of the aeroplane, and an analogue computer was also used for the Concorde flight simulator. The future lay with the digital computers, however, with their banks of tape decks and disk drives housed in expensive rooms with careful control over temperature and humidity. Just as the calculator replaced the slide rule, so too could the digital computer apply numerical techniques to analogue problems and the new technology soon made the analogue computer obsolete. The computer room had a console of twinkling lights, tape decks jerked into motion with erratic spins; card readers swallowed up hoppers full of punched cards; and printers noisily ran out reams of fanfold listings. Complex wind tunnel calculations and the equations of aerodynamics were solved numerically. Flight test data was recorded and analysed. Structural calculations were sterner stuff and it took the mainframe computer a full day and a night to perform a stress analysis on a large airframe. However, the computer was not reliable enough to run for long without a software failure and check points had to be set for recovery. The three-dimensional geometry of the aircraft profile was no longer stored as a set of drawings but was held on the computer as data for a mesh of lines and tiles, each with its own mathematical equation, and fitting perfectly together to form an aerodynamic surface. The geometric data was used to produce punched tapes. The tapes drove the numerically controlled machine tools, which carved a billet of titanium into a rib or a spar. The machined

part went to the assembly hall to be fitted to the airframe. The aircraft took shape in the great assembly bays of the Brabazon hangar.

The aircraft industry had long ago pushed aside shipbuilding as a major source of employment in Bristol. But on the evening of the 4th of July 1970 people came in their thousands from miles around to line the banks of the Avon to welcome back a rusty iron hulk which had been salvaged from the Falkland Islands and towed on a raft across the south and north Atlantic. They were disappointed. The wind was too high to bring the raft in on the evening tide and the faithful had to rise early the next day to witness the *Great Britain* passing beneath Brunel's suspension bridge for the one and only time in its long life. Eighty four years exposure to the wind and tides of the South Atlantic had taken their toll. All remaining fragments of superstructure had been removed, it was no more than a stained and battered hull which came back to its birthplace, its timber cladding peeling off the sides and barnacles thriving below the water line. But Brunel's decorative stern was still discernible, the prow and the classic swell of the long hull were easily identifiable as those of the greatest ship in the world which was launched from Patterson's yard in 1843.

The rusting hull of the *Great Britain* in 1970 after it had been towed across the Atlantic on a specially constructed raft from the Falkland Islands.

The new horned footbridge across the Floating Harbour, by Elias O'Connell, was named Pero's Bridge after a Negro slave who died in 1798. Pero is one of the few slaves about whom we know anything. He was owned by the Pinney family in Great George Street, and he appears in the family records.

Nearly thirty years later many of those who saw the return of the *Great Britain* took their children to witness the return of the *Matthew*, a full scale replica of Cabot's ship which repeated the journey to Newfoundland to celebrate the 500th anniversary of John Cabot's original voyage. The replica was built at Redcliffe Wharf in 1996 and was the centrepiece of the 'Festival of the Sea', a memorable maritime event when the sailing ships of all nations brought the waterside alive with activity and the great days of sail returned once more to the floating harbour.

In the last decades of the millennium it was the area near the M4 and M5 motorways which saw the most rapid new developments. The area was already the centre of the Bristol Aerospace industry. A new railway station was built at Bristol Parkway, complementing Temple Meads with high speed services to London as well as South Wales, the Midlands, the North and the South West. Business Parks and large retail centres opened near the new station. An even larger retail centre opened near the M5 at Cribbs Causeway and in 1998 the futuristic Mall shopping centre opened with what was, for a short time, claimed to be the largest indoor shopping mall in Europe. A second Severn Crossing was built to cater for the greatly increased volume of traffic between the Bristol area and South Wales. A short distance away the new housing development at Bradley Stoke was one of the largest developments of its kind in Europe.

Bristol Polytechnic was created in 1969 on a green-field site at Frenchay. It was an amalgamation of the Bristol Technical College, the West of England College of Art and the teacher training colleges at Redland and St Matthias. The polytechnic also contained the Bristol

College of Commerce which can trace its origins back to the Merchant Venturers' Navigation school of 1595. In the 1990s the Bath and Swindon College of Health and the Avon and Gloucestershire College of Health were amalgamated and the polytechnic became Bristol's second university, the University of the West of England.

Bristol was more fortunate than the majority of industrial centres; much of the aerospace industry was retained whilst new companies sprang up in the peripheral business parks but also in central locations. Insurance companies mushroomed along the inner ring road to bring new employment to the centre, and Lloyds Bank built a new head-quarters at Cannon's Marsh. It was a typical sign of the times that the city's derelict docks were redeveloped for housing and recreation. New developments at Merchant's Landing provided housing near the city centre with its yuppy marina next door. Warehouses on the old dockside near the centre were converted to create the Watershed complex, very popular with the young, with the much acclaimed Arnolfini Gallery opened across the water. The south side of the docks provided an excellent site for the Industrial Museum with the meticulously renovated Great Britain making a spectacular contribution further downstream. Queen Square and College Green were rescued from the ever-increasing city centre traffic, schemes so successful that it was hard to imagine either place despoiled as they used to be by the ubiquitous motor car.

What the guide books do not say about Bristol is that it suffers in varying degrees from all the problems of the late twentieth century. Unemployment varies greatly but is far worse in the poorer areas such as the Hartcliffe Estate and St Pauls. The eighties saw riots in both these places, and sociologists will debate the root causes for many years, but at the very least they indicated that the social divide is still very wide. In some parts of Bristol pub closing time generates drunken brawls and violence more akin to the unemployed sailors trying to avoid the press gang than the twentieth century.

Bristol has never developed a good local railway network. Bus services are much criticised for not running on time but at peak times the roads are so congested that schedules are virtually impossible to attain. The motorist persistently refuses to use buses, trains, bicycles or any other form of transport except his car. Car crime continues to increase and Bristol finds itself with a growing reputation as the car crime capital of Europe.

Yet it is easy to find statistics to prove the prosperity and success of Bristol at the end of the twentieth century. Employment, car ownership, property values, retail sales figures all point to a prosperous economy with many new business moving into the area. Bristol has always been a city in the forefront of technological progress and has always profited from the latest in communications and computing developments. The

The Lockleaze Tower stands near the site of Purdown Beacon and provides modern communications at a rate many orders of magnitude greater than the beacon.

Right: The Spectrum Building was a very controversial building when it was first opened, but the city has come to accept it as an exciting glass fronted building in keeping with the times.

Below: Poole's Wharf, an imaginative modern housing development close to the harbour.

unsolved question at the end of the century is why, with robots and computers so sophisticated that they can do the work of both the production line workers and the clerical staff, do the workers have to put in such long hours on top of the time spent in the traffic jams? Why has society become a slave to the machines which were designed to do all the work for them?

John Latimer described the reaction of a hypothetical resident transported from the Bristol of 1801 to that of 1901. If Latimer himself were to be transported a hundred years into his future then he too would be overwhelmed by the changes of a hundred years:

> The newspaper of 1901 gave limited coverage to local and national news, today's television network gives both local, national and international news bulletins with instant pictures from all over the world at every time of the day. The internet gives access to a virtually infinite world wide web of information available through a home computer and a telephone line. The flickering fantasy of the cinematograph has been superceded by a virtual reality world of sight, sound and touch where the user can interact with the characters and experience any kind of sensation he wishes. He can travel in luxury across the Atlantic at twice the speed of sound and arrive in America two hours after leaving England. Merchants transacting business anywhere in the world can hold meetings, see and talk with their opposite numbers in Japan by use of video conferencing without leaving their premises. [with apologies to John Latimer]

And perhaps in the first year of the new millennium we should write a similar piece for the Saxons of Brig Stow transported a thousand years into their future. They would find a world totally beyond their comprehension with miracles and magic to be seen around every corner. The last year of the old millennium is an excellent time to review the first thousand years of Bristol's existence.

The view from Redcliffe Bridge looking north along Welsh Back towards Bristol Bridge. Nineteenth-century warehouses still remain between the modern developments.

Castle Park is one of the best places in Bristol to contemplate the past. The ruins of St Peter's and St Mary le Port remind us of the days, still within living memory, when the narrow streets and the timber buildings of old Bristol burned to a cinder in the blitz of 1940. On the same site are remnants of the Norman castle and we know that the ruined churches stand on Saxon foundations where the town was born. The nineteenth century is still much in evidence with a wealth of Victorian buildings known to Elizabeth Blackwell, Mary Carpenter, George Muller and William Gilbert Grace from long ago. The *Great Britain* presides with dignity over the floating harbour and the façade of the original broad gauge terminus survives at Temple Meads, harbouring the ghost of Isambard Kingdom Brunel. The floating harbour now caters for a leisure and tourist industry but they take us back to the early decades of the nineteenth century. Hannah More and Robert Southey were familiar with the older buildings of Park Street and with the Georgian squares and houses surviving nearer the city centre. The home of the plantation owner John Pinney and other reminders of the slave trade are easy to find for the determined searcher, who can visit the back streets near the quays and follow in the footsteps of Thomas Clarkson. Chatterton's school and birthplace survive precariously where the traffic of the inner ring road roars incessantly past, where Samuel Johnson laboured up the steps to the then truncated steeple of St Mary Redcliffe across the road. Several of the timber-framed public houses were standing in the days when Samuel Pepys made his visit to Bristol, when he was entertained at the home of Debby Willet in Marsh Street. Tudor Bristol is harder to find but the Red Lodge of Thomas Young's great house remains and rare hidden gems of timber frame housing can still be found in unexpected courts and alleyways, a few of these were standing at the time of John Cabot's epic voyage across the Atlantic. It takes an effort of imagination to appreciate that for five hundred years Bristol Bridge was the busiest thoroughfare in the West of England, supporting merchant's houses and a chapel. Most of the city centre churches retain fabric and features which still answer to William Wyrcestre's descriptions from the fifteenth century. The gateway of St John's on the wall is old enough to remember the time when the Black Death ravaged through the town. Leonard Lane still follows the line of the ancient city walls. Broad Quay and the Watershed are part of the waterside of the 'wondrous trench' of 1240 which helped to bring the medieval maritime world to Bristol. The Norman Chapter House in the cathedral and the beautiful interior of St James survive to take us back to the beginnings of the market town where traders and travellers crossed the timber bridge over the Avon.

This is Bristol, the home of the world's first supersonic airliner.

The year two thousand. The Bristol Centre is built over the culverted River Frome. In its time the site has been a tramway centre and before that a shipping centre. It was redeveloped for the new millennium, the most prominent feature being the octagonal array of masts seen here as a symbol of a maritime past.

Bristol, an inland port with a suspension bridge to rank alongside the wonders of the world. This is Bristol, the city where merchants grew wealthy on the African slave trade. This is Brig Stowe, the Saxon market place on the border of Wessex and Mercia. Bristow, the town which discovered the American continent and never pressed the claim.

Green upon the flooded Avon shone the after-storm-wet-sky
Quick the struggling withy branches let the leaves of autumn fly
And a star shone over Bristol, wonderfully far and high.

Ringers in the oil-lit belfry – Bitton? Kelston? Who shall say? –
Smoothly practising a plain course, caverned out the dying day
As their melancholy music flooded up and ebbed away.

Then all Somerset was round me and I saw the clippers ride,
High above the moonlit houses, triple-masted on the tide.
By the tall embattled church-towers of the Bristol waterside.

And an undersong to branches dripping into pools and wells
Out of multitudes of elm trees over leagues of hills and dells
Was the mathematic pattern of a plain course on the bells.

John Betjeman

The Street Names of Bristol

The origins of many of the street names of Bristol are very obscure. In Saxon and Norman times the names were only used verbally and sometimes they do not appear in the written records until they are several centuries old.

High Street, Corn Street, Wynch (Wine) Street, Mary le Port Street, Broad Street and Small Street probably all existed in Saxon Bristol. The Little Red Book mentions Baldwin Street, Lewin's Mead, Broad Mead, Marsh Street, Redcliffe Street, St Nicholas Street, St Thomas Street, St Peter Street, Temple Street and Worship Street, with a similar number of long-forgotten names. William Wyrcestre's *Itinerary* (1480) and Millerd's map (1673) are valuable in naming many of the Bristol's forgotten streets.

Some degree of speculation is unavoidable, but I have tried to indicate where the origin of a street name is in doubt.

Alma Road
Named after the battle of Alma in the Crimean War, 1854

Anchor Road/Lane
A relic of the shipping industry. The area supported a ropewalk in the nineteenth century, which progressed to iron chains and anchors.

Anvil Street
Early nineteenth-century. A blacksmith's forge.

Baldwin Street
In 1160 Baldwin Allun was given a grant of land here. Baldwin was a miller whose mill-wheel was driven by the Frome before it was diverted in the 1240s. Baldwin Street was named after him.

Barossa Place
The Battle of Barossa was fought in 1811 during Wellington's Peninsular campaign.

Bathurst Parade/Basin
Charles Bragge Bathurst was MP for Bristol from 1796 to 1812. He changed his name from Bragge to Bathurst in 1804.

Bear Lane (Temple area, Millerd 1673)
Probably contained a bear baiting pit.

Bell Lane
Origins unknown, but shown by Millerd (1673). It is likely that the town bell hung here, or perhaps the curfew bell.

Birdcage Walk
Clifton Parish Church was destroyed in the Blitz, but Birdcage Walk runs through the ancient burial ground. The resemblance to an aviary is obvious.

Blackboy Hill
Named after the Black Boy Inn which was demolished in 1874. (See Whiteladies Road)

Blackfriars
Both the Benedictine and the Dominican monks wore black. The former were located near St James, the latter near Broadmead.

Braggs Lane (Donne 1773)
Charles Bragge changed his name to Bathurst in 1804. (See Bathurst Basin)

Bridewell Street/Lane
The bridewell is the term for a local lockup, used for drunks and casual misdemeanours.

Broadmead
Fourteenth-century or earlier; a wide meadow.

Broad Street
An original Saxon street, broader than its neighbour Small Street.

Broad Quay
Part of the new quay created by the diversion of the Frome in the 1260s. It still exists but it has looked out onto dry land since the Frome was culverted to create the tramway centre.

Broad Weir
Ancient. A weir where the castle moat overflowed into the Frome.

Cabot Street (St Paul's and Bedminster)
Named after John and/or Sebastion Cabot, long after the Newfoundland voyage.

Callowhill Street (Latimer XVIII p 318)
Penn Street area. Thomas Callowhill was a draper who built the Old Hotwell House in 1696 with Charles Jones. His daughter married William Penn.

Canynge Street
A belated nineteenth-century memorial to the Canynge family.

Carey's Lane
Previously Captain Carey's Lane. Eighteenth-century, now defunct.

Castle Street/Green
On or near the site of Bristol Castle.

Cherry Lane
A small cherry orchard existed here when the lane was in its prime.

Christmas Steps
The original name was 'Cutler Street' or 'Knifesmith Street'. The locals could not get their tongue around this and intermediate spellings such as 'Kynst-mass street', implying the reason for the change of name. The street was very steep, and was stepped in the seventeenth century and became 'Christmas Steps'.

Clare Street
Created in 1770 when St Leonard's Church and gate were demolished. A new road was made leading to a drawbridge over the Frome. Named after Lord Clare, MP for Bristol, 1754–74.

Cock Lane (*circa* 1600)
The site of one of Bristol's cock-fighting pits. Others were located at Pithay, Back Street, Redcliffe, Temple and the Ostrich Inn on Durdham Downs.

College Green
Named after the Cathedral Collegiate School.

Colston Street/Avenue/Parade
Edward Colston was one of Bristol's greatest benefactors but he was probably also the first slave trader to operate from Bristol.

Corn Street
Site of the first corn market from Saxon times.

Counterslip (Little Red Book)
A corruption of 'Countess Slip' – a slip down to the Avon where a ferry crossed to the north bank.

Crow's Lane (Welsh Back)
Shown by Millerd (1673). The only logical explanation is that it attracted scavenging crows.

Defence Lane
Long forgotten as the place where the rebellious townspeople built a wall across the town to defend themselves against the castle in the fourteenth century. (See Dolphin St)

Denmark Street
Named after George, Prince of Denmark 1653–1708.

Dighton Street
Shown by Donn (1773). The Dighton family were local brewers.

Dolphin Street
Formerly known as Defence Street, it was destroyed in the Blitz. It ran parallel to High Street on the east and was named after the Dolphin Tavern.

Exchange Avenue
Off Corn Street, it is shown as Corn Lane by Millerd. The corn exchange moved here from Corn Street in Tudor times.

Eyers Lane
Sir Robert Eyers (1666–1735) was the Bristol Recorder and a Judge.

Fairfax Street
A belated memorial to Lord Fairfax. The street was created when the Frome was culverted over in the nineteenth century (see Rupert Street).

Farrs Lane
After Samuel Farr MD, *c.* 1770. He was a founder of the Bristol Library Society.

Ferry Street
A relict of the ferry from Redcliffe Back to Welsh Back.

Fish Street (Millerd, 1673)
A seventeenth-century fish market near St Stephens, shown by Millerd.

Frog Lane, Frogmore Street
Frog Lane appear in Wyrcestre's Itinerary (1480) and Frogmore street appears as 'Frogmere' on early maps. The suggestion of a mere adds credence to the theory that the area was over-run with frogs.

George Whitefield Close
George Whitefield was a cleric with very advanced ideas who preached to the prisoners in Newgate and to the Kingswood miners. He was a great friend and influence on John Wesley.

Greyfriars
The Franciscan friars wore grey habits.

Guinea Street
A place where the traders to the Guinea coast lived and a relict of the slave trade.

Hallier's Lane (Millerd 1673, now Nelson Street)
'Haulier's Lane' was where the sledge hauliers had their premises. This reminder of Bristol's past was lost soon after 1805 when the council wanted to commemorate the hero of Trafalgar. There were plenty of new streets around at the time which could have been called Nelson Street.

High Street
An original Saxon Street. In Norman times it must have been the busiest street in Bristol.

Hobbs Lane
After John Hobbs, *circa* 1712. A wealthy merchant who was instrumental in improving the navigation of the Avon as far as Bath.

Horse Fair
The horse fair was held here from the middle ages until September 1837.

Jacob's Wells Road
A spring used by the Jewish community for ritual bathing from the eleventh century.

Jewrie Lane (Millerd 1673)
The original Jewish quarter was housed in the crypt of St Giles on the Wall at the end of Small Street. Millerd shows Jewrie Lane as just outside the wall.

Johnny Ball Lane
A mugging alley with eighteenth-century character, still existing behind the houses in Maudlin Street. Johnny Ball was an eighteenth-century local about whom we know nothing.

Johnny Ball Lane.

John Carr's Terrace
A belated memorial to John Carr, a soap-boiler, who left money for the foundation of Queen Elizabeth's Hospital in 1586.

King Square
Named after George II in 1737.

King Street
Named after Charles II, *circa* 1670.

King William Avenue
Situated off Queen Square. Named after William of Orange.

Leonard Lane
Mentioned by William Wyrcestre (1480) and still existing. It was named after St Leonard's Church and followed the ancient town wall. Several parish boundary markers can still be seen.

Lewin's Mead
Probably named after Leofwine, a brother of Sweyn Earl of Bristol around the eleventh century.

Long Row (Temple)
A long row of houses mentioned in 1250. Simon de Burton built almshouses for 16 women on the site.

Marsh (The)
The ancient name for Queen Square. It was drained

in the seventeenth century and became an area for recreation before it was developed for housing.

Marsh Street
Leading to the Marsh. Previously known as Skadpull Street, meaning stagnant pools of water.

Maudlin Street
Named after the Nunnery of St Mary Magdalene which stood at the foot of St Michael's Hill.

Merchants Street
Sixteenth-century, named after the occupation of the residents.

Moon Street (Latimer XVIII, p. 159)
Named after the Full Moon Inn, Stokes Croft. Latimer tells of two prize fights here in 1727, one pugilist was Mr Shiner, 'Champion of the West'.

Narrow Quay
Part of the new quay created by the diversion of the Frome in the 1260s. The Quay widened out to become Broad Quay to the south.

Needless Gate/Bridge (Millerd 1673)
The gate was not part of medieval Bristol. This bridge and gate were constructed in 1657, crossing the Frome at the end of Broadmead. The residents of St James' had to pay for it and they complained that the gate was needless. The rest of Bristol seemed to agree. (Latimer XVII, p. 256)

Nelson Street
Formerly Hallier's Lane. Re-named shortly after the Battle of Trafalgar (1805).

Newfoundland Road
A belated memorial to John Cabot's famous voyage but still very old. It is called Newfoundland Lane on Millerd (1673).

Old Market Street
The site of the castle market for the garrison in Bristol Castle. Thirteenth-century. The Pie Poudre Court was held here until 1870.

Orchard Street/Lane/Avenue
The orchard belonged to Gaunt's Hospital and was developed for housing early in the eighteenth century.

Park Street
Named after Bullock's Park which existed at the end of the eighteenth century.

Passage Street
The passage leading to the ferry for Counterslip.

Pembroke Road
Formerly known by the down beat name of 'Gallow's Acre Lane'. George Ashmead's plan (1849) shows Pembroke House and the southern part developed under the name 'Down Road'. The name Pembroke Road

was adopted in the 1860s when the remainder of the lane was developed for high class housing.

Penn Street
A belated memorial to William Penn and son, 'founders' of Pennsylvania.

Pennywell Road
The site of Penny Well which dates back to the reign of Henry III.

Perry Road
After the Perry family. Nicholas and William Perry were curriers (leather workers) c. 1713.

Petticoat Lane (near Temple Church)
A local market, stealing the name from its London namesake.

Phippen Street
Robert Phippen was mayor of Bristol in 1840.

Pipe Street (St Augustines)
Follows a pipe carrying water from Brandon Hill to St Augustine's Back.

Pithay
Thirteenth-century or earlier. The name probably means 'Cockpit hay meadow'.

Portland Square
Named after the Duke of Portland, Lord High Steward of Bristol 1786–1809.

Portwall
Follows the defensive wall built at Redcliffe in the 1240s.

Quaker Friars
The friary was that of the Domincan friars from 1229. In 1609 it was used as a meeting house by the Quaker Society of Friends. Hence the strange combination of religious bedfellows.

Queen Charlotte Street
Queen Charlotte was the wife of George III. The street was formerly known as Back Street.

Queen Square
This was Bristol's most prestigious address for much of the eighteenth century. It was named in honour of Queen Anne after her royal visit.

Redcliffe Street/Hill/Back/Pit
The suburb of Redcliffe was named after the red cliffs on the banks of the Avon.

Rodney Place (Clifton)
Completed in 1787 and named after Admiral Rodney who defeated the Compte de Grasse in the naval Battle of the Saints 1780. Rodney visited Bristol in 1782.

Rupert Street
A belated memorial to Prince Rupert. The street was

created when the Frome was culverted over in the nineteenth century (see Fairfax Street).

Shambles (Wyrcestre 1480, Millerd 1673)
Near Bristol Bridge, it has its own mini-history. It was the butchers' quarter, called 'Bocherew' by William Wyrcestre. It later became known as Bridge Street and was destroyed in the Blitz.

Silver Street (Millerd 1673)
The street of the silver smiths.

Small Street
One of the original streets of Saxon Bristol. It was small compared to Broad Street.

Temple Meads
Meadows belonging to Temple Church, that of the Knights Templar.

Tower Hill
This street originally ran further north towards the great keep of the castle.

Tower Lane
Follows the inner wall which had towers at regular intervals, Nightingale Tower stood on the lane and was of a much larger construction than the others.

Tower Street
Not shown by Millerd, but shown by Donn (1773) when the ruins of Tower Harratz were still very much in evidence on the bank of the Avon.

Trenchard Street
Shown as 'Trencher Lane' by Millerd (1673). It seems to have been a trench at one time, perhaps for drainage or possibly part of the Civil War defences.

Tucker Street
Very old. The tuckers were one of the trades from the woollen industry.

Wade Street
Named after a former town clerk, Nathaniel Wade. Wade was a conspirator with the Duke of Monmouth in the rebellion of 1685 and this made him very unpopular in Bristol. He built a bridge across the Frome which became known locally as Traitor's Bridge.

Welsh Back
Used by traders from the Welsh ports to unload and load their cargoes.

Whitefriars
The Carmelite friars were here from 1267, they wore white habits.

Wine Street
One of the original Saxon streets of Bristol, it certainly contained wine vaults but the original name, until the fifteenth century, was Wynch Street (see Wynch St).

Whiteladies Road
On the fact of it Whiteladies Road and Blackboy Hill seem to be the perfect setting for white ladies to parade with their small negro pages. This may have happened in Queen Square but Blackboy Hill is a mid-nineteenth-century name and Whiteladies Road was little more than a farm track at the time of the slave trade. Hammersley's map of 1746 shows that the upper part of the road was named at that time; he also shows White Ladies Inn at the junction with Oakfield Road.

Whitson Street
John Whitson died in 1629 after falling from his horse. He was a wine merchant and the founder of Red Maid's School.

Wynch Street
This was the original name for Wine Street, until about 1500. There would have been a winch to raise the drawbridge and portcullis on Bristol castle, but Wynch Street did not lead directly to the Barbican Gate. The older, motte and bailey, castle from 1087 did have a gateway on Wynch Street so this seems a possible explanation.

Zed Alley.

Zed Alley
This alleyway looks like the end of something. It has a 'Z' stagger where it crosses Host Street and this is the most likely derivation.

References

The information in this book is seldom obtained directly from original documents, but in most cases from professional publications of original documents. The exception is Latimer which is sufficiently reliable to be treated as an original source. Latimer's information is invariably compiled from council records, calendars or newspapers and his source is seldom stated but it is usually obvious.

Abbreviations for general references:

Latimer XVI: John Latimer, *Annals of Bristol in the Sixteenth Century* (1908, reprinted 1970)

Latimer XVII: John Latimer, *Annals of Bristol in the Seventeenth Century* (1900, reprinted 1970)

Latimer XVIII: John Latimer, *Annals of Bristol in the Eighteenth Century* (1893, reprinted 1970)

Latimer XIX: John Latimer, *Annals of Bristol in the Nineteenth Century* (Part I, 1897; Part II, 1902; both reprinted 1970. Page numbers are Part I unless otherwise specified)

B&G: *Transactions of the Bristol and Gloucestershire Archaeologocal Society*

Betty: J. H. Betty, *Bristol Observed* (1986)

Little: B. Little, *The City and County of Bristol* (1954)

LRB: F. B. Bickley (ed.), *The Little Red Book of Bristol*, 2 vols (1900)

McInnes: C. McInnes, *A Gateway of Empire* (1939)

Ricart: L. T. Smith, *Rikart's Kalendar*, Camden Society, New Series, V (1872)

Seyer: Samuel Seyer, *Memorials of Bristol*, 2 vols (1821–23)

Chapter 1

1. Douglas & Greenaway (eds), *English Historical Documents*, 11 (1953), pp. 123–4.
2. Anne Savage (ed.), *The Anglo-Saxon Chronicles* (Papermac edn, 1984).
3. Hamilton (ed.), *William of Malmesbury's De Gestis Pontificum Anglorium*, Rolls Series (1870), p. 292.
4. *Ibid.*
5. K. R. Potter (ed.), *Gesta Stephani* (1955).
6. *Ibid.*
7. N. Dermott Harding (ed.), *Bristol Charters 1155–1373*, Bristol Record Society, 1 (1930), p. 19.

Chapter 2

1. Rev. E. A. Fuller, *The Tallage of Edward II and the Bristol Rebellion*, B&G, vol. 19, p. 186.
2. *Ibid*, p. 184.
3. *Ibid*, p. 184.
4. Seyer, vol. II, p. 143.
5. C. E. Boucher, *The Black Death in Bristol*, B&G, vol. 60, pp. 31–46.
6. Oman, *The Great Revolt of 1381*.
7. *LRB*, vol. I, p. 115.
8. *LRB*, vol. II, p. 182.
9. J. H. Harvey, *William Worcestre – Itineries* (Oxford, 1969).

Other sources for this period include: E. Ralph (ed.), *The Great White Book of Bristol*, Bristol Record Society, vol. 32 (1979); E. W. W. Veale (ed.), *The Great Red Book of Bristol*, Bristol Record Society, vols 2, 4, 8, 16 (1933–53).

Chapter 3

1. Ricart, 1461.
2. Ricart, 1484.
3. Adams's *Chronicle of Bristol* (Arrowsmith, 1910).
4. J. H. Harvey (ed.), *William Worcestre – Itineries* (Oxford, 1969), p. 303.
5. *Ibid*, p. 307.
6. *Ibid*, p. 309.
7. Cumming, *Skelton and Quinn: The Discovery of North America* (London, 1971), p. 80.
8. *Ibid*, p. 80.
9. E. R. G. Taylor (ed.), 'A Brief Summe of Geographie' by Roger Barlow, Hakluyt Soc., 2nd series, LXIX (1931).
10. Ian Wilson, *The Columbus Myth* (1997). Other sources for this period include: J. Dallaway, *Antiquities of Bristol in the Middle Centuries* (1834); P. Fleming and K. Costello, *Discovering Cabot's Bristol* (1998).

Chapter 4

1. G. Townsend (ed.), *John Fox's Acts and Monuments*, vol. VIII (1839–43).
2. L. T. Smith (ed.), *The Itineries of John Leland 1535–43*, V (1910), pp. 86–93.
3. Latimer, XVI.
4. L. T. Smith (ed.), *The Itineries of John Leland 1535–43*, V (1910), pp. 86–93.
5. *Ibid.*
6. E. R. G. Taylor (ed.), 'A Brief Summe of Geographie' by Roger Barlow, Hakluyt Soc., 2nd series, LXIX (1931).
7. Latimer, XVI, pp. 28–9.
8. R. Gough (ed.), *William Camden's Brittania* (1586).
9. Ricart.
10. Adams's *Chronicle of Bristol* (Arrowsmith, 1910).
11. R. Gough (ed.), *William Camden's Brittania* (1586), pp. 86–7, 122–7.

Chapter 5

1. Adams's *Chronicle of Bristol* (Arrowsmith, 1910).
2. H. S. Burrage, *English and French Voyages 1534–1608* (New York, 1906).
3. McInnes, chapter VI.
4. Thomas Fuller, *The Worthies of England*.
5. Miller Christy, *The Voyages of Captain Luke Foxe and Captain Thomas James*, Hakluyt Soc., vol. II (1894).
6. *Ibid.*
7. *Ibid.*
8. Seyer, vol. II, pp. 287–8.
9. McInnes, chapter VI.
10. Captain Woodes Rogers, *A Cruising Voyage around the World …* (London, 1712).

Chapter 6

1. Ricart.
2. L. G. Wickham Legg (ed.), *A Relation of a Short Survey of Twenty-Six Counties in 1634*, Camden Soc. (1904).
3. Adams's *Chronicle of Bristol* (Arrowsmith, 1910).
4. Latimer, XVII, p. 130.
5. P. Mundy, *Travels in Europe and Asia, 1608–67*, Hakluyt Soc., Second Series, LV (1925).
6. E. Warburton, *Memoirs of Prince Rupert and the Cavaliers* (1849).
7. E. S. de Beer (ed.), *The Diary of John Evelyn* (1955).
8. Latimer, XVII, p. 338.
9. Latham and Matthews (eds), *The Diary of Samuel Pepys* (1976 edn), IX, pp. 223–36.

Chapter 7

1. Adams's *Chronicle of Bristol* (1910), pp. 33–4.
2. E. S. de Beer (ed.), *The Diary of John Evelyn* (1955).
3. Latimer, XVII, p. 29.
4. C. Morris (ed.), *The Journeys of Celia Fiennes* (1949).
5. Latimer, XVII, p. 156.
6. C. Morris (ed.), *The Journeys of Celia Fiennes* (1949).
7. Daniel Defoe, *A Tour through England and Wales*.
8. G. Sherbourne (ed.), *Correspondence of Alexander Pope* (1956).
9. *Ibid.*
10. Friends House Library, Norris MSS 10, quoted by Joan Day, *Bristol Brass: A History of the Industry* (1973).
11. Latimer, XVIII, p. 244.
12. Latimer, XVIII, p. 244.
13. A. P. Woolrich and Aden Ouden, *Ferrner's Journal 1759/60, An Industrial Spy in Bath and Bristol*.
14. *Ibid.*
15. *Ibid.*
16. *Ibid.*
17. *Ibid.*

Other sources: R. A. Buchanan and N. Cossons, *Industrial History, Bristol.*

Chapter 8

1. L. G. Wickham Legg (ed.), *A Relation of a Short Survey of Twenty-six Counties in 1634*, Camden Society (1904).
2. *Journal of William Schellinks in England.*
3. *Ibid.*
4. C. Morris (ed.), *The Journeys of Celia Fiennes* (1949).
5. G. Sherbourne (ed.), *Correspondence of Alexander Pope* (1956).
6. *Ibid.*
7. Latimer, XVIII, pp. 264, 311.
8. Latimer, XVIII, pp. 424.
9. *Ibid.*

Chapter 9

1. Latimer, XVIII, pp. 428–36.
2. R. Anstey & P. E. H. Hair, *Liverpool, the African Slave Trade, and Abolition* (1989 edn) pp. 91–2.
3. Published in the *Mariner's Mirror* (July 1951), edited by Prof. W. Minchinhampton.
4. J. Pope-Hennessy, *Sins of the Fathers* (1967), quoting from Alexander Falconbridge.
5. Letter in the *Boston Weekly News Letter*, 1737.
6. McInnes, p. 198.
7. Pinney Papers, Business Letter books, 1779–84.
8. Latimer, XVIII.
9. Thomas Clarkson, *The History of the Rise, Progress and Accomplishment of the Abolition of the African Slave Trade* (London, 1808).
10. J. and M. Collingwood, *Hannah More* (1990).

Chapter 10
1. N. Curnock (ed.), *The Journal of John Wesley*.
2. *Ibid.*
3. *Ibid.*
4. Latimer, XVIII, p. 64.
5. G. R. Powell, *The Bristol Stage* (1919).
6. J. Telford (ed.), *The Letters of John Wesley*, IV (1931).
7. G. R. Powell, *The Bristol Stage* (1919).
8. F. A. Kemble, *Record of a Girlhood* (1878).
9. *Ibid.*
10. *Ibid.*

Chapter 11
1. Latimer XVIII, p. 186.
2. *Felix Farley's Journal*, 28 October 1762.
3. *Ibid.*, 1 October 1768.
4. John Cranstone Nevill, *Thomas Chatterton* (1948).
5. James Boswell, *The Life of Samuel Johnson*.
6. J. & M. Collingwood, *Hannah More* (1990).
7. *Memoirs of Hannah More*, vol. I, p. 54.
8. James Boswell, *The Life of Samuel Johnson*.

Chapter 12
1. S. Hutton, *Bristol and its Famous Associations* (1907).
2. *Ibid.*
3. *Ibid.*
4. F. A. Kemble, *Record of a Girlhood* (1878).
5. *Ibid.*
6. L. T. C. Rolt, *Isambard Kingdom Brunel* (1957).
7. *Ibid.*
8. Mary Russel Mitford, *Recollections of a Literary Life*, Vol. III (1852).

Other source: Donald Jones, *A History of Clifton* (1992).

Chapter 13
1. N. Curnock (ed.), *The Journals of John Wesley*.
2. Latimer, XIX, p. 146.
3. *Ibid.*, p. 157.
4. *Ibid.*, p. 167.

Chapter 14
1. C. Morris (ed.), *The Journeys of Celia Fiennes* (1949).
2. P. Aughton, *Liverpool: A People's History* (1990).
3. L. T. C. Rolt, *Isambard Kingdom Brunel* (1957).
4. *Ibid.*
5. Charles Babbage, *Passages from the Life of a Philosopher* (1864), p. 325.

Chapter 15
1. Charles Babbage, *Passages from the Life of a Philosopher* (1864), p. 321.
2. Latimer, XIX, p. 191.
3. Charles Babbage, *Passages from the Life of a Philosopher* (1864).
4. *Bristol Standard*, 3 September 1840.
5. *Ibid.*
6. *Bristol Standard*, 8 July 1841, referencing the *Bath & Cheltenham Gazette*.

Chapter 16
1. Latimer, XIX, p. 296.
2. Agnes C. Vietor, *Elizabeth Blackwell: A Biography* (1924).
3. Arthur T. Pierson, *George Muller of Bristol* (1899).
4. G. H. Peters, *The Plimsoll Line* (1975).
5. *Ibid.*
6. *Western Daily Press*, 12 July 1935.
7. *The Times*, 1 October 1869.
8. Joan Rees, *Amelia Edwards* (Rubicon Press, 1998).
9. Amelia B. Edwards, *A Thousand Miles Up the Nile* (1877).
10. *Ibid.*

Chapter 17
1. Latimer, XIX, p. 369.
2. *Ibid.*, p. 101.
3. C. H. Barnes, *Bristol Aircraft Since 1910* (3rd edn, 1988).
4. G. F. Stone & C. Wells, *Bristol and the Great War* (1920).

Chapter 18
1. J. B. Priestley, *English Journeys* (1934).
2. *Ibid.*
3. *Ibid.*
4. *Western Daily Press*, 31 January 1935.

Other sources: Jack Steggles, *Joy of the Rovers* (1990); David Woods, *The Bristol Babes* (1994); David Green, *The History of Gloucestershire CCC* (1990); Simon Rae, *W. G. Grace – A Life* (1998).

Chapter 19
1. *Western Daily Press*, 26/28 June 1946, describing 24 November 1940.
2. Reece Winstone, *Bristol in the 1940s* (3rd edn).
3. M. Gilbert, *Winston S. Churchill*, vol. VI (1983).
4. C. H. Barnes, *Bristol Aircraft Since 1910* (1964).
5. *Western Daily Press*, June 1944.

Index

References in **bold italic** type indicate an illustration or caption on that page